Ralph Shaw, born near Huddersfield, finished his schooling in Rugby and in 1936 joined the Royal Army Service Corps—a move that landed him in Shanghai one year later.

After a short Army career he was 'bought out' by the *North China Daily News* and spent the next 25 years as a roving reporter in the Far East.

In this book, Shaw has graphically drawn on the experience of 10 of these valuable years—his profound knowledge of the political scene in China; his many sexual experiences and his close association with the Chinese people in joy and sorrow—to produce the frankest picture yet published of this decade in history.

D1262243

RALPH SHAW

Sin City

Futura

A Futura Book

Copyright © Ralph Shaw 1973

First published in Great Britain in 1973
by Everest Books Ltd

This Futura Edition published 1986
Reprinted 1986

All rights reserved.
No part of this publication may be reproduced,
stored in a retrieval system, or transmitted, in any
form or by any means without the prior
permission in writing of the publisher, nor be
otherwise circulated in any form of binding or
cover other than that in which it is published and
without a similar condition including this
condition being imposed on the subsequent
purchaser.

ISBN 0-7736-80209

Printed and bound in Canada
Published under license in Canada by
General Paperbacks

Futura Publications
A Division of
Macdonald & Co (Publishers) Ltd
Greater London House
Hampstead Road
London NW1 7QX
A BPCC plc Company

Eastward Ho

In 1937 the best people travelled out to China the 'posh' way – port out, starboard home aboard one of the ships of the Peninsula and Oriental Steamship Company.

Those were the days when British ships, unlike American liners, relied on fans and open portholes to keep passengers cool rather than emasculate members of the bulldog breed with such softeners as air-conditioners.

Britons then stewed in their own juices in the Red Sea in greater or lesser degree depending on position of cabin. A port-side cabin going out, so the old hands maintained, was eminently desirable in that it offered reasonable comfort compared with the Turkish-bath temperature of the starboard accommodation. Homeward bound the scramble was for starboard space.

I never got the choice. There was no cabin for me. I curled up banana-shaped in a swinging hammock. I shared, somewhere in the bowels of His Majesty's Transport *Dilwara*, a Black Hole of Calcutta reeking of sweaty socks and unwashed bodies with various odds and sods in uniform despatched by the War Office or the Admiralty to keep the Union Jack flying over lesser breeds in such places as Port Said, Port Sudan, Aden, Colombo, Bombay, Singapore or Hong Kong.

I was then a soldier – a private in the Royal Army Service Corps, though a superior one in that I was a clerk, a 'shiny arse', rather than a commonplace driver or butcher or baker or horse-transport minion. At fifteen shillings a week I was half-a-crown better off than they were though this financial superiority did not make my loathing of army life less intense.

The transformation from journalist to khaki-clad automaton was caused by my predilection for females and booze. After leaving school I joined the *Rugby Advertiser*, a Midlands weekly newspaper, as junior reporter – trainee they'd call me today. There was one other junior reporter – Mike Ardizzone, brother of the artist Edward Ardizzone. Unlike me, Mike led a reasonably

5

sober life and managed to eke out a precarious existence on what the board of directors decreed was a reasonable pittance for youngsters learning the ropes.

Jack Hudson, the chief reporter, told me that my brains were in my balls. He was right. I was at that time in a state of almost perpetual erection – even when going through musty files to write out each week the 'Peeps Into The Past' which consisted of extracts from the *Advertiser* of 50 years and 25 years back. I was susceptible to feminine charms – a lecherous young sod whose mind, if you could call it that, kept him standing on street corners outside the Lodge Plug works, or the Rugby High School, at going-home time to leer lasciviously at the remarkable expanse of thigh shown by girls on push-bikes.

I was also addicted to ballroom dancing which decreed that there was usually a girl to take home, to grapple with in some alley-way, to bring on to fruity responsiveness by nipple tweaking or, in moments of greater passion, a real feel between the legs. Invariably I got what I wanted – not the screw I always boasted about to my pals who were impressed by my expertise but a nice hand-job which spread over Rugby and district quantities of seminal liquid brought forth by the manipulative prowess of young ladies anxious to get indoors before dad came down in his night-shirt and laid down the law in forceful language.

Visits to pubs were a prerequisite to sexual virility. Mild, in half-pint jugs, was the aphrodisiac. Two or three pints from the barrel of Mitchells and Butlers mild brew, or Ansells, or anyone else's, dispelled my English reserve. I became a Latin Romeo – the Rudolph Valentino of Hillmorton, or Brownsover or where-ever the take-home larks deposited me. I kissed feminine hands as I'd seen them doing on the pictures. I got 'em gooey and simpering with complimentary remarks about their beauty. As a reward they tossed me off. I desired nothing else.

Advancement in terpsichorean technique resulted in my spreading my net further afield – at the Nottingham Palais or Victoria Ballroom, at the West End Ballroom in Birmingham, the Palais at Leicester, the Palladium at Hinckley or the Palace at Nuneaton. This meant that there were further emissions of seminal fluid induced by the physical efforts of young women dwelling in those places – in such spots as the local cemetery, at the back of the market, down by the canal or by dad's rose bushes at the bottom end of the garden.

It was a nice life but the trouble was that the miserable stipend the *Advertiser* bosses doled out to me could not possibly cover my weekly outgoings – even when I cooked, as I usually did, my expenses sheet. We were allowed a penny-halfpenny per mile cycling expenses outside the urban district as it then was. So in my sheet weekly there appeared the names of such villages as Newbold, Long Lawford, Church Lawford, Clifton, Barby, Crick or Easinghall which, to be truthful, I had never set eyes on for ages but which, if my erections were to be dealt with by other hands than my own, had to be brought into my money-making orbit.

I was responsible for the column, 'Pulpit and Pew', church news which necessitated visits to rectors, vicars and such-like good livers. I also had to pick up football reports after weekend games. All these gave me licence to 'cycle' to places well outside the urban boundaries. I charged lunches in the office on Tuesdays when we ran an afternoon edition for which I took down the racing results from the Press Association in Birmingham. But even at best I could not muster more than ten shillings on the 'swindle sheet'.

Nevertheless I managed to keep head above water until the editor, Tom Manock, decreed that I should go and live in Daventry as the *Advertiser* representative there. My salary was increased from fifteen shillings a week to £2 out of which I had to pay twenty-five shillings for lodgings.

Daventry – or Danetree as the natives called it – was the end of the world as far as I was concerned. It was a truly rural dump, a sort of penal settlement in which I was incarcerated until the paper came out on Friday morning to free me for a week-end of lechery in some more sophisticated spot where I could show off my new fifty-shilling suit and do some quick-step variations which would not entangle me in a pair of rural legs shaped like giant redwood trees.

On Monday mornings I was broke. I cycled the ten miles from Rugby to Daventry and spent the rest of the week trying to avoid landladies anxious for their money. This was nerve-racking and not good for my health but I survived.

I also managed to avoid, by skulking in back alleys or traversing little-used routes, various tradesmen to whom I was indebted – for cigarettes on tick, newspapers, toilet articles and so on.

I changed lodgings fairly frequently. I left one place when an irate parent discovered me with my hand down the blouse of his daughter, whose bust was intensely desirable but whose flesh I was touching because she had placed a packet of Craven 'A' between the two mounds of which she was inordinately proud It.

7

was the cigarette I sought – not a tit grab. I was broke, desperate for a smoke. She said I could have a fag if I got the packet out myself. 'Shit or bust,' said an inner voice. Hard shit it was when dad walked in, whacked my arse with his walking stick, told me to bugger off and never darken his door again.

Another establishment was run by a maiden lady, aged about 40 or thereabouts. She didn't smoke and her tits were nothing to speak of so there was no danger there. But she liked her money regularly and this did cause problems.

The crunch came when my indebtedness reached nearly £9 – and I gave the young servant girl violent hysterics.

I had managed to elude detection by my creditor by rising early every morning, dashing out of the house like a greyhound and making my way to the Conservative Club where I burrowed down deep in a remarkably large armchair for the remainder of the day.

Late at night I would venture out, walk up to the house to see if any lights were burning and if there was total darkness then I tiptoed in, soft-shoed my way to the kitchen, grabbed a handful of pickled onions, a slab of cheese and slice or two of bread and took them up to my bedroom. If any lights were still on I made one or two speedy sashays round the block until I was certain that the spinster was in bed.

This will-o'-the-wisp existence ended dramatically one night when I entered the darkened hallway to find the landlady, arms akimbo, waiting for me.

The good lady – for that she was – switched on the light and addressed me sternly. I had not paid her for seven weeks. I could not quibble over that. There was also the matter of a large jar of pickled onions the contents of which seemed to be disappearing at a phenomenal rate – not to mention diminishing stocks of cheese and bread.

The old Shaw phlegm stood me well. I did not flinch. Tongue well in cheek I assured the lady that I had arranged for payment to be made to her by my father and that she could expect his cheque within a day or two. My parents lived in Rugby and she knew their address – and phone number.

The landlady said she hoped this was true. I said she could trust my words. But I could see that she didn't. You didn't need telepathic powers to note that fact. I had an inkling what her next move would be.

As for the pickles, cheese and bread, I disclaimed any knowledge of their regular shrinkage. Again her face showed absolute disbelief. If payment was going to be as promised then I had better put in an appearance at regular meal sessions, she suggested. I said it was a good idea. I would follow her advice.

I reasoned that her next move would be to write to my father without delay.

The following night I went to bed early, rose at 3.0 a.m. the next day, dressed and sat myself down in the armchair in the lodgers' lounge. It was my intention to steal out at 5.0 a.m. and cycle the ten miles to Rugby and get hold of the mail at home before my father did.

At 4.30 a.m. all hell broke loose. The young servant, a simple country girl, entered the lounge and in the darkness spotted what she thought was a corpse in the armchair.

She let out a stifled scream, began to shiver violently and went into a foaming fit.

I jumped up from the chair, patted her reassuringly on the back – and she collapsed in my arms, out to the wide.

Just my bloody luck. I dragged her to the armchair, dumped her in it and then splashed her face with water from a nearby flower-vase.

She came round eventually, saw that I was the recalcitrant lodger and cheered up somewhat though her chest was heaving like a blacksmith's bellows. I told her not to worry and, for Pete's sake, not to mention the encounter to her employer. Another soothing pat, a soft-spoken sentence of reassurance and I was off to Rugby.

I met the postman at my parents' gate and tore the letter from the landlady into tiny fragments and made my way back to Daventry.

The reprieve was a short one. The landlady had been told of my early-morning brush with the servant, and had telephoned dad. I got the telling-off I richly deserved, my debt was paid and the landlady gave me marching orders.

As I left I saw the servant girl cleaning the steps. 'Bloody rotten sneak,' I hissed. 'Bloody country cow.' She burst into tears, looked at me as if I were Jack the Ripper and showed signs of having another foaming fit. I made myself scarce before the police were called.

The end came after several Daventrians and sundry country residents, who had sent me small ads for insertion together with the cash enclosed in envelopes, wrote abusive letters to the *Advertiser* demanding to know why bills had been sent to them. The fact was that I had sent the ads to my office but had borrowed,

9

'until pay-day', the cash. I never got around to depositing the money in the advertising department though, in my defence, I must make it clear that, when circumstances permitted, I fully intended to do so.

But good intentions are for ascetics. The thought of silky dalliance with Clementina in Coventry, Edna, Aggie or Vi in Hinckley, Gwen in Nuneaton or any of my Midlands dancing partners shattered honest aspirations.

I vanished from Daventry. My office sent out search parties and roped in Harold Mayes of the rival Northampton paper to cover for me until a substitute could be sent out. My parents, worried and fearful, joined in the search. They didn't find me – I was miles away in Keighley, Yorkshire, where my maternal grandmother, who loved me very much, lived.

Incidentally, I nearly got Mayes the sack. He was a photographer as well as a reporter. We were covering the annual Northamptonshire school sports at Weedon, near Daventry, when he asked me to mark his programme while he took some action shots.

I noticed there was a Baron Profumo among the patrons or vice-presidents. I forget now the designation. I marked in carefully the name of 'Baron Tossoffski'.

There was a minor earthquake when it got into the *Chronicle and Echo* in six-point type. But Mayes lasted out and the crime was attributed to some young teacher in a party of 12 or so detailed to revise the programmes before the sports.

I was born in Yorkshire. My mother's birthplace was the Brontë village of Haworth. My dad was a Huddersfield lad. Until I was about nine we lived in Shipley, near Bradford. Then my dad, who was a musician, took us to Newport, Monmouthshire, and from there to Rugby where increasing parental affluence enabled my brother and I to attend the school there founded by Lawrence Sheriff, the Rugby boy who made his fortune in London during the reign of Queen Elizabeth I.

I settled down with grandma, drew the dole and quickly found many Yorkshire lasses willing to take me in hand.

Unfortunately I had other relatives in the Keighley region who 'thought nowt' of my workless existence. They told me so forcibly in my grandmother's presence. They got on my nerves.

One morning in a mental stupor I walked into the army recruiting office in Cavendish Street and signed my life away – seven years with the Colours and five on the reserve.

A week later I was in Buller Barracks, Aldershot, the depot of the Royal Army Service Corps Training Battalion – a raw recruit, regimental number S/54897.

My misery started on the drill square in Grattan Squad – three months of sheer torture as we were knocked into military shape by bull-necked, raucous-voiced, indelicately-spoken drill sergeants, who quickly made it known that we were 'a fuckin' 'orrible shower of shit-order, ropey bastards' and that we probably sat down to pee. But, by Gawd, they'd make soldiers of us or have our 'fuckin' guts for garters'.

If we showed signs of strain in shouldering our rifles for hours on end we were given the sergeant's diagnosis. We had 'wanker's colic' or were afflicted with 'wanker's doom'. To wank was to masturbate. Our NCO, married and all right, Jack, grimly told us he'd be issuing boxing gloves at bedtime.

When we fumbled at the end of our rifles fixing bayonets we were told that we'd 'bloody soon find the 'ole if there was 'air round it'.

Standing stiffly at attention, body up to full height, we were bawled at to get off our 'fuckin' knees'.

One button undone and we were 'stark bollick naked'.

A flicker of rebellion in our eyes and it was 'bleedin' dumb insolence' and our feet wouldn't 'fuckin' touch'. This indicated such a swift removal to the guardroom that we'd be airborne.

Once we were standing easy after a particularly fearsome bout of quick marching, slow marching, forming fours and what have you.

Our sergeant spots a young woman carrying a basket from the NAAFI stores.

He looks at her for a time and then transfers his gaze to us, a diabolical smirk on his weatherbeaten countenance.

'Any squaddy 'ere like to fuck that lady?'

No reply – though we all would to be sure.

Again the question.

'Yes sergeant,' bawls out that nitwit West, 'I would.'

'Well you can't. That's my wife.'

A fusillade of barked orders and in seconds we are off on a doubling marathon – punishment for having the temerity to lust after an NCO's 'wife'. It was an old drill-square gag and, inevitably, there had to be one clot who fell for it.

We were not allowed civilian clothes. We had to be in barracks at 9 p.m. sharp daily except weekends when it was midnight. We spent innumerable man-hours 'boning' boots, polishing brass buttons, collar-dogs and other accoutrements with shiny surfaces. We blancoed our web equipment, we pulled-through our rifles, metal-polished our bayonets, arranged our bedding for inspection, numbered each item of kit, rolled on puttees, rolled 'em off again if they didn't finish right, polished our bed spaces with wax – in general gave our hearts and souls to that great deity of the services, Bullshit.

Conversation was well laced with the four-letter word and its variations: 'Fuck me' to indicate astonishment, 'Pass the fuckin' bread, mate' at supper time, 'Too fuckin' true' described by one wit as the 'army's split infinitive'. 'Fuckin' Hell', f . . . this, that, everything.

In the barrack-room practically only one topic for discussion – cunt, minge, twat, hole, tail . . . the female pubic region. Stories of erotic penetrations 'back home in Barnsley' invariably the invention of a fertile imagination. We were the most sexually frustrated crew in the country, living on erotic fantasies, masturbating regularly, thinking of women constantly – but never getting near them.

The local girls regarded us as if we were lepers, first cousins of Frankenstein or Count Dracula, untouchables, the lowest form of animal life. They had only to see a squaddy in uniform and they ran a mile. Accost them in the street and their icy stares sent shivers down your spine. Look at their legs or tits and they were ready to accuse you of instant rape.

I made a vow: come hell or high water, oath of allegiance or not, 'contract' for 'seven and five' notwithstanding I was going to get out of the army and return to journalism.

We passed off the square as smart as any guardsmen and split up to take our various courses. The drivers went to Feltham and the clerks remained in the barracks to attend the school there – shorthand, touch-typing, military law and other subjects.

It was well known that any aspiring clerk who failed to pass the final test could apply for transfer to a lower grade – driver, for instance – or take his discharge on the grounds that his educational ability was not up to the required standard.

Came the first test. I failed. So did two others. They got their marching orders. I did not.

I was told by the company officer to sit again. I did. I failed.

I was called in by the commanding officer. The gist of his message was that I would sit again and pass . . . or else. I took note, sat and passed.

A few weeks later Glasgow-born Private Jackson and I, fed

up to the teeth, got a weekend pass to visit London. We did not return. We were absent without leave.

Unfortunately the streets of London were not paved with gold. It was hard sleeping on a bench on the Embankment or in the crypt of St Martin-in-the-Fields, picking up butt ends in the gutters, feeding on hand-outs from the charities – a couple of homeless waifs.

Neither did we relish being picked up by homosexuals in Trafalgar Square – but we had to live and we were well paid for our services which meant that we could buy cigarettes instead of stealing them from the counters of kiosks or shops staffed by females, who could not run as fast as we could.

We lined up nightly at the Silver Lady mobile canteen and got free food and, sometimes, bed tickets which took us to a doss-house in Tooley Street. We knew all the other charitable institutions – the Catholic convents, the Salvation Army citadels, the Royal Scottish Corporation and several others. We didn't starve but the search for grub was certainly hard on our feet.

But the hopelessness of our situation certainly had its humorous moments.

There was the night we were sleeping in the crypt of St. Martin's where the Sisters of Charity cared for us. On the pew in front of us was an old tramp who suddenly disturbed the serenity of the hushed atmosphere by farting thunderously. The wooden bench acted as a baffle board, magnifying the rasping sound. In the cavernous depths it sounded like a thunder clap.

I burst out laughing. I was in the grip of uncontrollable mirth. Jackson was asleep – hadn't heard the fart – so he wasn't laughing.

Up comes one of the Sisters of Charity in high dudgeon. 'Get out,' she says, pointing to the exit. 'Get out this minute.'

'It wasn't me,' I spluttered. 'I didn't do it.'

'Get out,' she said, looking at me as if I were the Devil himself.

I spent the remainder of the night sitting miserably in Trafalgar Square while Jackson, oblivious of the commotion, slept if not comfortably at least warmly. All for laughing at a fart!

Worst of all was our experience in the 'advertising business' – carrying sandwich boards up and down Oxford Street. My contraption extolled the expertise of some passport-photo enterprise. Jackson's told the folk to 'Eat at Joe's' or was it 'Percy's' or 'Antonio's'? I forget. We soon got tired of the ceaseless parade, dumped our boards by Selfridges and made off to Hyde

Park to sleep in the afternoon sun. Our reward was to have been half-a-crown each.

'They can stuff it,' said Jackson – 'sandwich board as well.'

I made the decision to go down to Brighton to see my brother who was working in that area. My idea was to touch him for a quid or two and then return to London and rejoin Jackson. I made Brighton – walked it. I saw my brother, who had been visited by the police in their quest to discover my whereabouts. He gave me a pound and intimated that I was as welcome as a cholera epidemic. So I went off to enjoy myself.

Enjoy myself I did. My pound, though it went three or four times as far as today's piece of paper can manage, was spent by evening. I had no will-power. Money really burned a hole in my pocket. I visited various pubs, treated myself to non-charitable meals and enjoyed the variety show at the Hippodrome which featured singer Phyllis Robbins and Nat Gonella and his Georgians along with Teddy Brown, the immensely overweight but agile American xylophonist.

As darkness fell, completely broke, I was trying to crawl under a boat on the beach with the intention of spending the night there before starting the long trek back to London next day.

Suddenly the light from a torch made me blink. I looked up and there was an immense police sergeant, a Goliath in blue, looking at me quizzically.

'And what might you be doing, lad?' he said, kindly.

'Well,' I said, 'I missed the last train back to London. I just wanted to sleep here and catch the first train back in the morning.' I prided myself on my quick thinking.

'Oh, you did, did you?' There was something about his tone that made me nervous.

'Strange,' he said – 'considering there's a London train about every twenty minutes. And they're running now.'

Goodbye liberty. He searched me, discovered an army weekend pass for London well overdue (I hadn't destroyed it) and off we went to the police station.

A phone call was made to the RASC at Buller Barracks. Had they anyone called Shaw, who might be absent without leave? Had they? Most certainly they had and they couldn't wait to see him back – in the guardroom.

So I spent the night in a cell after a nice supper provided by the police. They gave me breakfast, too, just before I stood in court before a woman magistrate and was charged with being absent from my unit. I pleaded guilty.

14

Later a corporal and a private arrived to take me back under close arrest. They were a couple of decent chaps and fixed me up with some Woodbines before arrival at the barracks decreed that they should turn on the usual display of bullshit – arm-swinging marching, stamping feet, barked orders to me in tattered civilian clothes and a meticulously performed hand-over ceremony which saw me placed in charge of the quarter-guard NCO, anxious to thrust me into one of the guardroom cells.

I appeared before Colonel Boulter, the commanding officer. He took a dim view of my long absence. I would be incarcerated for 28 days in the Aldershot Detention Barracks and Military Prison, there to undergo rigorous reform treatment intended to ensure that when I came back to soldier on I would be a completely changed man.

They had me by the short hairs. Seven years I had elected to serve. Seven it would be. He didn't add. 'And may God have mercy on your soul.' He should have done.

The detention barracks, off Queen's Avenue – now demolished after being set on fire by the Canadians during the war – was manned by men of the Military Provost Staff Corps, all NCO's. all dedicated to the ideals of such historical characters as Nero, the priests of the Spanish Inquisition, the Marquis de Sade and Captain Bligh.

One month in their tender care and you emerged with respect for the kindliness of lions on a flesh-eating rampage, the cannibals of New Guinea, the hordes of Genghis Khan, of Attila the Hun, even of that loveable old soul, then making his presence felt on the European scene, Adolf Hitler, the concentration-camp specialist.

Everything had to be performed at the double, even crapping in doorless cubicles (just so that you wouldn't be able to commit suicide in darkened privacy). You were kept perpetually hungry – just enough grub to keep you on your feet. Laces, braces and puttees had to be deposited outside your cell every night – another anti-suicide measure. You had no knife, no fork. A spoon sufficed to eat the slop which they called meals. Razors were issued in the morning and you shaved with cell-doors wide open and MPSC morons watching every stroke. You handed them back when you had finished. It was purgatory. It was meant to be. Bullshit at the barracks was a Sunday-school picnic by comparison.

I returned to barracks, not in the least chastened but certainly a damned sight smarter than anyone else in sight. even the

Regimental Sergeant-Major. And, having survived 'glasshouse' treatment for 28 days, I was regarded by my fellow privates as a hero.

There followed a posting to 'G' company at Bulford on Salisbury Plain – like Daventry, the end of the bloody world. The only females we saw were four-legged Guernseys or Jerseys chewing the cud placidly on the green hillsides. The two-legged variety were in short supply. At night we lived in a world of sensual fantasy with visions of silken-clad legs, enormous bosoms and beautiful backsides urging us on to manual relief.

In the morning the usual admission: 'I had a wet dream last night.'

The invariable rejoinder: 'And I bet it made your bloody wrist ache.'

I was a clerk in the company office. I was in charge of pisspots, married families for the use of.

Once a week I roped together about half-a-dozen stout commodes, tied them to the handlebars of a green-painted army bicycle and pedalled carefully through Bulford village to the RASC married quarters.

I ignored the ribald comments of soldiers from other units who watched me pass by: 'Cor blimy, pisspots!', 'Try this for size' (pointing to genital region), 'What about a free demonstration, mate?', 'Go steady, China', etc., etc.

Then knocks at sundry doors to be greeted by blushing females, self-conscious and anxious to terminate contact. They would hand me pisspots in various states of disrepair, cracked, broken in pieces, minus handles, all leaky.

I exchanged them for shiny new commodes, got the women to sign receipts and made my way back to enter details in the barracks register.

Fed up to the teeth, I applied for a posting overseas. To my surprise, considering my record, it came quickly enough – to Shanghai.

I got fitted out with tropical kit: pith helmet, khaki drill tunic, shorts, stockings and, after leave spent in Keighley and Rugby, reported at Southampton docks where the *Dilwara*, externally spick and span, waited for me.

A band played on the quay as we boarded, were shown our quarters and where to stow our kit-bags. Going with me to Shanghai were the 1st Battalion, the Durham Light Infantry, some reservists of the Royal Army Medical Corps, who had rejoined after a workless existence in a country gripped by terrible depression, other odds and sods from the Royal Engineers and some sailors who would be manning the Yangtse river gunboats.

All aboard. A long blast from the *Dilwara's* siren. Ropes cast off and we are slowly swinging away from the quay. The band plays 'Auld Lang Syne' and a lump comes into my throat, my eyes are wet. I look down at the people waving goodbye. I think of my mother and grandmother, both of whom have died. For the first time in my life I am leaving dear old England. 'Goodbye Blighty.' After all, it won't be long before I'm back – three years. We get into midstream, the engines pick up power and we are off down Channel. The quayside crowd gets smaller and smaller and finally is out of sight as we encounter the choppy waters of open sea.

Life aboard the *Dilwars* was not a bed of roses. Getting into a hammock needed considerable agility. Staying in it in the Bay of Biscay needed great physical power. Lashing and stowing these contraptions was a chore that should have remained with the Jack Tars – our knots were apt to come loose at critical times.

Private Green of the Medics, among others, was deposited flat on his arse a few minutes after clambering in one night.

As the sailors laughed their bollocks off, Green, bruised and in high dudgeon, shouted:

'Shurrup, yer fuckin' matelot arsehole borers, yer wide-arsed shower of shit.'

This was meant to indicate that the jolly Jack Tars were renowned for their love of 'navy cake' – homosexual practices away from port. The army lads had the general idea that this practice was prevalent in the navy and that unwilling able seamen were forced to join in the debauchery by having their heads and shoulders stuffed into portholes as the erect organs of lustful petty officers penetrated them from the rear.

The sailors, in great merriment, told Green to get stuffed, that he was, no more, no less, a prize cunt, a fatherless product of a poxed-up Portsmouth whore.

Fisticuffs were only avoided by the arrival of a Durhams sergeant with Green, to use the expression of Private 'Jock' McDaid, also of the Medics, 'hopping around like a freshly fucked stoat.'

Our quarters, well below deck, served both as sleeping accommodation and dining room. After stowing hammocks we lowered from hooks in the ceiling great long tables which we fixed to the

17

deck. We hauled in benches and then ate our grub served by a giant Scandinavian cook.

After breakfast out with the buckets and swabs to sweep waves of sea-water from hose-pipes across the deck and into the scuppers. In other 'dungeons' below deck, the Durhams and the remainder of the human cargo were similarly keeping their quarters 'all shipshape and Bristol fashion' and mightily cursing the fate that had befallen them.

Above us the lascars of the ship's company, all devout Muslims, were similarly employed. We were a proud lot, bred on a liberal diet of Empire-worship, of our superiority over other less favoured races. We were exports from a country which owned most of the world; lands here, there and everywhere on which the sun never set. We sang – and believed – that dear old Blighty was the land of hope and glory, that God had chosen it as his instrument for perpetuating heavenly rule and that the King – God bless him – was Jehovah's right-hand man.

No wonder that we objected to doing the work of 'heathens' from India who prayed to some idol on mats. Our general knowledge did not extend to comprehension of the tenets of Islam or Judaism. Anyone who was not 'C. of E.' was, *ipso facto*, 'a bleedin' 'eathen'.

We were called on deck to do physical jerks so that we didn't lose the use of our legs which would be needed on flag-showing marches in various ports of call. We battled forlornly with salt-water showers and found that the salt-water soap we had bought in the ship's stores worked up as much lather as an 80-year-old bag taking on the Archbishop of Canterbury in an open field in the middle of a snowstorm. We found, too, that the daily evacuations posed hazards.

'The 'heads' were up in the bows of the ship. We squatted over troughs running on both sides of the ship. Sea water plunged down the troughs, which sloped from bows to scuppers – a distance of about seven yards each side. Thus, those of us lower down this 'canal' were apt to get whacked with the solid evacuations of the gentry squatting nearer the bows as the ship rose and fell in choppy seas. For all of us, except, perhaps, the matelots, it was the first time we had been assailed by turds.

'Look out, mate,' went up the cry, 'there's a turd on the way.'

Up would go our arses, waiting for the torrent to carry it down to the scuppers. Sometimes we were too late. We accepted the danger stoically as only men of the bulldog breed could have done.

Our duties over, we could go up on deck and play tombola

(bingo) or crown and anchor, or better still, peer aft beyond the quarters amidships allotted to our officers – single cabins and all mod cons – to catch sight of the women who were going out to join menfolk overseas.

We waxed lascivious as they sprawled in deck-chairs to sunbathe or emerged in various states of tropical undress to hang out their washing.

Our state of ebullience was aptly described by a private of the Durhams, who admitted in homely Geordie dialect, that sight of the ladies gave him 'the bloody 'orn'.

The women, wives and daughters of soldiers, knew damned well what effects their presence on deck had on us, the frustrated yoicks down at the blunt end. They exploited their charms to the full – beachwear parades in tight-fitting costumes out of which their tits bulged like gas-lamp globes, leg shows by the ship's rails, the exposure on washing lines of panties, brassieres, stockings and so on. They knew that the squaddies gazing their way were in full erection, penises straining against khaki drill, doing their damnedest to bridge the fore-and-aft gap that separated the sexes. But they were safe enough. Not one man would dare to traverse the amidships section where dwelt the commissioned men – gentlemen who would take a dim view of such prowling.

Nevertheless it was possible to visit the 'married pads' for an hour or two – on fire-watch. Each night we were detailed to stand guard at several points in the ship to watch out for fire or similar danger. We wore best service dress. We carried regulation cane – what for, God knows! And, if we were lucky, we found ourselves in corridors well laced with the small cabins occupied by the ladies.

Thus we could see them in the ironing-room, hot and sticky, with thin dresses clinging to fine, fat bums, revealing the bouncing softness of breasts or, better still, the swelling of pubic region. We watched them flit from cabin to cabin on social visits. We ogled them as they mounted the stairs going up to the deck. They knew, every one of them, that we lusted after them, were being troubled by enormous horns, that we could not, on guard duty, place hands in pockets to relieve ourselves – that we were well and truly 'up shit creek'. And they seemed to revel in our obvious signs of frustration.

'No fuckin' wonder,' said one of my colleagues on fire-watch, 'they're all the wives of bleedin' sergeants – 'orrible bloody shower.'

We passed Gibraltar and saluted the Union Jack there. We ropped in at Malta and saw it again. At Port Said it was in evidence everywhere. In the morning we marched behind the Durhams band through the town and were watched by large crowds of 'Gippos'.

In the afternoon in small groups we did tours, taking in the canal entrance and the statue of Ferdinand de Lesseps, who built it. We were importuned by the dirty-picture sellers, the small boys who lifted their gowns and exposed their penises or backsides, the shop touts, the bird-sellers, the fortune-tellers, the entire community, or so it seemed.

To each of them the order, 'Fuck off.' They didn't. We had to tolerate their presence until the time came to board the *Dilwara* for the journey down the canal to Port Suez.

On both banks we saw British troops who shouted that we were going the wrong way. We waved at them. They waved back. We saw them ordering the natives around and our hearts glowed with pride that we were Britons, that we should never be slaves as the 'Gippos' were.

At Port Sudan we marched again and saw the 'fuzzy-wuzzies' pushing railway trucks at the behest of sun-tanned Englishmen. Great big black-skinned men they were with crinkly hair coiled up aloft like guardsmen's bearskins.

At Aden we discovered that by staying below deck and getting a good porthole view we could look up the skirts of ladies gathered on the quayside above us to welcome friends aboard.

We were known as the 'wankers' brigade'. Our members were legion. There was always a mad scramble for a porthole peep as we entered port. The ladies, mostly officers' wives or the women of civilian expatriates, gave us splendid erections as the shore-side breezes billowed out their skirts and permitted us to get tantalising glimpses of long legs, rounded thighs and a variety of knickers.

In Bombay, where we did another march, pretty, seductive Anglo-Indian girls looking like Merle Oberon added to our enjoyment as they stood on the quayside beside the whiter pukka English women. We were thankful that our quarters were situated in such an excellent position.

We masturbated openly when wind and position at the quay-side offered us unhindered view up thin, summery dresses. There was no shame in the act. We were the most frustrated specimens of manhood marooned in sea-going celibacy. Who could blame us?

20

We repeated the performances at Colombo, at Penang, in Singapore. Then we reached Hong Kong.

I went ashore there and had lunch with a friend from Aldershot who had been posted to the colony.

After lunch we sat and talked in the cloistered serenity of the barrack-room with its highly polished floor and rows of small, steel beds. There was a young Chinese woman sitting in one corner of the room busily sewing away at shirts.

She was slimly built, had jet-black hair, shiny and thick, which she had coiled into a long pigtail hanging down her back. She was dressed in a tight-fitting tunic of black pongee silk with wide, flapping trousers of the same material.

I asked who she was.

'Oh, that's the sew-sew girl,' said my friend. 'She mends our kit for us.'

There was a gleam in my eye which he noticed.

'She's good for a toss-off,' he said with a chuckle, 'but she won't screw. Give her twenty cents and she'll get rid of your load. Shall I call her over?'

I did not hesitate. Six weeks at sea hand-reared and here was someone who would allow me to deposit my semen even further afield than the Midlands and Yorkshire.

He called across the room: 'Hey!'

The girl rose and walked towards us.

'You catchee my friend.' He pointed to my genital region and made masturbatory movements with his hand.

She nodded her head and beckoned me to follow her. No money had been mentioned. Twenty cents, it seemed, was the market price.

She entered one of the toilet cubicles outside the room, stood there holding the door and bade me enter. I did so and she indicated that I should stand over the toilet bowl. She locked the door.

'Takee out,' she said, gazing at my flies. Her tone was business-like.

I did so. It was stiff as a board, thrusting forward in rare erectile excitement.

She extended her right hand and grasped it. Gently she caressed it, fingers tickling the bottom of the glans which was the most sensitive spot. She was an expert.

As she stroked she pressed her small, soft body into me. Her movements quickened. I was on the way.

In enormous jerks I gave forth and the spurts fell into the

bowl. Expertly she held the stiff shaft so that its aim was true. There would be no tell-tale marks on the floor.

When I had finished she tore several strips of toilet paper from a container on the wall and handed them to me. I wiped the end clean. She wiped her hands with other strips and threw them into the bowl. As I buttoned up she flushed the lot away and as the water stopped gurgling inspected the pan. It was clean.

I took out thirty cents from my pocket and handed the cash over.

She counted it, smiled her thanks, unlocked the door and bade me go first.

As I joined my friend in the barrack-room she followed and took her seat in the corner. Immediately she commenced sewing.

'Great,' I told my friend. 'Just what the doctor ordered.'

'Good,' he replied. 'Trust the old corps to provide the service. All laid on for horny sods like you.'

After tea I said goodbye, took a last look at the sew-sew girl in the corner and made my way back to the *Dilwara*.

We ploughed our way into the China Sea, proceeding along the China coast until, wide-eyed in wonderment, we saw a straight line ahead of us dividing as clean as a knife-cut the ocean into two colours: deep, muddy brown and ocean blue.

For miles this brown sea heaved in muddy turbulence. Here was in mid-ocean evidence of the mighty power of the Yangtse river, rising in the highlands of Tibet to rush, wild and untamed, through the vastness of China and out into the sea – 3,400 miles of waterway, at its mouth some 22 miles wide. There it disgorged yearly millions of tons of the brown loess it brought with it in its mighty sweep southward.

We entered the estuary of the river and made for the Woosung forts where we dropped anchor prior to picking up one of the British Whangpoo river pilots who would guide us to our Shanghai anchorage.

Gliding past us were the dark-grey shapes of warships – cruisers, destroyers and smaller craft, including submarines. They flew the Japanese naval ensign and were on active service. In defiance of the League of Nations Japan had started hostilities against China and there was heavy fighting in the coastal region.

As we sailed up the Whangpoo we saw a veritable armada of Japanese shipping and the havoc caused by war on both banks of the muddy waterway. The Chinese were putting up a good fight but they were retreating inland. In the ruins of villages, of farmhouses, of barns, we saw the squat Japanese soldiery, steel-helmeted, grim of visage. They stood and watched us glide past. We waved at them. They did not return the compliment.

'Bloody short-arsed shower,' said one lad. 'Wait until they meet a real army.' I wonder if he lived to remember his cockiness after December 8th, 1941.

The *Dilwara* entered the International Settlement area of Shanghai – Yangtsepoo, Wayside and Hongkew – where we tied up at Holt's Wharf. We saw khaki-uniformed British police officers, turbanned Sikh constables, Chinese policemen. They all carried revolvers in holsters. The wharf coolies, thin and ragged, heaved ropes around the bollards. Long-gowned Chinese gentlemen, ledgers in hand, gazed up at us.

We thronged the decks and looked down at the scene.

Red-capped military policemen waited to board the ship. A posse of officers stood tapping swagger sticks against their legs. On the river side we could see long lines of Japanese warships tied up in midstream. Above them, White Ensign flying at the stern, was a British cruiser. Further upstream was an American cruiser.

Ominously, in the distance, we could hear the sound of gunfire. As we looked across the river we could see palls of smoke rising. Overhead Japanese planes returned from bombing missions. The rumble of artillery was clearly audible. For most of us this was our first sight of a real war. We had never fired shots in anger. We were excited, happy to be at the scene of hostilities which were earning world-wide prominence in newspaper headlines and in cinema newsreels.

'Welcome to Shanghai,' shouted a burly British police officer from the dock. 'I'm a Geordie, too.'

There were cheers from the Durhams. We were all raring to go.

Garrison Man

Shanghai was a cushy berth – dead easy compared with Aldershot and Bulford. For the first time in my life I had a manservant or, rather, I shared his services with others who lived with me in a barrack room at the British Military Hospital in downtown Shanghai, only a few hundred yards from the Bund waterfront.

The 'room boy' took over the chores that we did ourselves back in Blighty – making the beds, 'bumping' the floor, polishing our buttons, cap badges, blancoing our belts, cleaning our boots and so on.

So we lived like little tin gods, mostly prostrate on our beds reading such pirated literature as 'My Life and Loves' by Frank Harris while our man – an ever-smiling Chinese gentleman – bustled about the room and generally helped us to stave off exhaustion.

After leaving the *Dilwara* I had been assigned to the General Staff (i) office in the headquarters of the Shanghai Municipal Council on Kiangse Road, just beyond the Anglican Holy Trinity Cathedral. The 'i' denoted that we were an intelligence bureau and it was my job, as clerk, to type out on stencils a regular series of confidential reports which were sent to London, Hong Kong and other military nerve centres.

In charge was Major Timothy Gwynne of the Punjabis, a genial Irishman, hefty and ruddy. Second in command was Captain Davidson-Houston of the Royal Engineers, smaller, quieter, gentlemanly.

My immediate boss was Staff-Sergeant Carver, RASC, the chief clerk, easy-going but highly efficient – he knew the Manual of Military Law backward – and a dab hand at brewing a real 'sarnt-major's' cup of char, a job he always performed himself rather than let the likes of me serve up what he called witches' piss.

The fourth member of the staff was Sapper Mann of the Royal Engineers who, when I joined the office, was busy making a line drawing of a medium-sized Japanese shell picked up, unexploded, in the Chapei district where there had been some heavy fighting between the Japanese and the Chinese.

I had never seen a shell at close hand and I didn't like it. It sent shivers down my spine. I got into a blue funk when I saw the light-hearted way Carver and Mann treated it.

Maybe they knew more about shells than I but I did fancy that Carver was taking a bit of a risk when, with a hefty kick, he sent the missile rumbling along the floor to come to rest by the Sapper's desk. The shell, when it was not being inspected, stood on the floor by Sergeant Carver. At least six or seven times a day he booted it to the Sapper who returned it by the same method.

I was pretty near a nervous breakdown when the shell disappeared – sent, I believe, to some ordnance experts who were going to dismantle it and have a look at its innards. My health perked up in no time.

From time to time we were visited by furtive-looking gentlemen, speaking English in a variety of execrable accents. They had information to impart and were received either by Major Gwynne or Captain Davidson-Houston. Real cloak-and-dagger stuff it appeared to be when papers were burned daily in a metal dust-pan and I, on joining the office, took an oath of secrecy in the presence of the two officers.

Other visitors included American and French, hissing and bowing Japanese captains, and high-ranking police officials. They were received with typical British bullshit – cracking salutes by us, and much bowing by Gwynne and Davidson-Houston.

There was no bull in our barrack-room in the hospital. While the Medics, who operated the hospital with the women of Queen Alexandra's Imperial Military Nursing Service, were kept up to the mark by Regimental Sergeant-Major Hyson, RAMC, he left us of other units severely alone.

We had a sergeant with us – Unsworth of the RASC. There were a couple of RASC corporals, Robinson and Royal, both of whom had done boys' service in the corps, a Durhams corporal named Bradley, a few others of lesser rank and Sapper Mann and me.

Not a hundred yards away from us in Central Road was the Handy Bar run by an American, Jimmy James, late of the U.S. 15th Infantry, who had stayed on in China after discharge and had opened two restaurants both of which flourished under the title, Jimmy's Kitchen.

The Handy Bar – Hyson called it the 'Randy Bar' – owed its

popularity among hospital personnel to the fact that Jimmy had staffed it with a chorus line of Russian beauties, bar girls whose job was to entice solid cash from lecherous soldiers out on the spree.

Unlike British barmaids, the girls pulled no beer pump-handles. In fact there was no draught beer available. Drinks came in bottles and were served by Chinese 'boys' who could be any age from 20 to 70 or thereabouts. The girls decorated the joint, sat with the lads and coaxed by various means 'drinks – usually coloured water or tea – out of them.

Sapper Mann took me along to the Handy Bar where the long-legged, busty beauty of one girl, Nadya, had John Thomas up in appreciation long before she joined us at the Sapper's invitation. He had the cash. I didn't. He felt generous – willing and ready to play the host for a newcomer.

Legs! I loved 'em. Nadya had a pair that dazzled the eyes – long, shapely, stocking-clad, supported by high-heeled, shiny shoes. And her neckline was low enough to suggest that a couple of size 38s might break loose if she bent any lower over the table. I, for one, was ready to catch them!

Dark-haired, brown-eyed, she resembled Dorothy Lamour though it would have been a pity to cover up those legs with a sarong.

She noticed that my eyes were bulging and immediately found that there was something wrong with one of her shoes. She stood up, placed one foot on the chair so that I got almost a worm's-eye view up to suspender-belt height, bent forward, which temporarily had my eyes going up and down like a yo-yo, and began to fiddle about with the 'offending' footwear.

Like Olga Polovski, the Russian spy, she was in imminent danger. Poor old Olga, so the story had it, was going to be executed by a firing squad for conning Allied secrets in World War One. She appeared before the squad in a fur coat and, as the men in front of her took aim with their rifles, discarded the garment to stand completely and beautifully naked. She fell dead – riddled with fly-buttons.

Certainly the strain on my flies was intense, a point which Nadya had duly noted. Tumescence had to be maintained – it meant generosity, drinks. The leg show continued. She had considered the lure of bosom and, after weighing up my reaction carefully, had come to the conclusion that while I might be a tit man it was for certain that legs would arouse more benevolence as far as I was concerned. She was right.

Unfortunately, my financial embarrassment stopped me ordering another round and the Sapper was obviously reaching zero mark. He suggested we should leave. I had to make certain of seeing Nadya again so I told her, politely, that I would like to meet her at some future date. She said that she, too, would be enchanted but would I be in civilian clothes – a nice suit. Obviously His Majesty's uniform, as in Aldershot, acted as a female repellent. Hastily, I promised that I would be in at the weekend suitably attired.

Thank God for Tomes the Tailor, a bespectacled Chinese in long, traditional gown, who regularly visited us with samples, measured us and delivered the finished product within a day or two. And on the never-never, too.

Tomes turned me out in a double-breasted, grey, pin-stripe suit for 60 dollars – only five dollars down. It was the first tailor-made garment I'd ever bought and it certainly did not repel the ladies as I found out during a matinee performance at the Grand cinema.

I went in after the show had started. The usher lighted my way to the front of the stalls where a Chinese man on the end seat politely stood up to allow me to pass.

There were a couple of vacant seats next to him. I decided to sit in the centre of the row, intending to pass two European women, who occupied the fourth and fifth seats. I found my way blocked by a large thigh which pressed against my knee. I looked down and saw that the woman had both knees pressed against the seat in front, making access impossible.

Also visible was a skirt pulled back to pubic region, exposing two stocking-clad thighs with white flesh in clear contrast to the darker hue of stocking top. The woman followed my gaze but did not withdraw her knees from contact with the front seat. I was embarrassed.

I pushed again. No yielding. I tried again. Then the woman next to her said, 'Let him pass.'

Knees were slowly pulled back so that a small gap was left – enough to permit me to squeeze by. I moved. No sooner had I got in front of the woman when I felt a hand stealing between my legs. Then a firm grab of my genitals. The hand was withdrawn.

I stopped dead in my tracks – for a second or two. I had never been indecently assaulted by a female. I was at a loss but I had to do something – and quickly. I moved and sat down next to the other woman and stared intently at the screen as if nothing had happened.

The aggressor peered forward and looked across at me. She was a big woman, tall and busty, aged about 30 I guessed – desirable if you liked big bones and plenty of flesh. The other one was smaller and certainly less aggressive.

The big one gazed at me for a time and then reached over with her arm, resting her hand on my thigh. Had I got a light? Her fingers were gripping my thigh. I got out a box of matches, leaned over and lit her cigarette. She offered me a packet of Camel. I thanked her and took one.

She asked me: 'Are you English?' I nodded.

'We're Americans,' she said, pointing to the other woman, who had not shown any interest in my presence. 'We're killing an hour or two.'

I put two and two together. These two females had obviously been having a lesbian relationship in the cinema. My arrival had broken up the proceedings and the woman next to me was not pleased.

I had no idea what I should do next. Always I had been the lecher, the opener, the prodder, the dominant partner. I pondered over possible ploys – and did nothing.

The aggressive woman, speaking to her neighbour, said that I looked nice which boosted my ego somewhat. But I did nothing. We sat on and on. They both rose before the film ended and started to make their way out.

'Get cracking,' said a voice within me. 'For Gawd's sake do something.'

As the big female passed me I let my hand wander as hers had done. Up it went, right up her dress, between her thighs, touched her pelvic bone.

There was no visible response. Both women passed along the aisle and vanished through a red-lighted exit. Well, there it was. I had tried. What if she came back with a policeman and had me charged for indecency? Who would believe me when I said that she had launched the first attack? I was apprehensive and decided to make a quick move.

Just then, alone, the big woman re-entered the cinema. She walked to where I was sitting and started to search underneath the seats. She said that she had dropped a scarf and I had a quick look around myself. No scarf. But I couldn't let her go.

I reached out with both arms, grabbed her round the waist and guided her into the seat next to mine. No opposition. I placed my arm around her, drew her close to me and kissed her. Her breath smelt of whisky. She was randy. Her tongue played around in my mouth. Her hand alighted on my trousers where she groped until she had found the stiffness she sought. I followed suit and let my hand roam up her thighs.

Suddenly she pulled away. 'Let's go out,' she said in a southern drawl.

Go out? Where? I did a quick calculation. We wouldn't go far on 75 cents which was all I had until pay-day. Shanghai was cheap enough but my pay went not like water but with the speed of a raging torrent.

I decided to put my cards on the table. I told her I was a serviceman but she said that she had guessed that.

I added that I was 'financially embarrassed.' She had also guessed that and told me not to worry. She would finance us.

We left the cinema and walked the few yards on Bubbling Well Road to the Park Hotel which staggered me. The Park was well out of my league. It was comparable in social standing – though not prices – with the Savoy in London or the New York Waldorf.

The lady, now extremely haughty as she addressed the Eurasian reception-desk clerk, asked for her key. The clerk produced it with a flourish and took not the slightest notice of me standing in the background. As I followed her to the lift I caught the eye of the clerk and gave him a wink. A broad grin spread over his features. After all, we were in the same class – money-wise.

She had a single room with a shower and toilet. There was a single bed and plenty of cupboard space into which she quickly pushed her clothes. She was in a hurry although I was still limp – rather overawed by my surroundings. But the sight of her naked, eyes riveted on me as she beckoned me to undress and place my garments in a wall wardrobe soon had me rampant.

'Don't worry,' she said. 'We'll have a nice time, honey, and then a meal. Gee, you're cute.'

I felt like a small boy. She was about eight years my senior, may be more. But there was nothing childish about my John when I had undressed. She saw that. While her face had a certain coarseness, probably from too many cocktails or the hard stuff, her tits were large and bouncy. She had an over-size backside and her thighs were much bigger than most I'd seen.

She didn't exactly rape me but I emerged from the fray – for that it was – well clawed and with bleeding lip where she'd bitten me in orgasmic excitement. We adopted the natural posture but she did nearly all the work, thrusting, heaving that large backside up and down in great agitation. All the while she had me in a wrestler's embrace with finger-nails gouging my shoulders and

29

upper back. And the entire performance took no more than ten minutes. She came first, realised that I had not ejaculated and pushed me to the side of the bed. She took me in hand and brought me off quickly.

That was all. We dressed. She was pleasant and said that she was well satisfied. When we had dressed after showers she handed me ten dollars. She said she was hungry and we'd have a meal together. I was walking on air. Ten dollars and rations. Talk about a fairy godmother. What a tale I'd have to tell the lads in the barrack-room.

We didn't eat at the Park. She ordered a taxi and we finished up in the Chocolate Shop where I had a hamburger, served Shanghai style with fried egg on top, French fries and peas. She had, of all things, corned-beef hash. She paid the bill.

She never told me her name and I didn't ask. When we parted – I to get a bus down to the hospital and she a taxi to the hotel – we shook hands and we never expected to meet again.

We did, though. Maybe six months later I entered a lift in a large downtown office building and there she was, big and busty as ever, standing with a chap about 20 years her senior, bald, shrivelled, dried-up. No wonder she grabbed me in the Grand. Her husband, if that was what he was, couldn't have penetrated a wet paper bag.

She recognised me – her surprised expression showed that. But I did not betray her. I turned my back, waited until the lift reached the floor I wanted and walked out without a backward glance.

There was something in the Shanghai atmosphere, some sensuous ingredient, some aphrodisiacal stimulant, that seemed to maintain the female population, or a large proportion of it, in a state of perpetual heat. It wasn't the steamy summer. Nor could winter – with its ice and snow – take the credit. The women were aggressively sexy – apart from the missionaries and the do-gooders and they might have been privately for all I know. It could have been the spicy Chinese food, which was out of this world and which probably contained ginseng root or rhino horn, or perhaps it was just the normal female response to a male population which made no bones about the fact that it was the randiest in the world.

Another encounter with a female not long after the Park Hotel affair convinced me that I was indeed stationed in a seraglio of lust.

I was standing at the bus stop outside the Racecourse when I spotted a young woman just under the sign of the China General Omnibus Co.

She was a lovely piece of tail – medium height, nice legs, curved amply enough and pretty of face. She was European – probably Russian, I thought.

Too good to be missed. I spoke to her. Was she going anywhere? Nowhere in particular, she replied in good English, unaccented. Could we dally together for about an hour? She didn't mind. There was an hour to go to midnight when we were supposed to be in barracks – but nobody really cared. There was no check.

And then she posed a problem.

'Take me to your place,' she said.

My place? Tomes the Tailor had obviously given me the appearance of a young gent in possession of bachelor apartment.

'Go on, coward,' said that diabolical tempter within me. 'Have a bash. It's worth the risk.'

And so it was. She was good to look at and no more than 22 years of age, if that.

I unburdened my heart. She was lovely to look at. She was intensely desirable but the fact was that I was a soldier, a British soldier, and I lived not alone but with several others soldiers. Nevertheless, if she was willing then we could spend the night among them in what I hoped would be concupiscent privacy. Would she come along?

She agreed without demur which surprised me. She never mentioned money nor did I feel that she was 'on the job' – too clean looking for that, too well spoken in English, too much in possession of charming politeness.

She was not Russian but Polish and worked in the offices of one of the big British firms.

When we reached the hospital just before midnight there was a sentry of the Seaforth Highlanders on duty. His eyes opened wide when I ushered the girl past him, put my finger to my lips and looked appealingly at him. He smiled, nodded his head and said: 'Lucky bastard.' The first hurdle surmounted.

I took the girl up to the second floor, led her along the darkened corridor to the room of the attached details, carefully opened the door and listened. Not a sound except a snore or two. I took the girl by the hand, led her past the two rows of beds and halted by mine which was at the end of the room.

'Shhh,' I whispered. 'Don't make a noise.'

She got undressed quickly and got into the narrow bed,

31

hard and unyielding. I followed and, as we lay side by side, realised that my backside was in mid-air, about six inches of it exposed. If I wanted to avoid lumbago I'd have to mount her.

The girl was in a hurry. She pressed her soft body into mine and pulled me into a hot and passionate kiss. Still my arse jutted out. I got on top of her and the bed clanked ominously. I lay quiet for a moment and listened. Only snores. More than usual? Perhaps it was only my imagination.

'Kiss me,' she entreated. 'Kiss me.'

Her arms were clasped over my back. She was thrusting herself into me.

Hardly romantically I hissed, 'Shut up. Pipe down.'

'Kiss me,' she entreated. 'Kiss me.'

A pretty kettle of fish. There was I with a chatty nymphomaniac and a full-blown sergeant only six beds away – not to mention the corporals.

I kissed her – I had to to keep her quiet. She moaned, sought my rod and rammed it in. My lips were smack on hers. I daren't raise them. This had to be a quick job. The solid bed, not a spring anywhere, clanked like an old Tin Lizzie.

I went hammer and tongs. The girl reciprocated. Though I badly needed to come up for air I continued the marathon kiss. Finally, she jerked and then sank back contented. I let her have my load, clambered off her as carefully as I could, pushed her nearer the edge of the bed but still felt the night breeze playing over my backside. I decided to put up with the discomfort while she slept. After all I couldn't afford to go to sleep and allow daylight to expose us.

Shortly before dawn I woke her, told her that she'd have to get dressed and make herself scarce. She did not demur.

We dressed and tip-toed past the beds and into the corridor. Not a soul in sight. I took her down the stairs to the big entrance hall and held her back while I had a quick glance around. The sentry, it wouldn't be the same man, was obviously on his rounds and I got the girl to the doors.

I gave her a dollar. It was all I possessed. 'It'll pay your fare,' I said. She took it.

'Kiss me goodbye,' she said.

I shivered. This was a bloody waste of time. The blasted sentry would be back any minute and he might not be as understanding as the other Jock. You never knew with those kilted haggis-eaters. I kissed her.

Off she went, tripping gracefully on her high heels. I mounted the stairs in double-time and entered the barrack-room. Success. I was pleased with myself – too elated to go back to bed.

I had a shower, shaved, carefully hung up the grey pin-stripe and put on my uniform. I went up to the top floor and waited for breakfast to be served in the mess hall.

I was halfway through breakfast when I sensed someone behind me. Before I could turn round a rasping voice right by my ear said, 'Kiss me, you dirty bastard.'

I swivelled my head and gazed into the eyes of one of the senior 'stripers' in the barrack-room.

'You took a bloody awful risk, cocker,' he said. 'And you had half the room wanking themselves silly all night.'

He was joking. I breathed a sigh of relief. There would be no official report. I was safe.

Not so an unfortunate private of the Medics about a week later, who was found screwing a Chinese girl on the billiard table in the recreation room.

He went inside for six months – probably because he chose the table for his lecherous exercises. The table was the pride and joy of RSM Hyson whose breaks earned him considerable acclaim locally. Had the Medic chosen the old sofa or the top of the piano it's likely his sentence would have been much shorter.

Apart from the odd sexual foray life proceeded much along the same lines as any garrison town in Britain. The only difference was that we were part of an international force whose duty it was to defend the International Settlement of Shanghai.

Overall commander was Major-General A. P. D. Telfer-Smollet of the British Army. On the British side there were several battalions, among them the Seaforths, the Loyals, the Durhams, the East Surreys and supporting units. The normal British garrison was two battalions but the outbreak of war between China and Japan had led to the despatch of reinforcements from Hong Kong and Britain.

The Americans provided as regular garrison the Fourth Regiment of the United States Marine Corps, the Italians were represented by the Savoia Grenadiers and the Japanese a force of marines which they called the Japanese Naval Landing Party.

The British, the Americans, the Italians and the Japanese were the treaty powers committed to the defence of the International Settlement which had been formed by a merger of the old British and American areas of Shanghai.

The French, who set the pattern for General de Gaulle later to say 'Non' to any proposal for co-operation with the Anglo-

33

Saxons, chose to make the defence of their concession in Shanghai an entirely French affair.

In the International Settlement a reserve force in time of emergency was provided by the Shanghai Volunteer Corps (S.V.C.) which consisted of one professional battalion of young White Russians, superbly disciplined and impeccably turned out in British Army uniforms. The other companies were manned by volunteers from the civilian population. The commandant was a Briton, Colonel Hornby.

There was 'A' Company formed by Britons of pure-white descent. 'B' Company contained Eurasians. 'C' Company was the Chinese unit. There was no racial integration in the S.V.C. 'A' Company was exclusively white and it would have been impossible for a British Eurasian to have breached the strict racial barrier.

The most picturesque unit was the kilted Scottish Company complete with pipes and drums but the mounted American Troop commanded by a local lawyer, Major H. D. Rodger, ran the Scots a close second in their 'Boy Scout' hats and American-style cavalry uniforms.

Mercenary considerations – more so in Shanghai probably than anywhere else – played the chief role in assessing social standing. Affluence opened the top drawer – often to morons.

In the military world money also decreed what the role should be – caste-man or outcast. The American marines ranked, comparatively, in the millionaire class in joints which were not out of bounds to service personnel. American soldiers were still called doughboys and not G.I.s and it rankled the lesser-paid members of the international garrison, particularly the British lads, that the 'bloody Yanks' could fling the dollars about with gay abandon, grab all the 'tail' and buy a drink on a Wednesday while they were dying of thirst in barrack-room sobriety – and celibacy.

The Italians, too, had grave financial worries. Nevertheless, the Italians did have one asset – their Rudolph Valentino looks.

The Adonises among Mussolini's men appeared to be concentrated on a gunboat in the river, the *Bartolemeo Colleoni*. Compared with the homespun Geordies, or the rugged marines, they were the male chorus line of the combined services, particularly the petty officers who wore their caps at rakish angles and whose uniforms, nipped at the waist and well padded about the shoulders, looked like tailors' dummies.

While they were well favoured by the girls in such places as the

34

Majestic cabaret and its neighbour, the Little Club, which were the most popular taxi-dance ballrooms in bounds to servicemen, it was noticeable that during working hours they were scarce on the ground. Not so the American marines, who were noted for their generosity when there was a 'piece of ass' in prospect and threw around great wads of dollar bills.

It was this predilection by the girls for the bed-time favours of the Fascisti that transformed the Majestic into a disaster area.

Thursday was the marines' pay-day. They were out in full force in the Majestic in their grey-green walking-out uniforms, or in civvies, and they were spending heavily. They were also fully confident that their money, if not their looks, would buy them the rewards they desired. They were Uncle Sam's men. Their faith in the magnetism of the Almighty Dollar was supreme.

Sadly their patriotic faith was misplaced. The dollar – or its equivalent in local currency – was gladly accepted by the girls but when it came to knocking-off time at about one in the morning its purchasing power was greatly devalued by the Italians who appeared like a plague of locusts to abduct many of the taxi-dancers for romps between the sheets.

This caused international ill-will. It led one Thursday to an assault on an Italian petty officer by a marine corporal whose dancing partner spurned him by a waiting rickshaw for a dark-haired Romeo from the *Bartolomeo Colleoni*. And what irked the American was the fact that the goddammed wop hadn't spent a cent in the joint.

One blow led to another. In no time the ballroom floor of the Majestic was a seething mass of wildly flaying arms and feet and prostrate bodies as the Americans tore into the Italians, most of whom were from the Savoia Grenadiers.

It was after an Italian NCO had been flung bodily out of a window by a marine, to drop from second-storey height on to the Bubbling Well Road tramlines, that a call was sent to the Italian Grenadier barracks for reinforcements.

They came in trucks and burst in armed with clubs, knives, bayonets . . . anything handy. The gore flowed freely. The out-numbered marines, retreat cut off fought to the end. Screaming cabaret girls, dashing for the powder room, were sent flying. One poor Russian girl ended up completely out to the wide in the bass drum of the band. Others fainted dead away. Glass columns were shattered. Tables were reduced to matchwood. The floor was littered with the groaning wounded.

The carnage became even worse when the American military

police arrived and, in true New York style, began clubbing their own men to insensibility. They were joined by the Italian police who, less robustly, managed to herd off the Grenadiers and navy boys so that a fleet of ambulances could be loaded with the casualties who were, in many cases, in extremely dangerous conditions.

Poor Mr Wong, the owner of the Majestic, lost all his oriental inscrutability as he surveyed the damage, wrung his hands and estimated the colossal cost of the repairs that would have to be carried out. He let it be known that he would sue both the American and Italian governments for the havoc caused by the 'long-nosed barbarians' it was China's misfortune to have to accommodate.

One thing about the Americans in that mighty punch-up – they were certainly proof in solid bone and muscle that the United States had the highest living standards in the world and that Britain, proud owner of an empire on which the sun never set, had built its pre-eminent position on the shameless exploitation of its working-class population.

From the hovels of industrial slums there had emerged a stunted, sickly, under-fed and under-paid work force, born and bred in squalor, uneducated and in the 1930s more often than not unemployed at a time of great depression throughout the world. When the Durhams marched through Shanghai from the Dilwara to their barracks the *North-China Daily News* described them as 'stocky' men, a euphemism for 'under-sized'. Schiff, the Shanghai artist, whose black and white drawings adorned many of the city's night-spots, had produced a masterpiece which showed a pugnacious, kilted, Scottish soldier squaring up to a tall, gangling U.S. sailor. The young Scot's head was dead level with the sailor's upper chest.

There was much shamefaced heartburning in the British community when the Fourth Marines, who had been taught to play Rugby Union football by a coach from a Welsh regiment stationed in Shanghai, carried off the local championship – undefeated by any British team. They were known as the Thundering Herd because of their resemblance in action to a herd of African bull elephants on the rampage. Indeed, their eight forwards, garbed in the fashion of the American football squads we had seen on the screen, enormous padded shoulders, long knickerbocker-type shorts, each of them weighing no less than 220 lb, could have stopped, I fancy, in direct confrontation, a stampeding herd dead in its tracks.

The Italians, too, were bigger and stronger than most of their British counterparts in the international garrison. They were a touchy lot as well. I saw one Savoia Grenadier flatten a little chap from the Durhams in the Little Club after the Geordie had, most friendly-like, called him a 'funny old bastard'.

My knowledge of Italian is infinitesimal but obviously we share possession in our vocabularies of the word 'bastard' – to a British soldier merely a colloquialism for a fellow human being but to a good Catholic Italian, proud of legitimate parenthood, a deadly slur on his impeccable family antecedents.

The affliction of 'duck's disease' – possession of an arse too near the ground – among the British troops was most noticeable at the British Forces Recreational Centre in Ferry Road, where, on Thursdays, the wives and daughters of some of the city's well-heeled Britons charitably performed a slumming chore by dancing with us to gramophone records as well as feeding us on sandwiches, cakes and sweets.

Most of the girls had been born in Shanghai and had never known poverty. Thus, they towered above the short-arsed squaddies who pushed them around the floor. Still I enjoyed dancing with these females, despite the gap in social status. I won a quickstep competition with one of them and received as reward a pair of cuff-links. Usually, however, I tested their reaction to close contact with the hardness of an erection prodding them while the music played. Not one of them walked off the floor in high dudgeon. Rather I found that they all enjoyed the experience, pressed more closely against me and, in quarter-turns, landed against my pelvic region with solid bumps. Then they would go and join their groups, point me out and indicate that I was decidedly a horny individual. My ability to maintain a permanent stand got me more dances with the young ladies than any of my colleagues there.

I remember one woman, the mother of a girl there, who picked me in the ladies' 'Excuse me'. I gave her the full treatment, prodding her forcefully in close contact. At the end of the dance she looked at me, smiled and said, 'You didn't trip over, I see.' I didn't get what she meant until later; that I had in full bloom a long third leg which might have posed navigational hazards.

Though the Chinese formed the bulk of the city's population the foreigners, which included the armed services, lived in a cocoon of privilege as if they did not exist. We treated them as inferiors, worthy only of high-handed, often brutal, subjection to our territorial strength, established by force of arms in the previous century.

We insulted a courteous, hospitable people by barring them from front entrances, by insisting on their exclusion from the centre sports arena of the Racecourse, by rigidly insisting on a whites-only policy at the Shanghai Club and other social centres.

It was a common sight in the foreign areas to see drunken soldiers knocking Chinese pedestrians to the ground because they had had the temerity to be on the same pavement. Similarly, white civilians often attacked Chinese on the streets, hitting them with walking-sticks or bundling them off pavements into the road. I have seen Chinese pushed off buses by Europeans who simply wanted more standing room. I once witnessed a scene on a French tram in which an irate European forced an elderly, scholarly-looking Chinese to stand up and give him the seat he occupied. Everywhere – even in the missions – the Chinese suffered degradation at the hands of the whites.

I felt ashamed of the actions of my fellow nationals and of the other whites. Practically from the first moment of my arrival in Shanghai, when I saw a huge Sikh constable kicking an emaciated Chinese rickshaw coolie, my actions were dictated by the wish to prove to the Chinese that we were not all barbarians, over-bearing bullies, exploiters, racial bigots.

I always spoke kindly to the room servant, to the other Chinese employed in the hospital. I once gave up my seat on a bus to a young Chinese woman, who looked surprised – but not half so surprised as the seated Chinese gentlemen who obviously thought I had gone stark raving mad voluntarily to make myself so uncomfortable for the sake of a worthless female. I never shouted at, or threatened to strike, the poor rickshaw pullers who carried us at a fast, loping pace from the hospital to the Union Jack Club close to the Racecourse. During my first Christmas in Shanghai, made benevolent by booze, I even bestowed one dollar on the coolie who pulled me from Ma Jackson's Tavern to the hospital. His gratitude made the gesture well worth while though I could ill afford to lose the money.

There was one Chinese in the hospital who was always treated with a great deal of respect. He was the dhobi wallah, the washer-man, the chap who gathered up our dirty linen and returned it, spotlessly clean and immaculately pressed, a day or two later. He was also the unofficial moneylender.

The dhobi – we used the Indian army term – was good for

up to five dollars which, at least, ensured until Friday, when we were paid, the means to buy cigarettes, beer and dance-tickets at some cabaret or the other. The necessities of life in the soldier's scale of values were, in order, fags, beer and twat.

Sometimes the dhobi arrived late and the tension spread like a typhoon cloud throughout the building. Along the highly polished corridor on the second floor with jack-in-the-box regularity heads could be seen popping out of barrack-room doors. Never was a human being so eagerly sought, so warmly welcomed, so politely addressed.

Short, sturdily built, long-gowned and ever-smiling the dhobi handed out the dollars and made notes in his little black book. There were few defaulters. We needed him every week and failure to repay capital, with the few cents interest he charged, would have decreed complete ostracism by the man with the cash. RSM Hyson, too, who knew what was going on, would have had much to say in favour of the laundryman, who, no doubt, was generously inclined to those who ensured that the military hospital laundry concession did not stray into competitive hands.

I also discovered another method of increasing my income. This was by selling articles of kit to the owner of a clothing shop named Wang. Woollen articles had a high sales value in Shanghai – army-issue Long Johns, for instance, or short under-pants, heavy vests, worsted tunics, trousers and so on.

We owned a whole kit-bag-full of clothing, which back in England we would have had to produce at regular inspections. Not so in Shanghai. The officers, like us in the ranks, were too busy enjoying themselves. Though such transactions were illegal and, if discovered, were considered to be serious enough to warrant incarceration in the detention barracks, we flogged to the genial Mr Wang – and others – sundry items of clothing. In my case, over a remarkably short period of time, I found that I had an almost empty kit-bag. Gone was my best service dress – tunic and trousers, two pairs of Long Johns (which I never wore), short under-pants, vests, shirts, heavy socks and anything else that had a saleable value on the black market.

I wasn't the only disposer of Army property either. Half the Sikh watchmen, clutching their shotguns outside a variety of business offices, seemed to be wearing British Army tunics, dyed blue, it is true, but definitely traceable to some barrack-room or the other without much difficulty on the part of any shrewd investigator.

39

Thus daily I wore my second-best uniform, ink-stained and shabby. Best service dress was for the ceremonial occasion but I considered that, as a working 'shiny arse' I had said goodbye to parade-ground bullshit. I was wrong.

One morning Sergeant Unsworth, grinning broadly, informed me that I was undoubtedly 'a smart guy' because I had been selected as one of the guard of honour for the funeral of a corps non-commissioned officer. That meant best service dress, a spotless turn-out.

My problem was to obtain a complete turn-out of best service dress, which was non-existent in my kit-bag. I borrowed a cap from a chap whose head was the size of a gasometer. I stuffed it with paper and it stayed; more or less, in place. I wheedled a tunic from another lad four inches taller than I. It almost reached my knees. The trousers, from another source, were far too tight, and almost choked me. I had my own puttees and boots.

So I turned up at Ash Camp, the RASC headquarters in the western district of the city, ready to pay my last respects to the dead.

As we lined up on the parade ground the sergeant in charge of the guard of honour looked us over. He spotted me. His face changed. There was a look of hopeless bewilderment, of utter incredulity.

'Bugger me!' he exclaimed. 'It can't be true. Fred Karno in person.

'Come here, lad,' he said sternly.

'You look like a bag of shit tied up in the middle. What do you look like?'

I stood to attention and replied: 'I look like a bag of shit tied up in the middle.'

'You look like a bag of shit tied up in the middle – what?'

He was a stickler for rank.

'I look like a bag of shit tied up in the middle – sergeant.'

'That's better. Who dressed you? Buffalo Bill?'

'No, sergeant, I did.'

'Well, you're a fuckin' heap. You look like a dollop of cow-shit – only bloody worse and twice as bleedin' nasty.'

There was worse to come. We formed up in two lines ready to get our dressing. We were brought to attention and then the sergeant barked the order, 'Eyes right!'

I moved my head smartly to the right. My cap refused to obey the order. It swivelled round so that the peak covered my left ear. Over my nose there dangled a rolled up copy of the

Shanghai Evening Post and Mercury. The padding had come loose.

I thought the sergeant was going to explode. His face reddened. His eyes bulged. His mouth was wide open in astonishment. He was breathing hard. But he was speechless, which saved me a lot of abuse.

'Eyes front!' he yelled.

As we moved my cap became uncontrollable. The peak went round to the back of my head. The dangling paper covered my left eye.

He walked up to me. He looked me straight in the eyes – or, rather, my right eye.

'Fuck off,' he said. 'Get out of my bloody sight. Piss off before I have a fuckin' stroke. If I ever set eyes on you again I'll ask for my bleedin' ticket. Go on, fuck off before I start screaming.'

I left the parade ground, unloved, unwanted – but quite happy with an afternoon off in prospect.

I induced a corps driver to take me back to the hospital on his meat-delivery round to various units. After he dropped me he was due to visit infantry units manning the perimeters, barbed-wired, ringed with blockhouses and look-out towers. Although the fighting was no longer in sight from any point in the two foreign areas a relaxed state of emergency was still in force as the Japanese, flushed with their coastal victories and seemingly intent on provoking the Western powers, particularly Britain and the United States, created incident after incident intended to prove to the Chinese, whose hatred of the 'island dwarfs' was implacable, that their 'protectors', their white allies, were no longer powerful enough to challenge the might of Dai Nippon (Great Japan).

Militarily, the only force in the Pacific which could challenge Japan was that of the United States with its fleet concentrated at Pearl Harbour and with ancillary bases in the Philippines, Wake and Guam.

So Japan, condemned by the League of Nations, ran roughshod over China while the big Western powers stood fearfully by, insufficiently prepared for a test of strength, divided on strategies to be followed.

With scant regard for the supposed neutrality of the International Settlement, the Japanese flooded their defence sector in the Hongkew district with troops, warships on the river and massive armaments with which to launch attacks on the Chinese forces in Chapei, Kiangwan and other territory of the Chinese government. To all intents and purposes Hongkew, officially still part of the Settlement under the administration of the Shanghai Municipal Council, became a fully-controlled Japanese base.

The dreaded Japanese Kempetai (military police) imposed a reign of terror on the inhabitants there. The Japanese Consular Police took over street patrols in a direct challenge to the authority of the British-officered Shanghai Municipal Police. There were armed military and naval patrols on the streets and on Garden Bridge over the Soochow Creek, which was the boundary between Hongkew and the central area of the Settlement, squat Japanese army sentries stood only a few yards away from men of the Seaforth Highlanders on the crown of the bridge.

All Chinese passing over the bridge into Hongkew were forced to submit to the most humiliating and degrading forms of treatment. They had to bow deeply in obeisance to the Emperor, the Son of Heaven, whose divine person was represented by the 'soldier dwarfs'.

As the Seaforths watched from their side, helpless to interfere, Chinese men, women and children were mercilessly slapped, punched and assaulted with rifle butts because they had not shown enough respect to the men in the Emperor's uniform. Girls were 'searched' by grinning sentries, their hands running over breasts, buttocks and pubic region. From time to time, the Kempetai would drag away, screaming in fear, Chinese men who had aroused suspicion. Their destination was the infamous Bridge House, close to the river, where under the most diabolical forms of torture they would, if they survived, be forced to sign confessions admitting 'activities against His Imperial Japanese Majesty'.

There was little love lost between the allied forces and the Japanese. There had been several incidents involving the British and the Americans.

The Loyals were involved in one during a period of heavy fighting on Chinese territory divided from the Settlement by the Soochow Creek. In a large concrete godown (warehouse) a battalion of Chinese soldiers were engaged in a last stand against the Japanese. They had no hope of escape. With their backs to the creek they faced a well-armed advancing force.

The Japanese were confident that the Chinese were beaten – indeed the German-trained men holed up in the godown had been named the 'Doomed Battalion' or the 'Lone Battalion' in the

English-language and Chinese press. They had no doubt that the men's only avenue of escape – across the creek into the foreign area – would be barred by the British force there. And so as the Chinese were mercilessly battered by artillery and small-arms fire the Japanese waited for what they considered would be the inevitable result – either annihilation or surrender.

They were wrong. The heroic Chinese fought to the last round, left their dead behind and, carrying their wounded, swam across the narrow creek to the barbed-wire barricades of the Loyals, who, to the amazement and anger of the Japanese, allowed them in, disarming the men as they staggered to safety.

Then came a serious confrontation between the Japanese and the Loyals – facing each other, ready for action, across the oily, muddy water of the creek. The highest-ranking Japanese officer demanded the return of the 'Chinese bandits'. This was refused by a British officer, who pointed out that the men had surrendered to Settlement forces and would be given protection.

In the meantime, a call had been made for British reinforcements, which arrived at the perimeter posts in trucks. The vehicles were used to take the Chinese soldiers to Kiaichow Park, which had been selected by the Shanghai Municipal Council as a temporary internee camp, and British Army ambulances took the wounded to hospital.

News of the escape spread like wildfire in the Settlement and thousands of cheering Chinese turned out to give the men a rousing welcome.

At the scene of the escape, tension mounted as the Japanese carried out a series of movements which seemed to indicate an imminent assault on the Loyals and their reinforcements, grimly manning their blockhouses and hastily-dug trenches.

But the determination of the Shanghai Municipal Council not to hand over the Chinese soldiers and to intern them 'for the duration' was made known to the Japanese, and after instructions from their High Command, they lodged a firm protest but took no further action.

Another serious incident involved the American marines. A party of armed Japanese, chasing several Chinese, saw their quarry run to safety behind the American perimeter barricades.

The Japanese followed and stormed into the marines' sector where they were immediately set upon by burly Leathernecks, twice their size and raring for a fight in true Marine Corps tradition.

The marines' commanding officer, Colonel 'Sam' Price,

furious over the invasion of his territory, arrived on the scene. His actions were not diplomatic. Seizing the NCO in charge of the Japanese by the scruff of the neck, he frog-marched him to the barbed wire, thrust him unceremoniously into his own area and told him to stay there in future.

The remainder of the Japanese were similarly dealt with and, in order to stave off any Tokyo-inspired protest, a sharply worded account of the violation of 'neutral' territory was sent to the Japanese High Command with a request that the men responsible should be punished and that no further actions of that kind should be allowed. It worked. The Japanese let the matter drop, no doubt confident that, sooner or later, they would be able to deal in their own way with the foreign areas in China.

The first sign of foreign weakness came when the Japanese demanded – and were given permission – to stage a 'victory' parade of their armed forces via some Settlement roads. All leave for the Western troops was cancelled, the police were placed on a full alert and the Shanghai Volunteer Corps was ordered to be ready for mobilisation.

It was feared that anti-Japanese elements among the Chinese population would create 'an incident'. They did.

As the Japanese marched down Nanking Road, the Settlement main thoroughfare, a bomb was thrown, injuring several of the Japanese and a number of spectators.

The Japanese acted quickly. They sealed off the area with armed guards and stopped a street patrol of the Seaforth Highlanders, whose defence sector it was, from entering. Japanese soldiers were everywhere, even surrounding the British Military Hospital where I was quartered. British troops were not allowed to move. The situation looked serious.

On Nanking Road the Seaforths, under a junior officer, were surrounded by Japanese. Members of the Kempetai moved among the crowd and arrested several Chinese who were taken away in army trucks. All protests were rejected and, for several hours, the Japanese assumed control of a large section of the International Settlement.

Finally the Japanese moved out, taking with them many innocent Chinese whose fate, no one doubted, would be execution after weeks of torture in the Bridge House. The Seaforth patrol moved again and we in the hospital were allowed to circulate in the streets. The Chinese population assumed, quite rightly, that we had lost 'too much face'.

In August 1937 the Japanese decided to prove to the world

that it was the strongest power in the Far East and that Britain and the United States were mere 'paper tigers' unable and unwilling to retain their former pre-eminent positions in China, no longer reliable as allies, certainly without the teeth to emerge as protectors.

A deliberate aerial attack was made on the car of the British Ambassador, Sir Hugh Knatchbull-Hugessen, near Nanking. The car was clearly marked with Union Jacks and it was obvious that no mistake had been made. The vehicle had been shadowed by the planes and they knew that the Ambassador was in it. The usual apologies followed but they were empty and worthless.

Sir Hugh was hit by machine-gun bullets and narrowly escaped death. He had to return to England and it was more than a year before he was again fit for service.

Despite protest notes Japanese attacks on British and American citizens and property in China were frequently made and relations with Britain and America steadily worsened.

On August 13th, incidentally my birthday, two small Chinese planes appeared over Shanghai, flying high to avoid the barrage of anti-aircraft fire unleashed by the Japanese in Hongkew.

The target of the planes appeared to be the ancient Japanese cruiser, *Idzumo*, permanently anchored close to Garden Bridge, a former Imperial Russian warship captured during the Russo-Japanese war of 1905. This was the headquarters of the Japanese Navy in Shanghai, impotent as a fighting unit but useful as a monument to commemorate the country's victory over a Western power.

The Chinese planes manoeuvred over the *Idzumo* but at such a height that accurate bombing was out of the question. Then the bombs dropped to transform two areas of the International Settlement into flaming holocausts in which more than 1,000 people died.

The first bomb landed in Nanking Road between the Cathay and Palace Hotels. It created havoc. Hundreds of pedestrians of many nationalities simply disappeared in a whirling mass of dismembered bodies. Trams were set on fire. Motorists were burned to cinders in their blazing vehicles. The few who survived had not long to live.

There was even greater devastation on Avenue Edward Seventh, where the second bomb dropped. This was the Chinese theatre district, an area of street stalls, of pavement sideshows, always thronged with sightseers. The carnage was appalling.

It was the last attack launched by the Chinese in the Shanghai

45

area – an appalling débâcle that clearly proved to the world that China's material resources were not only scarce but that in quality they precluded any worthwhile offensive action against the well-armed Japanese.

I read of the death of Pembroke Stephens of the *Daily Telegraph*, London, who had been among the army of foreign correspondents covering the fighting from Settlement bases. Stephens was killed by a stray bullet while watching the hostilities from the top of a gasometer.

The big names in journalism were there: the American globe-traveller, Knickerbocker; Victor Keen of the *New York Herald-Tribune;* Hallet Abend of the *New York Times;* Sweetland of the *Chicago Tribune* and many more. I longed to be free of what I considered to be the degradation of army life – to be enabled once more to carry my notebook around and to record under my byline the stories of the day.

I thought about it for many days and a plan of action took shape. The first step was to write a graphic account of events in Shanghai for the *Rugby Advertiser* – the Rugby boy in the thick of it. I did just that and posted it off.

A cutting came back some weeks later from Jack Hudson who reminded me that although he still regarded me as 'Public Enemy Number One' he was willing to let bygones by bygones. Even Tommy Manock, the editor, sent his regards. I was touched.

One Wednesday I had the afternoon off from the office and, carrying the cutting with me, walked down to the Bund and to the imposing entrance of the North-China Daily News and Herald Ltd, a six-storey building of large dimensions with four towers at each corner of its flat roof to give it the appearance of a castle.

The editorial department was on the fifth floor, at the end of a long corridor of offices let out to various Shanghai companies. Behind a long counter at the entrance to the editorial department was an elderly Chinese gentleman in silk tunic and trousers, tied round the ankle with satin ribbon.

This gentleman, as I was later to discover, was 'Jim', the number-one boy, the king-pin of the large Chinese staff of messengers, copy-boys, coolies and cleaners in the editorial office. Who gave him the name Jim I do not know. But Jim he was to all of the staff, even the Chinese. I didn't know it then but he owned a terrace of houses in Hongkew. I discovered later where his wealth came from.

He asked me what I wanted. I said I desired to see the editor. He produced a pad on which I wrote: 'Ralph Shaw, former

Rugby Advertiser journalist, Rugby, Warwicks, now in Shanghai.'

Jim told me to follow him. He showed me into a spacious office. Behind a huge wooden desk, smoking a cigarette, was a man with an enormous pair of shoulders.

He handed me his card on which was written: 'R. T. Peyton-Griffin, Editor, *North-China Daily News* and *North China Herald*, 17 The Bund, Shanghai.'

He handed me a Ruby Queen cigarette from a large box on the desk. I noticed that he smoked his cigarettes only halfway down and then stubbed them to light others. This, I thought, was extravagance that would not be seen in any army unit anywhere in the world.

I came to the point. I was looking for a job as reporter. I handed him the cutting, which was well written in the descriptive, lengthy style of that day and age. It described me as a 'a former *Advertiser* reporter' and an ex-schoolboy in the town.

I could see that he was impressed. I told him that I wrote good shorthand and had been through the mill in Rugby – proof-reading, the printing side and general editorial duties, including sports reporting.

It was after I handed him a reference on *Rugby Advertiser* notepaper signed by a former editor, who had died before Manock took over, that he spoke. I didn't tell him that the reference, which extolled my virtues, had been written by me in Rugby and that I had forged the signature of the late editor.

He said that trained British journalists were hard to come by and that we might talk terms. I gave him the crunch line: I was a British soldier but that, on payment of £35, I could be his forever. I had looked up King's Regulations and, by my calculations, £35 was enough to purchase my discharge with no strings attached. I would be as a free as a bird – no reserve period to serve, out for good. I suggested that the firm could find the money and that it could be deducted from my salary in instalments.

My heart soared when he told me that I had impressed him, that probably I could be taken on and that he'd contact me again when he had had a talk with the 'management people'. I gave him the phone number of the general staff office. When I left the office I was walking on air – the end in sight of two bloody awful years of sheer purgatory.

Soon enough came the call to see him again. I had been accepted and would I set in motion the machinery to secure my discharge without delay and inform him what the paper was supposed to do.

Nobody in the barrack-room believed me when I told them

what had happened but Major Gwynne had a lot to say when I put in a formal application for my discharge under King's Regulations. For one thing, he said, it would cost me £65 and not £35. I had been trained as a clerk. That extra schooling in Aldershot had increased my value to the army.

I was absolutely dismayed but cheered up when Staff-Sergeant Carver told me that Gwynne was wrong. I was only worth £35 in view of the shortness of my service. With due respect I informed Major Gwynne that he was incorrect in his assumption that it would cost me £65. This produced an irate, Irish response and I was duly cowed but still determined, one way or the other, to get my blasted ticket and give the army a soldier's fond farewell.

The old shit-or-bust spirit came to the fore. I typed out a three-page letter on office foolscap to Major-General Telfer-Smollet. In it I told him what I thought of the army, that I'd never make a soldier as long as I lived, that Gwynne was being un-co-operative, that my record showed I was not good military material and that, after all, I had been trained as a journalist in the first place. All that and a lot more.

I took the precaution of sending the letter by the Chinese Post Office, which was extremely efficient, and not the Army Post Office. The envelope was marked with the general's home address and on the back of the envelope I made it known that the sender was: 'Private Shaw, General Staff (i) Office, Municipal Council Building, Shanghai.'

The following day a sergeant of the corps informed me that I was under close arrest and that my presence at Ash Camp was required forthwith. Bang went my hopes. I had visions of another spell in the detention barracks and I was not cheered by the fact that I had seen one of the Aldershot MPSC men, who knew me well, in the city. He was no friend of mine.

I appeared before the RASC commanding officer, who told me that I was on two charges: conduct prejudicial to good order and military discipline in that I, a mere private, had written a personal letter to the general officer commanding and that, worse still, I had revealed on the back of my envelope to all and sundry that where I worked was an intelligence office. How was I supposed to know that the 'i' part of the address was only to be exposed to official British contacts?

I gave up the ghost. That was it. To use an army term I'd had it – in the shit up to my ears. There was no escape.

Miraculously there was. Nothing happened. Some good fairy somewhere came to my rescue. Perhaps the army, looking over my record, came to the conclusion that they'd be a damned sight better off without me or it might have been that the *North-China Daily News* had had much to say on my value to them, a British newspaper flying the flag in difficult times. I was given my discharge. Total cost was £35. The paper agreed to pay the sum and to repatriate me on termination of appointment. I was a journalist again and could well afford to give the old two-finger salute to my MPSC friend when I saw him again.

I celebrated the red-letter occasion with a meal in Jimmy's Kitchen – hamburger, fried egg, French fries, peas and lashings of Jimmy's wonderful, tangy hamburger sauce. Alas no Nadya in the Handy Bar to rouse me with a leg show. In fact there was no Handy Bar any more.

Where Nadya had been and where she wasn't when I had gone to charm her on my first weekend in Shanghai, neat as a new pin in my double-breasted glory, was an annexe to Jimmy's main restaurant on Nanking Road. He had evidently decided that more money was to be made by dispensing food than by selling alcoholic beverages to one of the lowest-paid sections of the city's cosmopolitan community, the British Army.

I never did meet Nadya. I had no doubt that she had avoided me when I went in search of her, horny as a rhino. Perhaps she – like many other women – knew that the military hospital had more than its share of VD cases and that I might be a carrier. Silly girl. All I required was a manual service in some cinema or the other as I stroked those gorgeous gams. No danger in that I'm sure. Never mind, she wasn't the only beauty available in Shanghai.

Fourth Estate

The goal of every provincial journalist in my day was Fleet Street. Today I'm not so certain considering the precariousness of employment on a British national newspaper. The International Settlement was, in every respect, a transplanted Fleet Street – the centre of China's vast newspaper-publishing industry, the home of newspapers published in many languages, the Mecca of adventurous journalists from all over the world, the scene of a never-ending succession of turbulent events tailored immediately for front-page headlines . . .

There was a full-scale war on Shanghai's doorstep; death, doom and disaster were omnipresent; human suffering on a vast scale was visible in the city and far beyond; murder, brutality and cold-hearted inhumanity were part of the everyday scene; gangsterism, piracies, prostitution, opium-smoking – these and many more ingredients of that violent era provided for us, the journalists of Shanghai, the excitement and the danger that no Fleet Street man ever experienced within the parish of St Bride's.

The most influential newspaper in China – indeed over a large area of the Far East, including Hong Kong – was the *North-China Daily News*. Peyton-Griffin insisted on the hyphen in the title. This morning newspaper had grown from the old weekly *North-China Herald*, which was still published as the weekly edition of the daily paper, and its circulation – though small compared with the British nationals – was proof of its far-reaching influence not only in China but in London, Washington, Paris, Tokyo and other centres of government at a time of explosive delicacy in international relations.

The paper – and its many publishing enterprises – was owned by the Morriss family, British Catholics of Jewish descent. There were three brothers, Henry (Harry), Gordon and Hailey. The eldest, Harry, had his office on the second floor of the newspaper building and he was in supreme control of the company. Gordon, whose stockbroking firm, Lester, Johnson and Morriss, was situated in the Japanese bank building next door, also took a keen directorial interest in the newspaper. Hailey, alas, remained in England where he had blotted the family copy-book by a long series of sexual escapades that had taken him to court, to prison and to prominence in the *News of the World*.

Harry, a millionaire, was also a racing enthusiast. Steve Donoghue, whose fame will be everlasting, rode for him in Britain. One of his English stable, Manna, won the Epsom Derby in 1925. In Shanghai he and Sir Victor Sassoon vied for honours every week on the splendid Racecourse track.

He had a large mansion in Avenue du Roi Albert, where he kept a flock of servants and a small army of gardeners. He collected rare and expensive violins and 'commuted' often between China and Britain, where he also maintained a large and costly establishment.

Gordon, tall and rangy, lived happily with wife and family in Shanghai, which Harry did not. He was a frequent visitor in the editorial office where his Shanghai Club drinking pals, Percy Finch and Dickson Hoste, could always be found.

While Peyton-Griffin wielded considerable political influence as editor of the paper the greatest power in the company rested in the general manager, R. W. Davis, afflicted on one side of his face by a disfiguring lumpy growth which gave him a diabolical appearance, frightening to the lesser-paid juniors who held him in perpetual awe.

Under him were such men as Davey of the Hong List, a profitable directory of China business firms; Haslam, the blunt Lancashire-born newspaper printing manager; Woodhead, a Yorkshireman on the advertisement side; Mockett, a Londoner, also on the business staff, and several more expatriates.

In the editorial department, Percy Finch, from Sheffield, occupied as city editor the number-two position. He was a tall, dark-haired man of about 40 then, moustached and smartly dressed, a good newspaperman whose job, which he did well, was to cover with reporters and photographers the Shanghai scene.

The night editor was Dickson Hoste, the son of a missionary who had given up a commission in the British Army to preach the gospel to the Chinese. Dickson was born in China and married the daughter of a missionary. Educated at a British public school and at Cambridge he had served as an officer in the Royal Artillery during World War One, mostly in Mesopotamia.

There was little of the missionary in him. Dickson could 'put it

51

back' with the best of them. Often he appeared speechless after a bout at the Shanghai Club, which boasted the longest bar in the world, but this in a community of heavy drinkers brought no stigma. He did his job well and though his wife and family rarely saw him sober he was a likeable, gentlemanly chap, aristocratic in appearance, definitely from the top drawer.

While Hoste had never been active in the missionary field, the entertainment-page editor, Calvin S. Hirsh, had arrived in China as a converter of heathen souls. Somewhere along the line the lure of the high life of Shanghai had eroded good intentions and Calvin had slipped badly.

Star of the office was 'Sapajou', the cartoonist. He was a White Russian ex-officer named Sapojnikoff, a brilliant artist with a wonderful sense of humour. Tall, thin, bespectacled he limped badly as the result of a wound received in an engagement with the Bolsheviks during the Russian Revolution. In Shanghai he had quickly earned fame through his brilliant political cartoons and, for a stateless exile, his membership of the Shanghai Club classified him as a rare specimen.

In charge of the *North-China Herald* was 'Dooley' Dunne, a bearded Irishman, middle-aged and affable. He was a former Shanghai jockey and he had a fund of dirty jokes, most of which he had picked up from the bar of the Shanghai Race Club where he lived. He was a widower but he showed enough interest in sex. He collected boxes of Japanese aids to sexual pleasure which included various gadgets to fit the male penis. These were intended to rouse the female to speedy climactic joy thus saving the penetrating male much muscular effort. I don't think he ever used them on a woman. Any man who had lived in Shanghai as long as Dooley had usually exhausted all his steam by the age of forty.

The sports editor was Randolph Raven, lean and tall, a graduate of Stanford University in California. His father had been President of the American-Oriental Bank which had collapsed, a disaster which had led to criminal proceedings being taken in the American court against Raven senior, who was jailed.

The cables man was Charlie Bruce, German-born but adopted by a British family in Shanghai. His job was to handle all the international news which, in those days, came into the office from the news agencies by hand after being received by radio and typed out on stencil sheets. Oriental news from the agencies went to Hoste. The remainder stayed with Bruce – copy from Reuter, the

Associated Press, United Press, the International News Service, the French Havas organisation, the German Transocean service, Tass, the Italian news service Stefani, and several more.

We had rivals the chief of which was the *Shanghai Times*, owned by a Briton, Nottingham, who was supported by Japanese money.

There was one large-circulation evening newspaper, the *Shanghai Evening Post and Mercury*, a copy of which had proved to be inadequate as cap-padding towards the end of my inglorious Army career. Its editor-publisher was Randall Gould, outspokenly anti-Japanese.

Fearless, also, were two other Americans, J. B. Powell, editor and publisher of the *China Weekly Review*, and broadcaster Carroll Alcott.

Powell was anti-Japanese and pro-Chinese. Week after week, he printed eye-witness accounts of Japanese atrocities against the Chinese, of the mass murder of Chiang Kai-shek's soldiers.

Alas, Powell, the brave American, later tasted the savagery of the Japanese, who settled old scores with inhuman brutality.

Luckier was Alcott, who had left the *China Press* to become a news broadcaster and commentator over the American-owned radio station, XMHA.

Publishing in English as I found out on the *North-China Daily News* had its hazards. The printing staff were almost entirely Chinese. Thus the linotype operators followed the copy letter by letter as did the men setting up the headlines. They did not speak or write English and it was amazing to me that they attained such a remarkable degree of accuracy.

Nevertheless mistakes did occur. There was the time when Harry Morriss entered his horse, The Knut, for the big Autumn Champions Sweepstake race. It was highly fancied. It won, to the great joy of the proprietor, who looked forward to seeing the feat commemorated by a nice banner headline across the sports page. He got one:

'THE KUNT WINS AUTUMN CHAMPIONS'

The sports page seemed to be particularly vulnerable to howling blunders by the printing staff.

There was the report of a football match part of which read: 'Then Loh, the Lido outside-left, dropped a great shit right in the goalmouth. . . . '

We also had examples of what Peyton-Griffin called pisspotical prose written by various staff members whose knowledge of English left much to be desired.

We took on a young American globe-trotter who assured us that he had worked on a newspaper in Massachusetts. Finch sent hime to cover a wedding at Holy Trinity Cathedral conducted by the incumbent, Dean Trivett.

One sentence in his report sent Peyt charging into Percy's office as if a red-hot poker had been jammed up his arse.

The sentence read: 'After the ceremony the happy couple signed the register in the vestry and applauded by 150 guests consummated the marriage on the lawn.'

Peyt summoned the American into his presence. He asked him if any pictures had been taken of the impatient bridegroom screwing his wife on the lawn – in the presence of the Dean and the guests.

The reporter hastily assured Peyt that nothing of that kind had occurred. The bridegroom had merely kissed the bride.

Well, why had he in his report declared that intercourse had occurred – on the lawn which was probably damp and damned uncomfortable.

What did 'consummation' mean?

It meant the act of kissing.

The reporter's services were quickly terminated and he went on his way to the Philippines where, we heard later, he amassed a sizeable fortune in the cigar and cheroot business.

We were a happy crew although the political situation gave us little to smile about. Japan was on the rampage and though we did not realise it at the time the end of our long era of privileged existence in China was not far distant.

The two foreign areas of Shanghai had become vast refugee camps as thousands of Chinese from the hinterland fled from the scene of hostilities where the Japanese were committing diabolical atrocities against Chinese troops and the civilian population.

A French Roman Catholic priest, Father Jacquinot, had established a camp at Siccawei, on the French Concession perimeter, where thousands of fear-ridden Chinese were accommodated in temporary huts. At least they were safe there though they existed on starvation rations and lived in absolute squalor.

In the Settlement a large, dilapidated cinema, which was to be re-opened later after de-bugging and renovations as the Roxy, accommodated about 500 refugees, mostly women and children. Food was delivered to them in trucks by various charitable societies but their plight, particularly that of the children, was pitiable.

There were beggars everywhere – the professionals and the refugees who, without money, would soon be at death's door. In winter, when ice and snow covered the central China region, the death carts did their rounds, picking up the frozen bodies from the pavements.

Daily I passed the bodies, frozen stiff in their rags. I tried not to look at the corpses but when I had to step over dead babies, many of them thrown away in utter desperation by starving parents, a great surge of anger swept over me.

Japanese barbarity reached its peak in December 1937, when the troops of General Matsui in six weeks of bestial savagery accomplished what has become known as 'The Rape of Nanking'. More than 200,000 Chinese civilians and prisoners of war were slaughtered.

After entering the city on December 12th the Japanese troops were let loose to ravish and murder.

Even women of 80 years and more were not spared. They were raped many times and then killed by the sword or by bayonet thrusts.

No less than 20,000 cases of rape were known to have been committed. The exact total is probably much higher. The soldiers looted and like sadistic beasts continued their orgy of killing everywhere. Not satisfied with the results of their savagery they set fire to houses, shops and offices. At least one third of the city was gutted by fire.

I visited the country districts around Shanghai that had been the scene of fierce fighting.

All the farmhouses had been burned down by the advancing Japanese. I listened to stories of Japanese atrocities: the arrest of Chinese civilians who, after abominable torture, were tied to trees and bayoneted to death; the raping of all the women in one village and the wholesale slaughter of the male inhabitants; how the countryside had been littered with the bodies of farmers and their families, killed in cold blood with their hands tied behind their backs – everywhere a trail of blood and devastation.

Looting and murder occurred everywhere on the line of march. In the city of Soochow, famed for its waterways and beautiful girls, many inhabitants were lined up against walls by the Japanese troops and shot.

The Japanese steadfastly refused to admit that they were making war on China. The hostilities were merely an 'incident'. Therefore any Chinese soldiers taken prisoner were denied any rights under the Geneva Convention. Most of them were shot. Others were made to dig pits, their hands were tied behind their backs and they were bayoneted to death as hundreds of grinning warriors of the Emperor, standing on the rim of the pits, watched the inhuman slaughter. Chinese men, both soldiers and civilians, were buried alive. Others were deliberately blinded. The Chinese, said the Japanese propaganda machine, were 'bandits' who were defying Japan's 'righteous role' to establish the 'Imperial Way' in the land. They were being taught to see the error of their ways.

General Matsui was later recalled from China by the Tokyo government after the outcry against the Nanking horror but he was decorated for his services in China. After the war he was sentenced to death for war crimes.

In the two foreign areas we lived in selfish exclusiveness while an entire nation was being ravaged. The cinemas were crowded. The bars did a roaring trade. Taxi-dancers plied for hire in the cabarets. The brothels, here, there and everywhere, served the males of many countries. The restaurants offered expensive repasts. Everywhere there was luxury.

At a salary of 360 Chinese dollars a month I lived like a lord. A self-contained apartment cost me 60 dollars a month, food no more than 20 dollars, a young and shapely amah only 15 dollars and incidentals, perhaps, another ten. I was in the money. As usual it burned a hole in my pocket. But I had learned my lesson. There would be no repeat of the Rugby débâcle. The job would come first and that having been done then I could hit the high spots. I steadfastly followed this precept all the time I was in China. It paid dividends.

I was appointed court reporter. This was an important assignment as the *North-China Herald* was the offical court record. Previously there had been much dissatisfaction by H.M. Supreme Court in China of the work of the reporters sent to cover cases. Mistakes had been plentiful and a lack of knowledge of court procedures had, in some cases, resulted in ludicrous coverage.

The Chief Justice of H.M. Supreme Court in China was a South African, Sir Alan Mossop, stocky, soft-spoken and phlegmatic, scarlet-robed and bewigged in true Law Courts tradition, a firm upholder of the dignity of the law.

The fun and games were provided by his assistant, Judge Penrhyn Grant-Jones, a fiery little Welshman, who could always be relied on to bring light entertainment into the courtroom, which was situated in the extensive grounds of the British Consulate-General on the Bund.

He was not an ardent supporter of the press – at least the newspaper fraternity in Shanghai, who had misquoted him badly on many occasions. Nor did he ever believe that a Sikh could tell the truth – and the Sikhs in Shanghai occupied much of his time in court.

The Sikhs had a large community in Shanghai. Most of them were in the police. Others were watchmen. They were British subjects because India was part of the Empire. The ex-soldiers amongst them had been recruited for police service, on traffic duties, in the riot squad or the mounted section, and on retirement from the force they found their services in demand as bank guards, security men on the wharves, at the city's warehouses and the big business hongs or as commissionaires at hotels, restaurants and night-clubs.

The Sikhs loved money. They lent it but at such exorbitant rates of interest that their debtors, who were plentiful, were likely to remain insolvent for the remainder of their natural lives. Every other Sikh had a sideline – moneylending. This produced many appearances in court as plaintiffs against Empire citizens who had defaulted on promissory notes.

Judge Grant-Jones administered the law in conformity with the strict principles of British justice. Nevertheless he never missed an opportunity to express astonishment – and stern condemnation – of some rates of interest levied by the Sikhs or to question their veracity under oath.

On one occasion a big, bearded Sikh moneylender was addressed by the judge:

'The extent of your extortion has only been equalled by the amount of the fabrications you have given in evidence. One day I will meet a member of your community who will tell me the truth, the whole truth and nothing but the truth, an occasion which I shall celebrate as the miraculous attainment of the impossible.'

Then the judge would look over to me – he knew me as a shorthand writer – just to make sure that I'd got down what he wanted to be printed. A slight nod from me and he would continue the hearing.

There was the Sikh on a charge of indecency. A British woman had given evidence that while watching the races she had felt a hard object pressing into her bottom. On turning round she had seen the Sikh. There was no doubt that what she had felt was his penis.

57

The Sikh hotly denied the lady's story. What she had felt, he said on oath, was a bottle of beer he kept in his trousers pocket.

'Pint or half-pint?' asked the judge.

'Half-pint.'

'No hyperbole there – modest,' commented the judge, sober-faced.

A Chinese witness told the court that he had seen the Sikh with his hand in his pocket definitely prodding the lady's bottom.

The Sikh said that he had been about to withdraw the bottle to take a swig from it. Accidentally the bottle may have touched the lady's person. It was no more than that.

The judge was no fool. He knew his Sikhs and their sexual reputations. Had it not been a fellow judge once who, when asked to give a definition of a virgin in India, had replied, 'A goat that can run faster than a Sikh'?

He said that he did not believe the defendant's tale. Indecency there had been and a large fine was imposed.

I was in court once when two Chinese men in blue overalls carrying a ladder pushed their way through the swing doors. They stood at the back of the court and bowed low to Judge Grant-Jones. Always a stickler for politeness he bowed back.

Then they padded past the benches to stop underneath the court clock – a product of English craftsmanship that was the pride and joy of the court staff, who were inveterate clock-watchers, particularly when they were dying for a smoke or a cup of tea.

The two workmen, for that is what they appeared to be, placed their ladder against the wall. One of them mounted it and care-fully unscrewed the clock which he handed to his mate. He de-scended the ladder and carrying ladder and clock in their arms, the two Chinese walked toward the door. There they stood facing the judge. They bowed low. He bowed in return. They left the court with the clock. It was never seen again. For a barefaced act of skulduggery it had no equal – a clock pinched right under the eyes of a stern British judge, who had sent many to jail for lesser crimes.

Judge Grant-Jones took it in good part. He was heard to remark that if he ever set eyes on the two lads again then he would tell them the time in no uncertain terms – and it wouldn't be in seconds, minutes or hours but years.

In the office I met the Chinese foreman printer, who was known to all and sundry as 'Bollocky Bill' because of the immense size of his testicles. No amount of clothing could disguise the gargantuan proportions of his balls. They were the size of footballs. The poor chap – though he was an ever-smiling, jolly worker – suffered from elephantiasis, enormously enlarged testicles. They thrust themselves into rounded, bouncing magnitude every time he appeared on the editorial floor. The girls in the building, particularly, could never take their eyes off his genital region.

Finch said he reminded him of the chap from St Paul's who used to do turns in the halls. His favourite trick, so the limerick had it, was to stand on his prick and roll off the stage on his balls!

Fairly frequent trips to the printing floor were made by the girls from the business department every day – just for a glimpse of a pair of balls they were never likely to encounter in bed.

We also had a buxom girl proof-reader of mixed American-Russian parentage who came on duty at nights.

I saw her one evening diligently reading copy to a young Eurasian chap who sat opposite to her at a small table. He seemed to be in turmoil. Was the story one of those heart-tugging tales from the human-interest lobby or a crime report of such violent proportions that he had been overcome?

Overcome he had been. In fact he had come all over. I saw the girl, left hand under the table, jerking him off as she read the copy for him to correct the galley proof. No wonder we had our quota of printed howlers.

Once a week I went on duty as night reporter ready to cover any story that broke during Dickson Hoste's session.

The duty entailed a visit to the Central Police Station at midnight to find out if there had been any crime worthy of recording. In the courtyard of the police station was a notice board on which the armed robberies of the day were listed. There were never less than sixty.

We left them alone. They were so commonplace that we could have filled the entire paper with them. There was little variety in the teleprinter reports received at the police station and stuck on the press board:

'Three men speaking Kompo dialect, all armed with Mausers, entered No. 5 Chiaotung Lane, Sinza district, at 7.30 p.m. today, held up the occupants at gunpoint and escaped with money and valuables worth 500 dollars.'

Strange it was that the Kompo area seemed to provide Shanghai with its rogues, its bad men. Every armed robber, it seemed, spoke Kompo dialect just as the best cooks conversed in Cantonese or the sailors in Ningpo dialect.

Mauser automatics were everywhere – loot from the battle-fields. The gangsters had a field day after the Chinese army retreated inland. Lawlessness, never scarce, increased a hundred-fold. The overworked police had their hands full.

So had the station officers at times. 'Paddy' Self, a British sub-inspector, was on duty behind the counter one night when I called in.

He informed me that there was nothing doing except that a newcomer, a probationary sergeant named Williams from Welsh Wales, had got himself 'well and truly pissed up in French Town' and was being delivered to his quarters in the station by the French police. Mr Williams, Self told me, had once been sparring partner to the British heavyweight champion, Tommy Farr, who had gone the distance with the mighty Joe Louis in New York.

Probationary-Sergeant Williams was delivered in a sidecar of one of the French police motor-bikes. He was dumped at the bottom of the stairs leading up to the charge-room and it appeared that several Chinese constables would be required to heave his well-padded, six-foot frame into his bed.

Before Self could summon a couple of big Shantung men to lug the Welshman up the stairs and along the corridor leading to the foreign officers' bachelor quarters the ex-boxer recovered consciousness, staggered to his feet and lurched his way up the steps and into the charge-room where he stood by the wooden notice board. He was a powerful specimen, muscular and lithe. Even in his drunkenness the way he moved indicated that, sober, he would be a match for any man.

Suddenly he went stark-raving mad. Uttering a wild cry he adopted a boxing stance and rammed his right hand into the notice board – and again. The noise of the impacts was ear-shattering, but Williams, who could have broken his knuckles, seemed oblivious of any pain. He spotted one of the Chinese constables and advanced menacingly, fists ready to lash out. The Chinese moved behind the counter where Self, quite unper-turbed, said to me – I was well behind the counter – 'Ah well, I suppose I'll have to deal with the daft bugger.'

He drew his truncheon, and advanced from the counter to face Williams in the centre of the room. The Welshman lunged at him. Self brought the truncheon down on his shoulder. No effect. As his fists were rammed forward Self side-stepped smartly and let him have the full weight of another truncheon-blow on the same shoulder. Williams was knocked clean off his heels, falling heavily on the floor.

Self leaped on him, called for the Chinese constables to help him and flashed out his handcuffs. As the two Chinese held the raving Williams down he clasped on the handcuffs and closed them quickly. In less than 30 seconds the Welshman was behind the bars.

A few days later Williams was on his way home – an inglorious end to a remarkably short career in the Shanghai Municipal Police.

Self was to find himself in an even tougher situation on December 8th, 1941 – but that eventful day was still a long way off.

It was a sad reflection on international harmony in Shanghai that the defenders of foreign privilege displayed a lamentable dearth of goodwill to one another when they were off duty.

The Seaforths – short-arsed though most of them were – were a fearsome crew when they were on the rampage. The Glasgow mobs of that time were renowned for their razor-slashing attacks – razor blades being inserted in cap peaks or in the brims of trilby hats which were used as weapons in gang fights. The Seaforths used their belts which contained heavy brass buckles and these could split open a man's face.

I reported one clash between the Seaforths and the American marines in the Del Conte bar in Bubbling Well Road in which victory went to the belt-wielding Scotsmen. This was a mode of attack to which the Leathernecks could not reply as they were not equipped with belts that could be used as weaponry. The Seaforths simply swept down the bar of the Del Conte and, in skittle fashion, laid recumbent at least ten Americans.

The Italians, too, could be bad tempered, particularly when they lost a match in the local football league. The Seaforths trounced them on the Racecourse and the Italian spectators, most of them from the Savoia Grenadiers, decided that the time had come to express militant opposition to the referee. They attacked him *en masse*

The Seaforths present came to his rescue, sent word back to the stands, which were being used as barracks, that reinforcements would be appreciated and these appeared wielding belts, hockey sticks, cricket bats, anything likely to be lethal. In no time at all there was a first-class riot.

The French showed similar belligerency from time to time, particularly in the 'Blood Alley' dives which regularly were placed out of bounds.

The French police, however, handled troublesome situations

with a fearsome efficiency that the more lenient Settlement force did not employ. At the first sign of violence a call would be made to the police headquarters in Avenue Joffre and, within minutes, with sirens screaming down would come a truckload of steel-helmeted riot squad men, all young Russians. Wielding truncheons with remarkable accuracy they would proceed to carpet the floor with a covering of prostrate bodies placed there on the premise that anybody standing on his feet had no right to be in that position.

It was not that the Settlement police riot squad was softer. Just as the British 'Bobby' today is supposed to demonstrate the democratic, gentler approach to mass violence than, say, the Parisian police riot squads, so the British-controlled and officered Sikhs, Chinese and Russians, who were on call to deal with the mobs, were never used unless it was imperative to do so.

When they did go into action then the lathi-wielding Sikhs, the clubbing Chinese and the well-armed Russians were as ruthlessly efficient as their French counterparts.

I was engaged in one 'action' with the riot squad. I was doing the night call at Central Station when the alarm bell rang. In poured about 20 Chinese policemen who rushed to cupboards in the charge room, hauled out bullet-proof jackets, donned them and, pulling out their revolvers from belt holsters, speedily loaded them and dashed downstairs to board the emergency vans.

I went down with them and sat with the British officer in command in front of one of the two vans being sent to an armed robbery.

A large gang, all armed with Mausers, had entered a large commercial and residential building. There they were holding up the residents and grabbing large amounts of loot. But before they could escape the alarm was given and by the time we arrived they were firing at other police from behind the low walls enclosing the flat roof.

I dashed for cover with bullets whining down from the roof to splatter or to richochet from the road or the walls of other buildings. With a probationary sergeant named Meyer I ran down an alleyway at the side of the building, to shelter behind a large stack of empty kerosene cans.

Meyer and I crouched down. It was bitterly cold – this was the Shanghai winter season – and it began to snow, covering the officer and me with a white shroud. My feet were frozen. My teeth were chattering – and it was not entirely due to the bitter conditions. Every move we made brought down a blast from above. It was so everywhere else. The police on the ground, sheltering wherever they could, were drawing fire. The advantage clearly was with the armed robbers.

Then from a backdoor entrance further down the alley in which Meyer and I sheltered we saw two British detectives, Bernard Warman and Richard Moir, late of the Grenadier Guards, enter the building, Mausers ready for instant action. They wore bullet-proof jackets, which probably saved their lives. They reached the entrance to the roof where they were fired on and hit. Both went tumbling down the stairs, but their injuries were not serious.

The decision was taken to call out the riot squad under Assistant Commissioner Fairbairn. He took command and within minutes his men, armed with sub-machine-guns, were stationed on the roofs of buildings overlooking that on which the robbers were still sending a steady stream of fire in every direction.

He mounted searchlights which showed the robbers crouching behind the walls. His men opened fire and, through the steadily falling snow, a hail of bullets struck the walls of the roof, whistled over it or landed on the solid concrete on which the gang were crouching. They returned the fire – they seemed to have an inexhaustible supply of ammunition – but this time their targets were the riot squad men.

Down in the alley Meyer and I, blue with cold, covered in snow, made a rapid dash to join the force in the main street. It was gone three a.m. We had been pinned down for more than three hours.

While the riot men above drew the fire of the gangsters a force was assembled below to rush upstairs from the two entrances of the building and to gain access to the roof.

Down on the street we heard the rapid exchange of fire as the robbers, all hope gone, unleashed the last of their ammunition to hit as many of the police as they could. The riot squad men replied and the battle lasted well over half an hour. At the end of it eleven gangsters were dead and not one police casualty.

Frozen stiff, I rushed off to the cable office and sent a story to the London *News-Chronicle* for whom I had been appointed China correspondent. With an eye on British readers I vividly described what I called 'The Sidney Street Siege of Shanghai'.

This recalled the occasion before World War I when two anarchist gunmen barricaded themselves in a house in Sidney Street in the East End of London. With a supply of bombs they fought it out with the police and a detachment of Guards. Mr (later Sir) Winston Churchill, then Home Secretary, appeared on the scene, top-hatted and astrakhan-collared, to take a hand in the operation which ended in both anarchists being killed.

The story was published on the front page with my byline, one of many that I sent from China.

Another time I was walking along the Bund to my office when, behind me, there was a burst of gunfire. I looked back and saw heading in my direction about seven Chinese, revolvers in their hands. At times they turned round and let loose a burst at several Chinese policemen in pursuit. The bullets were flying everywhere. I saw two pedestrians crash to the pavement, hit in the exchange of fire. I ran like hell with the Chinese gunmen not far behind me. Once I reached the entrance of my office I dashed inside, pressed myself against the solid concrete of the hallway supports and peered carefully along the street.

I saw that the gunmen, hotly pursued by the police, had turned up Kiukiang Road, a street leading off the Bund. I heard more gunfire and, seeing the last of the policemen turn into Kiukiang Road, decided that it was safe to investigate. By the time I entered the side street the gunmen and their pursuers had turned into Szechuan Road, another major thoroughfare, and were heading towards Nanking Road. There was still the sound of heavy firing.

Passing a large Japanese bank building in Kiukiang Road I noticed a blue-clad Sikh watchman lying in a pool of blood. He had been shot in the stomach and was still feebly tugging at his holster in an effort to draw his revolver. He looked to be gravely injured and I didn't give him long to live. Luckily I was wrong. He did recover eventually and was back on duty some months later.

As I gazed down at the watchman, who had been shot by the gunmen, I was joined by Mike Nenchew, the paper's chief photographer, a White Russian. He took several shots of the wounded man and then, together, we ran toward Nanking Road where, with sirens screaming, several police vans had arrived.

I questioned a British officer, bullet-proof jacket over his uniform, Mauser automatic in his hand. I got the details: a gang had attempted to rob a truck carrying a large amount of money to the large Chinese Maritime Customs building on the Bund. They had been foiled by a combined force of constables from the River Police, from the SMP and Chinese and Sikh watchmen. They had turned and fled, firing indiscriminately in a desperate attempt to escape.

The officer dashed away when the sound of firing came from the Cathay Arcade, built beneath the towering majesty of the Cathay Hotel from Nanking Road to a small side street, Jinkee Road. In the arcade, which was a popular shopping centre, the bandits had been cornered. At one end of the enclosed shopping precinct a large force of police barred the exit to Jinkee Road. On the Nanking Road side, pistols drawn, another large detachment of blue-clad, winter-uniformed police closed the trap.

The bandits were brave. They were trapped but they were not going to give up without a fight. As women in the exclusive shops cowered in terror and pedestrians dashed for shelter anywhere the arcade became a battleground.

It was all over soon enough. One by one the bandits were cut down, fired at from both ends of the arcade. Four of them were dead and the other three badly wounded.

The risk of sudden death was omnipresent in Shanghai – as it was, indeed, everywhere else in China then. Violence was commonplace. There were more gangsters in Shanghai than Chicago ever saw in the heyday of Capone. It was common to see a rich Chinese in his private rickshaw being protected by an armed bodyguard, often a Russian, loping at the side of the two-wheeled vehicle pulled by its 'human horse'.

But, despite the prospect of sudden death, Shanghai offered the journalist many pleasant assignments.

One was the commencement exercise at the Shanghai American School. This was the school-leaving ceremony – the commencement of life in the outside world for the senior scholars. It was made pleasant by the presence on the stage of the girl leavers, white-clad, high-heeled, long legged and eminently desirable.

Compared with the gym-slipped, blue-knickered girls of the British Cathedral School in their black stockings and clodhopper shoes the American schoolgirls offered the male the sophisticated appeal of modern hair-dos, of brassiered uplift, of well-tailored femininity in flouncy white – and, for me, the leg lover, stocking-clad symmetry over all-white high-heeled shoes.

I found it easy, covering the farewell speeches, to set my eyes on one girl on the stage, to stare unceasingly at her legs, to fidget uncomfortably as if in the throes of great passion and then to watch her reaction.

Females love to be admired, to feel that they are desired by a male. The message comes through – they are exciting a male, perhaps giving him an erection. They must entice him to greater passion.

65

So it was at the American School. The girl of my choice would note my unceasing stare at limbs, smile, change position to expose more length of leg, note my obvious increased passion and, provocatively, give me as much encouragement as possible without drawing tutorial attention to her display. Often a whispered remark to the girl seated next to her and a nod in my direction to draw attention to a young chap who had fallen prey to feminine charm. All very stimulating and certainly mutually rewarding.

Home life had its benefits, too. My amah was a pretty little thing. She looked to be about 15. She was 19 or 20. She was the daughter of the 'boy' of a German-Jewish family in the same apartment building and so I had to stifle certain incessant urges which bade me display my baser nature.

Nevertheless by sheer accident I discovered that she was willing to cooperate with me in certain sensual experiences.

I was in bed after night duty one morning, behaving myself properly as befitted a young British gentleman employing a 'native' servant. The girl wished to open a tin of rice but could not do so. I was lying on my back in the bed watching her. I asked her to bring the tin to me and I began to wrestle with the lid which was firmly embedded. Suddenly it came off and the rice spilled out over my genital region, covered by a thin white sheet.

The girl rushed over and began scooping it up. I noticed her little hand, delicately feminine. It was brushing my penis. In a few seconds I had an erection.

The girl continued scooping up the rice. She felt my hardness and smiled. Suddenly I threw back the sheet, scattering the remainder of the rice all over the place and exposed myself.

I guided the girl's hand towards it. She made no move of opposition. Her hand closed around its thickness but before she began to move she undid my pyjama cord with her other hand and, as I raised my body, drew the trousers down so that they reposed just above my knees. She knew what was coming and did not want semen to soil the garment.

Then, slowly at first, quickening her strokes as my passion mounted, she brought me off in great spurts.

She quickly withdrew her hand and ran into the bathroom where I heard the water running. In a moment she was back with a soapy hand-towel to give me a thorough cleaning, no sign of embarrassment. She had masturbated a male before, that was obvious. Who? Perhaps a former employer. Perhaps a younger brother who needed pacifying. The Chinese female well knew the soothing quality of masturbation. Crying boy babies could be made happy little creatures simply by playing with their penises. This was common practice.

The bed session led to even greater enjoyment in the bathroom. The little amah would soap my genital region into a foaming lather as I stood in the bath. There was an indescribable feeling of pleasure as, with soapy hand, she moved up and down my erect organ, thrusting forth towards her. And then when the climax arrived she would hold it steadily so that the sperm dropped into the bath water below me.

She cooked well, too. Strange that the Chinese servant, who scorned the barbarian's diet as an atrocious murder of God-given ingredients, could produce the most delicious Yorkshire puddings, steak-and-kidney pies, tripe and onions or any of the countless varieties that had sustained generation after generation of stolid, sturdy Europeans.

Involvements with women in Shanghai produced many embarrassing situations for some foreigners. I was involved in a murder case at the apartment of a high-ranking police official in the International Settlement. His Chinese cook-boy savagely attacked his Russian girl-friend with a kitchen knife and her body was found there horribly mutilated.

The Chinese servant disappeared and, as far as I know, was never caught. While we gave the case good coverage in the paper the real reason for the crime – jealousy on the part of the cook-boy – was never mentioned. Undoubtedly the relationship between master and servant had been more than that of employer and employee.

But who cared in broad-minded Shanghai? If a chap liked boys then that was his business.

Sodomy was rife in the country. So was transvestism – and in Japan also. Male courtesans, dressed as girls, dedicated themselves to homosexual functions. There was a cabaret in the Sinza district in which all the taxi-dancers were transvestites – delicately slim youths, painted and powdered and certainly undistinguishable from any of their female competitors in the other night-spots.

They could be seen sitting on the knees of the big westerners who regularly patronised the place. Occasionally, however, discovery of the fact that, though they looked like beautiful girls, they possessed 'a handle' led to unseemly behaviour on the part of normal customers in search of a genuine piece of tail.

In Hongkew, too, male courtesans plied for hire. It was well known that the Japanese Samurai, a martial caste of sado-masochistic inverts, believed it to be a matter of chivalry to love a strong and handsome comrade in place of an unclean woman. They sought violence and pain to induce orgasms and they ranked high on the huge list of Oriental flagellants and suicide cultists.

Women were considered to be unclean by both the Chinese and the Japanese. Thus a Chinese woman during her menstrual period was not permitted to enter a temple to burn joss sticks and pray to her gods. Women were pack-mules, she-studs, fit only for the most menial tasks. Neither could she produce semen which was considered to be 'good medicine' for the elderly in search of erectional rejuvenation.

Thus elderly Chinese men, desperately anxious to satisfy lusty young concubines, went in search of youths who would offer their semen as a medicinal beverage. In one establishment off Avenue Joffre more than ten young Chinese males either mastur-bated or offered their penises for sucking to the seekers of vitality who paid well for their services. It was firmly believed that this juice from the loins of vigorous males would fortify not only the over-forties but even senile gentlemen who would never see eighty again.

One old Chinese gentleman, travelling by train from Nanking to Soochow, found himself in a compartment alone with a youth of about sixteen years who fell into a deep sleep. The elderly one noticed that the young man's penis had made a bell tent of his thin, silken trousers as he slumbered away on the seat. Gently the old man placed his hand inside the lad's flap and pulled out his organ which was, indeed, in a state of tumescence. He then proceeded to suck it in the hope that the semen he was about to bring forth would take years off his aged shoulders and put some zest into his withered loins. Unfortunately his exertions awakened the young lad who took umbrage and demanded cash for the service he was providing. The old man refused whereupon the lad reported the matter to the station authorities in Shanghai who had the elderly one arrested. He was charged in the Mixed Court and fined. Strange that he should have forgotten, or ig-nored, the unwritten law of China that a cash hand-out made a virtue of crime and closed a protesting mouth.

A cash hand-out to an irate Eurasian mother once saved me a lot of bother. I had taken her daughter to see a cinema show. She was a shapely lass of about fourteen years and for thirty cents, with which she bought sweets and ice-cream, she tossed me off in the stalls, handling my rampant tool delicately but with much interest. I did nothing to her. Alas, she told her sister of the ease with which money had come her way. Sister told mother and mother accosted me in the street. A sum of thirty dollars, however, and a promise not to do the act again left her in a happy frame of mind and she did not bother me again.

A regular assignment that I covered was the daily Japanese press conference held in the residential Broadway Mansions, just across the Soochow Creek in Hongkew.

Here we were served tea and cakes while Japanese navy and army spokesmen told us of the progress of the fighting in China, answered our questions – mostly evasively – and smiled blandly when some of us became downright rude.

Bob Horiguchi, a tall journalist from the Domei agency, born of a Japanese father and a South American mother, was the official interpreter. He spoke excellent English with an American accent and handled the questions superbly – never ruffled, always polite and smiling.

We were a mixed crew. There was Hallet Abend from the *New York Times*, sometimes with his ex-Marine assistant, Robinson. Hallet, who lived in the Broadway Mansions, made no secret of the fact that he preferred male company always. He had many boy-friends to whom he was said to be most generous. He was also a good newsman, a real professional who maintained the high standard of journalism for which the *New York Times* was famous.

For the London *Times*, then a much more powerful organ than it is today in this age of British decline, there was Ian Morrison, China-born son of Dr Morrison of Peking. Cambridge-educated Ian was killed later covering the Korean war. It was well known in the post-war years that this tall, handsome young Scotsman (for his father, though Australian-born, was of pure Scottish descent) was the hero of Han Su-yin's book, *A Many Splendoured Thing*. I met them together many times in Hong Kong in the late 1940s and early 1950s before Morrison was sent off to Korea.

The *China Press* was not friendly towards the Japanese. Nor was Charlie Tombs, its representative at the press conferences. He was Horiguchi's thorn in the flesh. I remember a heated Tombs working up such a rage at one conference that he lost his top set of dentures which slid over the polished table to come to rest right in front of the army spokesman. To his credit.

the officer did not bat an eyelid and politely shoved the teeth back across the table to Tombs, with the end of his pencil.

We were given the usual accounts of Japanese victories over the Chinese and of the results of bombing raids on Chungking and other cities still under Chinese control, but our questions usually dealt with some incident or the other that involved either the British or the Americans – the bombing of a mission hospital or interference with British shipping on the Yangtse. The answers were evasive and if regret was expressed by consular representatives at the conference we could sense the insincerity of their statements.

The Japanese entertained us at garden parties where we were served saké or Japanese beer by kimono-clad waitresses. We were taken to sukiyaki parties at Japanese restaurants in Hong-kew, and on one occasion the army spokesman, a lieutenant or captain (I could never fathom Japanese army insignia), invited me to spend an evening with him at the Tiger Ballroom which catered for service officers and Japanese businessmen.

The Japanese girl who, at the army's expense, became my dancing partner was a tall girl dressed in long, white European-style ballroom dress. She spoke some English and was a marvellous dancer which suited me well.

I could feel her lithe body pressed against mine. She was leading me on. Her thighs swished silkily against mine. Her pubic mound was thrust into my pelvic region. There was no gap between us. We were glued together.

The inevitable happened. I got an erection, which was what she had been working for. Cleverly, as we danced, she manoeuvred her body so that my hard shaft was thrust between her thighs, right under the pelvic bone. She swayed as she rode me – for that was what she was doing – round the floor. I pushed myself hard against her, to feel more of her, to savour the eroticism of her movements as she mounted herself over the sensitive glans, held back only by the thinness of summer cotton trousers.

The band was playing a Japanese tune in foxtrot time when I shot my load. Violent shivers ran through my body. She knew what was happening, pulled me closer to her and we stopped dead in our tracks. Then, wet and uncomfortably sticky, I danced on until we reached our table where we broke contact and sat down.

The army spokesman was still on the floor with his girl, shorter, stockier to match his size.

With true oriental politeness by a female in the presence of the

70

superior male the girl stood by the table until I had sat down. Then she poured me a glass of beer. She looked at me and smiled.

'I please you, yes?' she asked.

I was embarrassed. My steam had gone. I was all wet down below and it felt cold. But I had to admit the truth: 'Wonderful,' I said. 'You are beautiful, very good.'

She purred with satisfaction and then, diplomatically, excused herself, realising that I would want to get to the toilet as quickly as possible to do a renovating job on my white trousers. This proved to be an impossibility. I couldn't wet them. I cleaned up inside and stood by a fan to let it blow on the wet stain on the cotton. It dried but the tell-tale mark was still there when I rejoined the officer at the table. He didn't notice it. I never lost the rim-mark by my flies that paid tribute to the sensual movements of that Japanese girl. It stayed with me as a reminder of a fabulous night until the day came when the trousers had to be discarded because of old age.

The girl and I danced again before the night was over. There was no more sexual play. We concentrated on steps and variations and we attracted a lot of attention from patrons watching us from their tables. All of which pleased me as I liked to show off. I still do.

While the Japanese girls were renowned for their ability speedily to arouse lust in males, the Chinese cabaret taxi-dancers were no less skilful in employing their bodies on the dance floor to encourage a whopping hard-on.

They made a joke of it. A raised forefinger on the hand resting on a partner's shoulder indicated to a giggling community of girls sitting around the ballroom floor that a dancer was being prodded by a mighty horn. The Chinese girls, who could not expect an indecorous show of carnality by their own menfolk bred on the Confucian precept of modesty in all things, always showed amusement at the instant and unmistakable sexual response of the white man. They loved to lead on a big American or an Italian to hardness and they got many a laugh by playing the forefinger game.

The Russian girls, whose bodies were bigger and who no doubt were as much used to the instant horn as their Chinese colleagues, did not play the game. If a partner had a hard-on then there it was. There was no signal to other girls not dancing. They either coaxed it to greater degrees of sensual generosity or ignored it, depending on their response to the attractiveness of a patron.

71

Where the Russian girls scored was in bustiness. Possession of big breasts in the Chinese had, for centuries, been considered extremely vulgar. This had led to chest-binding so that the growth of breasts was restricted.

Thus the tit-loving westerner, ever ready to grab a large handful, could always rely on the Russian girl to provide naturally the largeness and softness that he sought. The Chinese girl rarely could measure up to the standard required by the white man and this deficiency had to be remedied by resort to artificial aids which included padded brassieres and such gadgets as false tits blown up like balloons. French products they were, well shaped to cup over nature's tissue, nippled and beneath a dress realistic in appearance.

I was dancing with a well-busted Chinese girl at the Little Club when I heard a hissing noise. It went on for about a minute and I had the idea that my partner was issuing what in the army we would have called a rubber-heeled fart. It was not so. When we finished dancing I noticed that the girl had a lopsided appearance. The right breast was in full prominence but the left one had vanished. She had had a puncture and was highly embarrassed. She left me quickly and fled to the ladies' room to carry out instant repairs with a rubber patch and some sticky fluid provided by the manufacturers.

But in the leg stakes the Chinese girls scored heavily over the Russians. They had no need to resort to shaving or depilatories. Their skin was smooth and hairless – no stubble to put you off. A grope up the silky thigh of a Chinese girl was one of the great pleasures of life offered by the Shanghai cabarets.

While the cabarets offered erotic relaxation at night there were mundane, everyday assignments on the office diary and they included such events as the annual general meetings of the St Andrew's Society of Shanghai, the St David's Society or the Royal Society of St George.

Because Jardine, Matheson and Co. was a Scottish firm and the Keswick family were involved in the doings of St Andrew's Society, which had its headquarters in the Jardine building, the Scots always got full coverage in the columns of the *N.C.D.N.* There was the case of poor Abe Frank, a Russian Jew who, when he was marked to cover the a.g.m. of the society, decided that it was not worth attending and that he could pick it up later. It was a mistake. Peyt fired him instantly when, on the following day, not a line appeared in the paper.

John Keswick (now Sir John), product of Eton, and W. J.

Keswick, educated at Winchester and a former chairman of the Shanghai Municipal Council, were the taipans of Jardines, founded in the previous century on the lucrative opium trade. The firm had immense interests throughout China and its trading name, 'Ewo', was known in every corner of the land.

The firm was founded in 1828 when the export of opium to China by the East India Company was making fortunes for those engaged in the nefarious trade. William Jardine, a 44-year-old Scot, who was a surgeon aboard an East Indiaman running the opium into Canton, established himself in business in London and later met James Matheson, son of a Scottish baronet, in Canton and took him into business with him.

The firm of Jardine Matheson was founded and quickly became pre-eminent in taking Bengal opium into China despite the objections of the Chinese government of that time which was too weak to challenge the might of such Western powers as Britain. Jardine and Matheson soon became the ablest men in the opium trade and they established a fleet of ships running between Bengal and Canton.

Britain's victory in the Opium War against China, which resulted in the take-over of Hong Kong, firmly established Jardine Matheson and Co. elsewhere in China and they transferred their headquarters to Shanghai where a massive building on the Bund waterfront testified to their economic ascendancy in the China trade.

While opium was a dirty word in Shanghai in the 1930s and most firms shunned the trade like the plague, the port was still an entry point for the drug and, as a result, had become the centre of gangsterism. Like the Mafia, the Shanghai underworld was engaged in drug-pushing – opium and its derivatives, particularly heroin. There were opium dens everywhere and though the police carried out many raids with the object of eradicating the drug from the local scene they were never able to accomplish more than a few arrests of smokers and small-time pedlars. The big boys, particularly the number-one gangster, Tu Yueh-sen, remained unassailed and lived in privileged luxury.

Among those who had made immense fortunes by bringing in opium was the 'Baghdad Jew' Hardoon. Starting life as a watchman he had risen like a phoenix from the ashes of the millions of pipefuls of the drug he had provided for the emaciated sots who were in its deadly grip. But, as if to atone for the misery his trading success had caused, he adopted a family of about nine orphaned children of many races who lived with him in a palatial mansion on Bubbling Well Road.

There were few old-established British firms which at one time or another had not had a stake in bringing Indian opium into China. The Indian drug was considered to be superior to the native-grown product.

The day had to come, of course, when the export of Indian opium to China had to be banned by international agreement, but this was of little importance to the British firms which had built vast trading empires on the drug. They had made their money. Opium had enabled them to diversify their trading activities – into shipping, textiles, mining, railways, finance and so on. Opium-smoking was made illegal in foreign-controlled Shanghai but it could never be stamped out. Fortunes were still made smuggling the drug into China and the gangsters took over the nefarious trade – the gangsters and the Japanese.

The policy of the Japanese was to undermine the morale of the Chinese nation by the wholesale introduction of opium. In the wake of their armies – in the north, in central China, everywhere under their military control – the opium dens were introduced. Some of them were lavish affairs intended to emasculate in luxurious surroundings the wealthy Chinese, the men who mattered in regional influence – the officials, the businessmen, the industrialists, the men whose craving for the drug could be converted into active support for the Japanese cause.

Along with the opium the Japanese sent thousands of beautiful girls to work in the dens or to become prostitutes. As far as the Tokyo High Command was concerned it mattered little whether the women were Japanese, Chinese or of any other race. They had the utmost contempt for members of the female sex, whose only duty, as they saw it, was to serve the dominant male. So the daughters of Japanese families might find themselves serving opium pipes in Peking or working in a brothel in Harbin. They were told that what they were doing was a patriotic duty in the service of the Emperor whose blessing of their sacrifices would ensure in the next world immortal life. And they believed it. After all the Emperor was the Son of Heaven, direct descendant of the sun goddess, Amaterasu, who founded the royal line in BC 600.

In Shanghai the Japanese were more circumspect. They ran their brothels for the fighting men but Japanese women, in general, were not on open sale as they were in the Japanese-controlled areas of China. Here and there it was possible to find a brothel offering only Japanese females – they had a reputation for expertise that ensured constant popularity – but they were scarce on the ground and expensive. Not so, however, the Japanese massage shops which flourished everywhere – in Hongkew, in the Settlement central district and in the French Concession.

Cal Hirsh introduced me to the proprietress of one of these establishments in Avenue Edward VII. He was good for a free advertisement in the form of what we journalists called 'the puff paragraph' and he was on the free list. This, as the proprietress well knew, meant liberal helpings – prior to treatment by one of the girls – of whisky from a John Haig bottle, the real stuff.

The owner was a large Japanese woman – at least twelve stone, all muscle in a power-packed frame. She was reputed to be a ju-jitsu expert and she needed to be to deal with some of the patrons, who permitted lascivious impulses to goad them into acts of violence when they discovered that the masseuses who had stroked them to the point of no return were definitely not going to open their legs.

'Play-play' yes; 'fuckee' no. That was the rule of the establishment and the lady owner was big enough, tough enough and determined enough to see that the commandment was obeyed. According to Cal as a bouncer she was ferocious but as a masseuse gently feminine – the best of the beautiful bunch she employed.

She asked me as we sat at a small table in her office, glasses in front of us, if I'd like to have the entire treatment – entirely free of charge as I was a friend of Cal. I could pick my own girl and she'd do the rest. The proprietress smiled at Cal, who gave me a knowing wink.

She asked me what type of girl I fancied – big and strong, medium-sized or small and feminine. I said that I liked hefty girls if they had good figures and were not ugly. Ugly? She was upset. All her girls were hand-picked. They were beautiful. Why, if she employed ugly girls then she'd be out of business. Her English was fluent enough, the result of long association with patrons from the Western powers.

She called in one of the girls from a group I had seen briefly sitting in a large room just off the entrance hall. She wore a kimono-style dressing gown and walked on wooden clogs which raised her height from about five feet eight to five feet ten. I could see that she had strong, shapely legs. Her shoulders were broad and her large hands denoted strength. Her face was well

75

painted Japanese style which I thought was a pity. They always laid it on thick and heavy but she had pleasant features and a pearly-toothed smile. She suited me and I said so.

The girl, who spoke some English, led me to a steam-filled room where the hissing of showers blended with the soft cadences of piped music. Gently taking me by the hand she drew me towards a cubicle. We pushed open the curtain and entered.

I was still fully dressed and the girl asked me to strip off, which I did. I handed my clothes to her and she took them outside where she placed them in a locker, the key of which she produced from a pocket of her dressing gown. She locked the container and returned to the cubicle.

Once inside the girl doffed the dressing gown and hung it on a coat-hanger fixed over a wooden box by the entrance. The box had a lid and could be used as a seat.

She was tall and powerfully built. Her shoulders were muscular and so were her arms, which suited me well. No doubt the muscles had been developed by a thousand-and-one massage sessions with males like me.

She told me to stand under the shower. I looked at her. She wore only the briefest of shorts, figure-clinging and erotically revealing. Her breasts were encased in a flimsy brassiere, one of the see-through type which clearly outlined the deep hue of her nipples.

The girl turned on the cold water. The spray hit me in stinging iciness. My breath was taken away. I gasped. The girl laughed. I had no doubt that the cold water was intended to defuse high-powered loin voltages.

Gradually she adjusted the taps so that the spray warmed up and I was able, once again, to breathe normally and to take an intelligent interest in the proceedings.

When I had been thoroughly soaked she turned off the water and, arming herself with a cake of sandal-wood soap and a hard loofah, proceeded to lather me all over and to scrub in the soap with great vigour. No wonder she had muscles. The vigour with which she performed the exercise was indicative of the strength she possessed. I could see her breasts bouncing with her exertions. My loins filled with desire. Within a moment or two I had an erection. It stuck out there, thick and throbbing, moving stolidly as the loofah swept over my body.

The girl took no notice. She was evidently used to masculine expansion as soon as the cold-water treatment had worn off. She soaped me all over the genital region, through the hair, between the thighs and around the scrotum. I loved the touch of her long, strong fingers. But she left alone my rampant rod. This she did not touch. She bade me to take the soap and to wash behind the foreskin. This I did, pulling the foreskin back and well soaping the glans. I handed back the soap. She continued to loofah my legs and feet and then told me to stand under the shower again.

This time I was assailed by a fairly hot spray of water which hit my skin fiercely and removed all traces of the sandal-wood soap with its musky smell. The girl opened the wooden box and took from it a large towel which she draped over me as I stood clear of the shower.

Leaving her dressing gown in the cubicle she led me, hard as a rock, to a small room in the centre of which was the padded massage table – long and narrow, sloping slightly from head position to base. She pulled the towel away and told me to lie down on the table.

For about thirty minutes the girl worked me over. I watched the muscles of her arm flexing and relaxing. Expertly and unerringly she found my muscles and nerves, massaged them, pounded them, pulled them, stroked them. The feeling was delightful. I became languorous, sleepy, particularly when her long fingers gave me a soft facial massage. Tingles of intense pleasure swept through my body. She worked on my neck, shoulders, chest, back, hips – and thighs.

It was when she reached my thighs that she first touched my penis. Working on one thigh with the right hand she pushed its stiffness out of the way with the left hand. Similarly on the other thigh the hard shaft was gently moved clear of the massaging hand.

The sight of the muscular attractiveness of this tall Japanese girl as her arms, hairless and shiny with beads of sweat, worked over my body roused me to fever-pitch.

Not once had I touched her body though I greatly desired to do so. I wanted to feel her biceps as she kneaded my yielding flesh. I desired to cup her breasts in my hands. I wanted to stroke those rounded thighs, silky and hairless. But I did not do so. I had an idea that she would object. It was well known in Shanghai that the massage girls, like the geisha girls, were not prostitutes. They gave their services to men as experts – the geishas as entertainers, sing-song women; the masseuses as fully trained (which most of them were) physiotherapists, specialists in their own line.

Nevertheless, the girls knew that males, lustful animals that they were, needed relief if future patronage was to be ensured. Relief there was – but only by one method: masturbation.

Once she had finished the massage the girl looked at me. Her eyes took in my erection. She gazed at it for a few moments and then, walking over to a cupboard by the wall, took out from a drawer there a bottle of talcum powder and liberally sprinkled the contents over both hands.

She came over to me, carefully rubbed in the powder between her palms and in a slow, sinuous movement raised my shaft so that it reposed between her palms. Then, slowly rotating her hands in different directions, she gently massaged the palpitating thickness so that as excitement increased it jerked and shuddered with each silky movement she made. This rotating caress was delightful. For one thing, the build-up was slower. The feeling was ten times more lascivious. The talcum powder gave the palms a silky sheen, smooth and erotic.

As the girl increased the speed of the rotary movements I arched my body and gasped. I was approaching climax. She continued the movements, carefully watching the glans. In a moment it was all over. The sperm shot forth – burst after burst. She continued the movements until it was obvious that I had spent all my reserves. I lay back in sensual delight, sated, semen still trickling down my penis.

Before I rejoined Cal and the proprietress, still tossing back whisky and water, ice cold from the distilled-water container which every establishment in Shanghai contained, I gave the Japanese masseuse one dollar as a tip. She bowed low and expressed her thanks in hissing English. I told her I would see her again – would be, in fact, a regular customer of hers. Again she thanked me.

Strange, I thought, that these demure, soft-spoken, man-pleasing females, so anxious to satisfy, should belong to the same race as the brutal savages who wore the Emperor's uniform. Perhaps it was all a facade and, in different circumstances, Japanese women could be as violently sadistic as their menfolk. I doubted it, though. All the Japanese women I met seemed to be genuinely feminine, gentle creatures – thought I had to admit that there had to be exceptions. The proprietress, for example. I fancied could be cruelly belligerent when the occasion demanded. She needed a weight-lifter as a husband or a gigantic Sumo wrestler.

I visited the establishment several times later and was completely satisfied with the attentions of the big Japanese lass but I transferred my custom permanently to a Chinese massage house within a month or two. The reason was that the girls there, all Chinese, all hefty country wenches, not only washed you thoroughly before a massage but, completely naked, got into a deep bath with you, played with your balls under the water and worked you up to voluptuous voltage before the actual massage started. And then if you wanted manual masturbation they provided it or, better still as far as I was concerned, placed your rampant penis in the mouth and sucked you off as you touched their breasts, stroked their legs or worked yourself into a mighty lather by other forms of contact. But again only 'play-play'; 'no fuckee'. I never entered one massage establishment where the girls would permit intercourse.

Cal never accompanied me on these visits. And he never came to Blood Alley after the paper had been put to bed at about one o'clock in the morning. Women were the lure and a certain amount of drink, of course. But Cal always excused himself.

One of the joys of night duty was the thought of Blood Alley after all work had been completed. Nowhere in the world, I'll bet, was there a carnal fleshpot so universally popular as that little street.

79

Blood Alley

With war, famine and pestilence never more than a few miles away, the Shanghailanders' motto was, 'Eat, drink and be merry for tomorrow we die'. Though it was not apparent in the general demeanour of the foreigners, the prophetic words of Sir Robert Hart in the previous century summed up the feelings of those who could read the portents of events in China in 1937: 'The day will come when China will repay with interest all the injuries and insults she has suffered at the hands of the European powers.' In the meantime, it was in the establishments of Blood Alley where the foreigners lived for the present.

Blood Alley, or to give it its proper title, Rue Chu Pao-san, was a short street off Avenue Edward VII – a thoroughfare entirely dedicated to wine, women, song and all-night lechery. The only 'business' of Blood Alley was the easy pickings to be had from the drunks, the sailors, soldiers and cosmopolitan civilians, who lurched there in search of the joys to come from the legion of Chinese, Korean, Annamite, Russian, Eurasian, Filipino and Formosan women who worked the district.

Here were the Palais Cabaret, the 'Frisco, Mumms, the Crystal, George's Bar, Monk's Brass Rail, the New Ritz and half a dozen others – opened in the case of the cabarets around 6 p.m. daily and closed, depending on the staying power of the customers, any time after 8.30 a.m. the following day.

Some of the bars never seemed to close. The cynical attitude of their owners toward their patrons, many of whom might be boozing there one day and halfway to Yokohama the next, was summed up succinctly in the New Ritz, owned and operated by American ex-marine 'Yen' Yenalevicz, a burly, tobacco-chewing extrovert who had erected over his extensive bottle-shelves a notice which would have done a missionary's heart good: IN GOD WE TRUST. This in enormous black letters. Some way underneath in small print: Everybody else cash!

In midsummer, when swing-doors were left open in the Turkish-bath heat, the cacophony of wailing saxophones and strident trumpets thumping out the hits of the day in discordant competition gave no pleasure to music-lovers but, inside the dives, kilted Seaforth Highlanders, tall U.S. Navy men, the seamen from the Liverpool tramps, the French poilus, Savoia Grenadiers, had ears only for the girls clinging to them in the half light of dance-floor alcoves: 'Darlink, buy me one drink, please.'

For the girls a 'drink' meant coloured water or cold tea from a bottle bearing such respectable labels as John Dewar. For the guzzler, wood alcohol or doctored meths in what appeared to be unopened, brand-new imports of John Haig or Old Kentucky were planted on the table. But, if he knew, he didn't care, stimulated as he was by his girl's adroit caresses.

The penis was under constant watch by the girls. From time to time, it had to be stimulated by soft bodily contact on the dance floor. Behind the tables in the alcoves its tumescence could be maintained by 'accidental' brushes with a well-manicured hand. But these inducements to unflagging stiffness were never carried too far. A premature ejaculation lowered resistance to the whisper, 'Buy me another drink, darlink.'

'Drinks' played an important part in the livelihood of the Shanghai taxi-dancer. Half the cost of a glass of 'Scotch' was her commission. The more she coaxed from the customer the better her prospects of making ends meet in a calling which, to say the least, was precarious.

If she was young and beautiful, she had little to worry about – provided she kept the 'girl-manager' happy with his squeeze. But if she was past the first bloom of youth the struggle to exist could be fraught with pitfalls. It was imperative that the 'girl-manager' should be bribed to favour her and this meant larger handouts than those expected from her younger sisters.

'Girl-managers' regulated the traffic in every taxi-dancer establishment in Shanghai. More often than not these were American-speaking Chinese gentlemen with George Raft hairstyles and zoot suits. They, and they alone, decided whether a girl would eat or starve. Each man had his 'district' of cabaret. In this area he was responsible for introducing patrons to the girls who sat demurely, like slaves in a Baghdad market, on high-backed chairs all around the dance floor. Through the oily offices of the 'girl-managers', they could be induced to sit at table with a gentleman ready to invest dollars for dance and sit-out tickets. This meant commission for the house, for the girls and a cumshaw (gratuity) to the go-between.

And if drinks were supplied at the customer's request to the dancing girl then a slice of this revenue had to go into the manager's pocket. He couldn't be fooled. Eagle-eyed Chinese 'boys' behind the bar kept careful tabulation on the abacus of the amounts of cold tea or coloured water sent to the girl. They, in turn, got their rake-pff from the gentleman squeezing the dancers.

Any dereliction by a girl in meeting the demands of the American-accented sharks only resulted in her utter isolation – hours of hopeless waiting on the rim of the dance floor for patrons who never materialised. This 'solitary confinement' inevitably brought rebels to heel.

Introductions could also mean buy-out tickets at a cost then of about £3. These had to be paid for by customers in a hurry to let off steam if they wished to take their partners from the establishment before their usual 'clocking-off' time.

Most of the Blood Alley girls, the lowest caste in Shanghai's cabaret society, lived mostly in the French Concession, usually alone in single rooms of terraced houses in the densely populated side-streets. Many of them clustered around Avenue Joffre, with its trams and buses, its European-style shops, its restaurants, bars, cinemas and its thronged sidewalks.

It was in a tenement on Joffre Terrace that Anna, the Korean, lived.

Anna was one of the most popular girls at the Palais Cabaret, the biggest of the Blood Alley night spots.

She was about five feet three, slim but with big breasts, which, if not exactly of Russian proportions, were certainly larger than those of the average Chinese girl. Her legs were long and elegant and she enjoyed exciting the 'red-haired devils' with the sight of them.

She had the high cheekbones of the northern Mongol. Her eyes were slightly more almond-shaped than those of the Chinese but her nose was straighter, more European. She generally wore her jet-black hair swept up to show off her delicate ears. Sometimes she would let it down around her shoulders in silky contact with the cheongsam she invariably wore with its figure-hugging provocation and thigh-revealing slits.

Anna was something of a linguist. In addition to her native Korean and Shanghai dialect she was fluent in Japanese, which was not surprising as her homeland had been a Japanese possession since 1895 when it was seized from China. She could speak some Mandarin, too. Her English, however, left much to be desired.

It was a mixture of the Bronx and the Orient and had been learned through much contact with 'sleeping dictionaries' – mostly enlisted men from various units in the United States Asiatic Fleet with whom she had shacked up from time to time. They were forthright fellows who believed in calling a spade a fucking spade. No wonder, then, that Anna's English at times would have brought blushes to the cheeks of a Billingsgate fish-porter.

Anna's English hit me with the force of a piledriver when I first met her at the Palais.

I danced with her. She was soft, seductive, definitely desirable. I got a hard-on – couldn't help it. It made its presence known to her. I suggested she might do something about it.

She showed righteous indignation and her words flowed.

The purport of her message was that if I thought she was a goddam easy lay then I was sadly mistaken. She wasn't the sort of bum who opened her goddam legs for anyone. She certainly wasn't going to be screwed by me and I'd better piss off or, better still, jack myself off because that, as far as she was concerned, was the only solution if I desired relief from my urge.

Nevertheless I knew that Anna, indignant or not, was no virgin. No, it was all part of the cabaret-girl's facade – face demanded that they should be demure, hard to get, worthy of wooing before being bedded.

So I wooed Anna. I was infatuated by her. She said that she knew I wanted to screw the ass off her (her own words) but that I'd have to prove my worthiness first.

I should have got danger-money. There was more excitement in soft-soaping Anna than I bargained for. For instance, she liked strong liquor – no coloured water for her; the real McCoy. Six or seven brandy-cokes and she was ready to take on Joe Louis.

Taxi-drivers seemed to bring out the worst in her. I took her out of the Palais one night, walked her down to the Ford Taxi Co. garage nearby and ordered a driver to take us out to the Ali Baba night club in the western district.

The driver seemed to be a nice, quiet Chinese chap – very polite and soft-spoken. To my surprise Anna started to abuse him in Shanghai dialect. The driver looked pained but he bore it man-fully. Then, suddenly, she hit him across the face with her bag.

This was too much. The driver took up a stance that indicated that Anna was going to get the works – a fistful in the jaw to start with.

I stepped in. I grabbed Anna and heaved her bodily out of the way. I gave her the bum's rush, one hand grabbing her neck and the other in the middle of the back. I rushed her out of the garage, down the street and didn't stop until we came to Monk's Brass Rail.

'Why the hell did you have to do that?' I asked Anna heatedly.

'Balls,' replied the Korean. 'Me kill the bastard.'

'No you don't,' I said, pushing Anna into the Brass Rail. This was kept by an American ex-sailor, an enormous bladder of lard who turned the scales well over 280 lb.

A quick brandy-coke and Anna had recovered some sort of composure. Monk knew her. He cracked a joke (I'd heard it before): his belly was so enormous, he told the girl, that he hadn't seen his tool for years. He could only grope for it. Now, however, he was happy. He'd bought a periscope and no longer was he forced to rely on the memories of long-past youthful slimness. He could see it, admire it for the beauty it was.

Anna fell into paroxysms of violent mirth – that was after I had explained what a periscope was and how it worked for the rotund Monk.

There was the night that Anna took umbrage over the remarks of a tiddly Russian cabaret girl who had insinuated that all Oriental girls 'no have got tits'.

To give Anna credit her breasts were all right, a good handful long nippled and worth caressing. She was hurt – and annoyed.

Anna picked up her glass of brandy-coke and heaved it over the taller European. She spluttered and screamed in rage.

Then the two women were at each other like wildcats, clawing, scratching, grabbing hair and hurling abuse in two languages.

I grabbed the Korean round the waist, heaved her ungracefully across the floor to the door, which was opened wide by a Chinese servitor, dragged her out, hailed a taxi, bundled her in and then relaxed.

Anna was heaving like the sea in a force-eight gale. I put my arms around her, pulled her close to me and planted my lips on hers. I thrust my tongue inside her mouth. This always worked. She responded quickly. We were soon fondling each other on the way to a real climax in bed.

'Russian cocksucker,' hissed Anna. 'She say my tits no belong proper.'

'Forget it,' I whispered. 'Your tits belong number one. Give me hard-on.'

But that was not all. There was the incident at the Roxy,

84

another western-district night club when I went a bit berserk and gave Anna her come-uppance.

The Roxy was a well-kept establishment. There was Austrian refugee Harry Fischer on violin, leading a trio of excellent musicians. Anna and I danced beautifully together to the tunes they provided.

All went well until I spotted Abe Franks, then with the *Shanghai Times*, in an alcove with a Chinese woman partner.

I went across to talk to him and left Anna at the table to watch over my whisky-soda and drink her brandy-coke.

I was introduced to the Chinese lady. She said that I was a good dancer. An easy victim of flattery, I purred with enjoyment. I asked her if she would like to join me on the floor. Abe readily nodded approval and off we went.

It was a mistake.

As we moved over the ballroom floor I saw Anna approaching us, a glass of brandy-coke in one hand, my whisky-soda in the other.

I tried to steer my partner clear but it was too late. Anna raised both arms, poured both drinks over our faces and spat insults at the female.

My partner screamed. Up rushed Abe ready to do a Sir Galahad act. I broke contact with the Chinese girl and, in violent rage, sent Anna sprawling against a table in one of the alcoves. Over it went, glasses smashing on the floor.

Anna got up somewhat shakily and dashed for the door. I followed, caught up with her outside and smacked her down. She hit the ground with a bump. She screamed for a taxi and lurched towards it as it drove up. I hit her again. She fell against the taxi. Suddenly she opened the door, scrambled in and as the vehicle turned round to head downtown she lowered the window, stuck her head out and screamed at me: 'Shaw, you bastard! You bastard. You goddam sonovabitch!'

I was firmly convinced that my love affair with Anna was over for good. I was wrong.

The next night I visited the Palais. There was Anna. She greeted me lovingly. Not a word was said of the Roxy fisticuffs.

The first night I slept with Anna in her room in Joffre Terrace was a disappointment to her.

I was naked in the bed. I watched her undress in front of the wardrobe mirror. She let her cheongsam fall to the ground. Slowly she undid her brassiere and as her breasts bounced free she held them in her hands, slowly caressing them.

85

She stepped out of the cheongsam, sat on the high-backed chair and raised one leg high. Delicately she undid the suspender clips, rolled down one stocking and took it off. The same with the other leg. This was strip-tease finesse – tantalising, feverishly exciting.

Off came the suspender belt and then panties. There she stood completely naked, smooth flesh glowing in the light from the centre-ceiling bulb – long limbs, rounded buttocks, upthrust breasts and a face wreathed in smiles as she watched me jerking my rampant tool against the blanket.

She put out the light, clambered into bed alongside me. I grabbed her and pulled her towards me. I could feel the softness of her thighs pressing against me. Her breasts were thrust against my chest. She flung her arms around me, planted her lips on mine and her tongue darted in and out.

It was too late. I felt the familiar surge sweeping up from my innermost depths. I was coming. I heaved myself half over Anna so that my penis, jerking furiously, was over her thighs. It gave its all in jolting spurts. It was all over. I lay back panting, wet, uncomfortable but happy.

'Shaw,' said Anna quietly, 'you sure needed a woman badly.'

'Sorry, Anna,' I replied. 'I couldn't wait.'

She said, 'Never mind, I frig myself. Next time you more better.'

And Anna did just that. She lay on her back. She put her right hand between her legs and for ten minutes or so the bed jerked furiously as she brought herself to a climax, legs kicking out and then contracting. She sighed, breathed heavily, turned towards me and said, 'Shaw, we sleep.'

And we slept, arms around each other – wet but happy.

Next time I was not 'more better'.

We were in bed after an energetic night of dancing and drinking at the Hungaria night club and mutual gropings in the taxi on the way from the western district to the French Concession.

Anna was naked. So was I. My hands were running over the softness of her breasts. Her skin was silky, lovely to touch. She had one hand on my balls, stroking, slowly caressing the hot scrotum. The feeling was indescribably erotic. We lay face to face, our hands exploring sinuously each other's bodies. I fingered Anna. She sighed and jerked as the passion mounted.

'Put it in,' she sighed, turning over on her back. 'Come on, put it in.'

I mounted her. Her hand grabbed my swollen organ, found

86

the entrance and thrust it in. I pushed and it was received by a vagina gripping it in lubricated lust. I started thrusting wildly, bringing my body ever closer to hers. I could feel my balls moving against the softness of her flesh. I was in as far as I could go. Excitement mounted within me. I could no longer have controlled myself than a stallion straddling a mare. Madly I thrust into her as she pushed and twisted her body to meet my movements against clitoris.

In mad sweeps of delirious joy the signal came. I was coming. The seminal fluid had been released. It flooded my whole being with heart-pumping, breath-taking sensations. The sperm, in full spate, was thrust out into Anna's vagina, the muscles of which were gripping me in exciting stimulation. She took it all.

I sank down across her, exhausted.

From the darkness there was a grunt of sheer disgust.

'Shaw,' said a voice hissing with absolute frustration, 'you're a bum fuck.'

She got out of bed, squatted herself over the chamber-pot and commenced rinsing operations.

By the time she got back I was asleep. But dimly I could hear Anna's voice: 'You selfish bastard!'

Anna was tolerant when it came to male sexual idiosyncraises.

She knew that her legs excited me as they did most of the westerners. At cinema shows she would pull back her dress so that I could savour their full shapeliness.

'You like my million-dollar legs?' she would ask. 'Make you happy, yes?'

I would stroke their stockinged smoothness. My other hand would be on my tool, hard and eager to go.

'O.K. Shaw, you feel goddammed good. Can jack off.'

And, as Anna watched me, I'd do just that – bring it out, grasp it and, with the other hand stroking her thighs, bring myself off.

As Anna once told me, 'Too much men jack off look-see me. My legs belong good. You look-see.'

With that she would hoist her dress and give me full view of those long and lovely limbs, stockinged up to high-thigh level.

She was willing, too, to please the others who had different ideas of sexual fulfilment.

She told me of the chap, a Frenchman, who could only come when she slapped him good and hard across his backside – resounding thwacks which made her arm ache. And, as her hand fell on him in rapid succession, he would madly toss himself off.

All this standing in a corner of her bedroom, she belabouring his arse from the back and he going hell for leather on his tool as the blows stimulated him to full enjoyment of an ejaculation.

She thought nothing of it. If men wanted it that way, then it was all right with her. Who was she to stand on ceremony – happiness was where you found it.

There was a Frenchman, a high officer in the Concession police force, who was renowned for his toughness with crooks – the Gestapo or the Japanese Kempetai were in the same league – and, as far as Anna was concerned, for his 'crazy' method of attaining sexual relief.

'He makee me piss on he,' Anna told me. She was forthright and made no secret of the quirks of her men friends who, no doubt, paid her well for her co-operation. Certainly in the case of the French police official Anna sensed that here was protection – and the Shanghai cabaret girls, often bullied and exploited by Chinese constables and such renowned extortioners as girl-managers or landlords, were ever in need of high-placed male guardians.

All she had to do was to undress, as she put it, 'bollock naked', squat over the neck of the officer lying prone on the bed – 'and makee piss'.

From his position he could see all of Anna's genital region. This gave him an erection, got him ready for greater joy to come. And, as the warm urine flowed from Anna to cascade all over his upper chest, he violently masturbated. That was all.

Anna was paid for regular pissing sessions which the Frenchman enjoyed. Strangely enough, he was married but was evidently bereft of this urinary solace from his wife who, perhaps, had no inkling of his desires.

I asked her how she managed to do it every time. It was easy – drink Cocoa-Cola and keep it inside for a long time. Then let it all go over him. No trouble at all.

I was tickled pink. 'I'm forever pissing bubbles,' I sang. The joke was lost on Anna.

Whenever Anna turned up at the Palais – she was absent on many occasions; no doubt with other male friends of whom I was particularly jealous – I took her out and laid her in her room.

As far as she was concerned I was a 'bum fuck'. For the love of me I couldn't extend the waiting period to allow her to achieve an orgasm.

But Anna had other friends who managed to do what I never could do.

One of them was well-built, tough, Chinese cabaret girl named Lily. She was bigger than Anna, more coarse-looking. Like the Korean she was no stranger to men. She had been shacked up with half the U.S. Navy but, inevitably, there comes the time when the female, sated with penetration after penetration, seeks the gentler, more refined stimulation of a Lesbian association.

It was well known that many of the cabaret girls had their girl-friends either in their own establishments or in some other night spot. While they gave their bodies to males for some financial security, the real sensual delights came when they paired up with girl-friends.

Anna and Lily made no secret of their association. They admitted it to me and, on one occasion, allowed me to watch their performance. It came after I had taken both of them to a matinée performance at the Cathay cinema and had treated them to tea and cakes afterwards.

I had not sat between them. During the show I had noticed that their hands were roving over each other's bodies from crotch to breasts. They were feeling each other and evidently enjoying the sensual stimulation the gropings provided.

Back in Anna's room it was soon evident that my masculine attentions were not desired as Lily and the Korean, fully clad in tight-fitting cheongsams, hugged each other and rubbed their crotches together. I noticed the flushed face of Lily and the heavy breathing of both girls.

'Wanchee woman,' said Anna, addressing me. 'You sit – maybe jack off.' At which Lily laughed heartily and came over to me. She placed her hand over my flies, felt the erection I'd raised and said. 'Him no can pee.' At which both girls doubled up in sheer mirth.

It was summer-time. The room was hot and steamy. I undressed down to under-pants which was usual at that time if you wanted to keep cool.

Anna and Lily stripped off entirely and lay face to face on the bed. They snuggled up close together so that their breasts met in yielding contact, flattening out under the pressure. Lily, broader, more fleshy, thrust her face close to Anna's and with mouth wide open sucked in the Korean's lips. Her right arm moved over Anna's back and, pressing firmly, drew her closer. Left hand in front of her chest, she eased backward a little so that I could see fingers delicately stroking Anna's right nipple. She was assuming the dominant role.

89

The love play continued for several minutes. Lily's mouth was closed entirely over Anna's lips. She was using the tongue as stimulus. She continued to caress the nipple. Anna was breathing hard with mounting excitement.

Then Lily broke off contact completely. She lifted her face from that of Anna. Her hand moved away from the Korean's breast. She rolled away, stayed on her back a few seconds and then slipped off the side of the bed. Anna still lay there breathing hard, legs tightly closed but jerking convulsively in muscular stimulation of the clitoral region. Her eyes were closed. Her mouth was open wide.

Lily crossed over to the dressing-table near which I sat with the finest hard-on I'd ever raised but which I was leaving severely alone. I was intrigued. This was the first lesbian encounter I had seen.

Lily opened the top drawer, rummaged under a pile of clothes and brought out a massive, life-like penis replica in tremendous erection, veined, stiff but yet pliable, large, bulbous head 'circumcised' – an above-par tribute in moulded rubber to the magnificent craftsmanship of some Japanese creative expert.

Lily took not the slightest notice of me. Her eyes were on Anna whose right arm had slipped over her body so that knuckles, taut and white, were over her mound of Venus. Rapid movements indicated that fingers were erotically engaged in stimulation of the clitoris.

Lily, huge penis in hand, fingers clenched around the blown-up scrotum, walked over to the bed and stood for a moment or two watching Anna masturbating. Then, quite roughly, she clasped the Korean's wrist in a steely grip and pulled her arm away. Anna opened her legs wide to reveal under pubic hair, fully lubricated, vaginal lips, distended, receptive, stimulated to the point of intense desire.

The Chinese girl, still standing by the side of the bed, held the artificial penis in her left hand. Slowly she manoeuvred it into position between Anna's thighs and then, suddenly, finding the opening, wet and admissive, thrust the huge cock inside – right in so that only the scrotum, securely held, was visible.

There followed the most bizarre performance I have ever witnessed – one I shall never forget if I live to be as ancient as Methuselah. Lily, vigorously, commenced pulling the organ out until almost its full length was exposed and then strongly thrusting it back. It filled Anna entirely – an enormous weapon. Quicker and quicker Lily thrust it in, pulled it back, shoved it, withdrew it. She panted with the exertion of the operation. In it went, massive, wet, bulging, pushing the lips apart. Out it came. In again.

Anna, lips wide open, was sighing loudly. With each thrust her face twitched, her body jerked to meet the strokes. Her hands were closed over her breasts. She was tweaking her nipples wildly.

I watched Lily. She was sweating in the steamy atmosphere. I could see the beads on her forehead as with athletic strength and precision she held the great weapon and used it as an erotic piston, bringing on contortions from Anna as the monster filled her, constantly collided with clitoris and brought her ever nearer to the climax Lily was vigorously seeking in rapid but smooth arm movements.

And then it happened. Anna cried out, jerked her body stiffly upward, chest heaving, tongue thrust forward over lips, fingers clawing erect nipples. She remained taut for several seconds. Her legs shivered in the ecstasy of passion. I could see thigh muscles flexing and contracting.

Lily thrust the giant organ in and left it there to be gripped by violent muscular contortions inside the vagina. I could see the scrotum moving. Deep sighs and Anna sank back on the bed where she lay for several minutes until her heart-beats returned to normal. The entire operation, perhaps, had taken five minutes – perhaps a little more or less. I didn't time it. I was holding my own which had burst out of the fly opening of my cotton under-pants – a dwarf compared with the Japanese monster. No wonder I could never please the Korean. She needed an elephant. But I was holding back. Obviously there was more to come.

There was. Anna rose from the bed, accepted the great dildo from Lily and waited until the Chinese girl had laid herself down near the bed edge.

The repeat performance differed from the first in that Anna, holding the penis in her right hand, straddled Lily who was lying flat on her back. legs partly opened. With left hand Anna found the opening and for several minutes manipulated lips vigorously with her fingers. From time to time she leaned forward and let her breasts drop on Lily's chest so that nipples came into contact. Both girls then jerked spasmodically. Anna then worked the phallic emblem into position between her body and Lily's thighs and, still lying over the Chinese girl in breast-to-breast contact, manoeuvred the bulbous head so that it was ready for entry. A sudden thrust and it achieved penetration. Her pelvic mound rested over the great dildo so that it appeared to be part of her. As she thrust it in and pulled it back her body moved in rhythmic grace, reposing as a man's would on top of the Chinese girl. Her hand was making the great thing go in and out. Her body was thrust close as the vagina enveloped its enormity. It was withdrawn as the wet monster was pulled back.

'Screw me! Screw me!' moaned Lily in her American English. Anna increased her motions. She rammed it home. Back it came. Body movements were co-ordinated with the phallus's entry and exit. Here was a girl screwing the ass off another girl. Lily squirmed and kicked. Anna pressed down on top of her. I could see the Chinese girl's hand roaming over Anna's buttocks, down her thighs.

And then as Lily's movements increased in feverish spasms Anna dropped her body so that her face hovered over that of the Chinese girl. Lips wide open she began to kiss her passionately. Her hand was thrusting the giant penis in to its base, withdrawing it – quicker and quicker. Lily was ready. She was coming. Her arms pulled Anna down in even closer embrace. She moaned in ecstasy. Two or three sudden kicks, a heaving of chest and it was all over. The two girls became motionless, resting after what had been a physically exhausting erotic episode.

After a minute or two, Anna withdrew the phallus, got off the bed and placed the wet object in a towel on the dressing-table. She donned a Japanese kimono and slippers and, carrying the penis in the towel, left the room, no doubt to wash it thoroughly.

On the bed Lily, still on her back, looked over at me. I had my whole apparatus out – testicles as well. My hand gripped the hard shaft which was raring to go.

'Poor Shaw,' said Lily. 'You come.'

I got up and went to the bed, stood there and looked at my tremendous erection pointing at the Chinese girl.

'Come,' she said.

I drew closer.

Lily thrust out her arm, her hand closed over the bulbous tip. Her fingers played delicately with the glans. I began to heave.

'Get tissue,' said Lily.

There was a box of paper handkerchiefs on the dressing-table – Shanghai-made in imitation of the American product unheard of in England. I drew one out and took it to the bed.

Lily placed it over the tip of my rod. Her hand closed over it again and in rapid motions she brought me off, withdrawing the handkerchief, now wet and sticky. She rolled it into a ball, handed it to me and told me to deposit it in the commode under the bed. This I did.

Anna returned with the dildo which she placed in the dressing-table drawer.

'Me jack-off your sweetheart,' said Lily.

Anna pretended to get angry. She didn't give a damn really. But she put on a show.

'Cocksucker,' she said. 'Goddam, he belong me. No can jack-off my sweetheart. You savvy?'

Lily said that she savvied and then both girls burst into peals of laughter – just to show me that they had been play-acting. There was no ill-feeling. We were just one big happy family.

I had another experience of Lesbianism among the cabaret girls not long afterwards.

The Venus, about a quarter of a mile from Blood Alley, was owned by Sam Levy, a British subject. His establishment had formerly been in Hongkew but since the unofficial takeover of that Settlement area by the Japanese after the outbreak of hostilities with China he had transferred his business to the French Concession.

There he had three Korean girls who were among his prize possessions – good money-makers. He reserved them for his best customers and I was thankful that he regarded me in that light.

I went home with them one night. They shared a room and a big bed in Avenue Joffre – the bottom end which was less exclusive than the top stretch.

I got into bed with one of the girls who was going to provide me with her service. The other two snuggled in at the side of us – four of us in one big bed, a bit of a crush but room enough, nevertheless.

We kissed, I played with nipples, stroked the soft body offered to me, and, in time, mounted it normal style. I was thrusting away when action at my side indicated that something was going on there, too.

In the darkness I could dimly perceive two shapes in close embrace, one girl on top of the other. They were making a real party of it – we were a foursome. The bed shook as they rubbed bellies together, mutually explored each other's bodies, kicked and panted in excitement. Erotically aroused, I launched thrust after thrust into the vagina that was enfolding my rigid organ.

The girl under me, while she regularly jerked her body or wriggled so that it seemed as if she was enjoying penetration, certainly did not possess the enthusiasm of Anna. The cabaret

93

girls were fine actresses when it came to stimulating passion, making a man feel that he was good on the job, virile and exciting. I fancied that she envied the two girls feverishly embracing each other in the darkness next to us.

From time to time the two bodies at my side touched mine, sending an electric shock racing through my frame. I could hear them moaning, grunting, kissing wetly and loudly. I could hold myself back no longer. I let it all go. The Korean beneath me took it all, let me stay inside her until my penis had softened and fallen out and then she got out of the bed, squatted over the commode and gave herself a thorough rinsing. Still the Lesbian wrestling match proceeded. I could feel legs jerking in spasmodic motions. From time to time searching arms brushed mine. The two girls rolled about, twisted their bodies, moaned and sighed. I had no idea what was really going on. I couldn't see a damned thing. Then, suddenly, it all ceased. There were gasps, a lessening of the action and the sound of violently heavy breathing. My girl re-entered the bed after her ablutions. I placed my arm over her breasts and lay back. I soon fell asleep.

One thing I'll say for the patrons of the Blood Alley dives is that they were good for a giggle.

There was the cadaverously built Scotsman, who regularly appeared in the Palais after a Burns Nicht celebration or the annual dinner of the St Andrew's Society and settled the question for the girls of what may or may not be seen under the kilt.

He was the kind of chap – and there were many in Shanghai – who was led to the bright lights of the all-night dives by a skinful of alcohol. Normally his everyday respectability would guide him to the higher-class cabarets such as the Paramount where the girls were all Chinese, hand-picked and expensive, or to the night clubs in the western district or French-town. But, as in my case, a surfeit of the hard stuff produced a sort of Mr Hyde complex with concomitant wicked desires and the Scotsman was no different from me.

In full regalia – 'pissed as a fart', to use the expression of Charlie Tombs – the Scotsman would whoop his way into the Palais, subside into a seat close to the ballroom floor, order a slug of Scotch and then, quite alone, absolutely unpartnered, join the dancers on the floor to do a Highland fling – no matter whether the band was playing waltz, foxtrot, quickstep, tango or Palais Glide.

His performance, if not particularly graceful, was certainly athletic. His wild cries soon had all eyes on his frenzied cavortings, particularly those of the girls who knew what to expect.

Suddenly down would go his hands, up would come his kilt and there was the answer to the question that had intrigued women – and non-Scottish males – for generation after generation. Shaking like semi-solidified jelly it was all there to see – a great dangling tool and a scrotum gyrating madly with each mad leap he took.

Screams from the women – not of disgust but of sheer mirth. Great guffaws from the males. And wild war whoops from the Scotsman as with kilt completely exposing entire genitalia he set out to prove that not only was he another MacNijinsky but a revealer of the truth so far as the great kilt mystery was concerned.

And, as Charlie Tombs pointed out after witnessing the Scotsman's spirited performance, the occasion was unique so far as the girls were concerned in that he'd lay odds of 100 to one that not one of them had ever seen a cock, Scottish or any other breed, in 'the soft state, not even bloody half-hard'.

Why, continued the little Australian, who had a fund of tall stories, there was the case of the cabaret girl who took up nursing and had her first examination.

She was asked what would be the first thing to do if she had to perform an amputation job on a male penis.

'Easy,' she said. 'Simply saw through the bone.'

'Bone,' said the examiner, startled. 'Why a penis has no bone.'

'Everyone I've seen has had one,' replied the girl.

Tombs himself could also have you in stitches – quite unintentionally from time to time.

He was one of us who could not resist the lure of a dram or two – or three or four or more – after night work. There were also Max Chaichek of United Press, Adolph Goldberg of the *Shanghai Times*, Randy Raven of the *N.C.D.N.*, and several others. We met after one a.m. at the Frisco, second in size in Blood Alley only to the Palais, where we congregated in front of the bar and guzzled the hard stuff as if it were no more potent than mother's milk.

Tombs, whose favourite tipple was Scotch, was apt to get belligerent although he was no bigger than a jockey.

There was the morning – about four a.m. it would be – when after trying to hit a good-natured Yank from a merchantman in port and missing him by about a foot the diminutive Tombs disappeared from view. In the excitement of the occasion we had all suddenly latched on to the American, who was twice the size of the Australian, in an effort to keep him from replying with a fist the size of a garden spade to Tombs' wild swing. The joint move had been successful. There was no retaliation – and when we looked around there was no Tombs. It was as if the floor had opened up and engulfed him.

We searched everywhere – high and low, on the ballroom floor, underneath the tables and even in the gents' toilet.

But he hadn't left the building. We knew that. We were standing right by the exit which was close to the bar. Where the hell was the little bleeder?

Suddenly I had an idea. We hadn't really searched the toilets thoroughly. Could it be that he was on a throne in one of the cubicles?

In we went again – *en masse* as a search party. 'Tombs!' we yelled, 'where the bloody hell are you?'

I heard a strangulated moan from the end cubicle which was closed. I tried to push the door open. It was locked. Max Chaichek, who was short but who had shoulders like Charles Atlas, joined me and we launched a concerted assault on the woodwork. It gave way.

There was Tombs, kneeling on the floor, back to us, right arm well down inside the toilet bowl and hand frantically groping somewhere out of sight beyond the bend.

'What's the matter, Charlie?' I asked.

Tombs looked round. Never have I seen such a woeful expression on a human face. Come to think of it never have I since seen a face so completely changed in a matter of ten minutes or so. The Australian's cheeks looked as if they had been sucked in by a vacuum. His lips curled inwards. What jaw there had been seemed to have completely disappeared. Sags, bags and wrinkles had taken the place of firm flesh. He looked like a senile coelacanth. And then he spoke. Or, rather, he lisped, splashily and definitely incoherently.

'I've lost me fuckin' teeth.'

His toothless gums met with a sort of a swishing sound as he spoke. I thought his lower lip was going to engulf his nose. He looked like my granny after she had taken out her false teeth at night to put in the water-glass.

I burst out laughing. So did Chaichek. We rolled about in feverish glee. Never was there a funnier sight than toothless Tombs on his knees groping about in a lavatory bowl.

'Rotten bastards,' he mumbled. 'I was spewing me guts up when me bloody teeth came out. They're here somewhere – must be.'

His arm dived deeper into the bowl and his hand explored the watery wastes beyond the bend. But no teeth.

'They're probably in the old Whangpoo by now,' said Chaichek, still doubled up.

'Or biting the balls of a deep-sea diver down at Woosung,' I volunteered.

Tombs was not amused.

'Time you got some glue or something to keep those bloody teeth of yours in your mouth,' I added, remembering the great table-slither of the Australian's top set at the Japanese press conference.

'Bollocks,' spat Tombs. 'It was an accident.'

Alas, the teeth had vanished somewhere in the sewers of Shanghai. We got a great army of cabaret coolies, armed with bamboo rods, suction pumps and anything else handy to scour that lavatory bowl and its mysterious bends. No teeth. They were gone forever.

Tombs, looking thirty years older, on a diet of slops or some sort of mush that did not require chewing, was minus his dentures for about a week. Then, suddenly rejuvenated, he appeared sporting, dazzling white, evenly spaced, the pearly molars that restored him to full circulation among the girls of whom he was particularly fond. Confidence restored, he rejoined us at the Frisco sessions.

Lip Service

When sex raised its bulbous head for me in England it had usually been hand-reared – either a do-it-yourself job or the charitable effort of a girl anxious to do her bit to keep the birth-rate down.

In Shanghai I quickly became more versatile and added several variations to my repertoire – rolling between a massive pair of Russian tits, the lascivious delight of being brought off by a Japanese cabaret girl just through bodily contact on the ballroom floor, normal coition with the girl passive, the more exciting penetration with the female dominant, anal entry, the sensual joy of the massage table – and, by far the most rapturously ecstatic of the lot, fellatio, oral stimulation of the penis.

As an art of love it had been practised in the Far East, including China, from time immemorial but, in the puritanical society of Britain at that time, it was regarded as an obscene sexual deviant.

In the foreign enclaves such as Shanghai the suckee-suck girls were plentiful.

For 30 cents there were the 'schoolgirls', as the rickshaw pimps called them – small, delicately boned Chinese damsels whose ages could have been anywhere between 12 and 18. It was hard to tell the age of a Chinese girl because even at 40 and over the women of the Han race looked 20 years younger. Nevertheless most of the suckee-suck girls gave me the impression that, if they had been British or American, they would still have been at school sucking pens and not penises.

They dressed well, these young purveyors of sex – tight-fitting cheongsam, high split revealing most of the thigh, small breasts made more appealing to the tit-loving westerner by a padded brassiere, faces skilfully made up and hair cut and permed western style. But they did not wear lipstick. At that backward time its hue was transferable by the act of kissing or sucking and there weren't many gentlemen in the city who relished the decorative imprint of lips around their tools.

My first experience was a stand-up affair. A Chinese girl, whose age I estimated at about 14, had spotted me emerging from the Del Conte bar in Bubbling Well Road.

'You wanchee suckee-suck?'

She looked sweet and innocent – about five feet one, deliciously fragile, enticingly smooth-skinned as bared arms revealed in the summer heat. She wore stockings because she knew that the big westerners liked a silky feel. When she smiled her even teeth sparkled and there was sensuous magnetism in her deep-brown eyes. She wore the inevitable cheongsam, fitting her lithe little body like a glove.

The usual query from me.

'How much?'

'Fifty cents.'

Obviously higher than the recognised market price.

'Fuck off!'

The girls knew that this was an English expression meaning that their presence was not required.

'Forty cents.'

Better but still leaving ground for further negotiations in a land where the person who did not argue loud and long over prices was considered by both purveyor and lookers-on to be a complete ass.

'Chi-la.'

Another injunction by me, this time in Shanghai dialect, for the girl to get lost.

'Thirty cents.'

More like it. But why not have a go at making a real cut-price bargain?

'I fuckee you. Thirty cents.'

'No can do. No belong fuckee girl. Belong suckee.'

Obviously a strict trade-union demarcation line to be observed.

'Okay, thirty cents.'

She takes me by the hand, presses close into me to get me steamily horny and leads me into a dark alleyway not far from the Union Jack Club.

She pushes me against the wall, swishes her little body against mine so that I feel her pelvic mound. I place my arms around her, pull her in tightly. She giggles as she feels the out-thrust hardness pushing its way between her legs, over her flat stomach, across her thighs as I jerk in rising excitement.

'You likee me?' she asks.

'Belong number one,' I reply.

She is pleased. She pulls herself back, looks down at my flies and then her lovely little hand travels downward to open each button slowly, caressingly. I've got the jack to beat all jacks – a big stiff beast, wet and sticky already. Can't wait much longer. It jerks convulsively as she grasps its unbending rigidity. She pulls it out and her fingers move in delicate rhythm over the glans.

I'm panting, huffing and puffing like the 'Flying Scotsman' starting off from King's Cross on the non-stop Edinburgh run. My body jerks convulsively as the little hand plays around the tip and she strokes my balls with the other. She looks at me and smiles. I get the idea that she wants to toss me off to avoid the gobble job if she can. Or, perhaps, she's a real professional properly working me up to near-ejaculatory enthusiasm before she gets those little lips around my cock. Whatever her motive for the manual titillation I can't wait much longer.

'For Christ's sake get it in!' I yell. 'Get it in. Put it in your mouth.'

She bends down so that her head brushes my rampant hardness. The touch is satiny. My cock jerks in responsive excitement. I look down at her as she crouches below me. Still holding and stroking my balls she lifts her head a little, guides my enormous shaft to a position in front of her lips. Suddenly she opens her mouth wide and thrusts it in. I start jerking backward and forward so that the glans brushes those soft lips now firmly closed over the throbbing thickness of my erection.

As I move her tongue darts under the glans and the sensation is fabulous – heavenly. I grip her small shoulders and shove into her more strongly than ever. I can see her body quivering as the enormous power of my thrusts into her mouth calls forth all her reserves of strength to keep her lips in vice-like grip.

I slow down as her tongue darts in perpetual motion to caress the sensitive glans. I feel great surges of passion sweeping up from my balls as she strokes them. She senses the great hardness swelling. Her hand tightens its grip. She holds on with her lips like grim death. Her tongue goes hell for leather underneath the tip.

In massive bursts the semen floods out – spasm after spasm flinging out the sticky fluid into the softness of the cavern in which she has imprisoned my rod.

As the last burst issues forth she holds it in her mouth for a second or two to allow for the final ecstasy and then she pulls back so that wet, shiny with semen, I can see the great gun that has exploded into violent action. I look at her. Over her bottom lip there are trickles of seminal fluid. Her mouth must be filled with my sperm. I wonder if she has swallowed any of it. She must have. I was thrusting deep into her mouth. She never let go. She took it all.

She spits what's left on to the ground, wipes her mouth with a cloth which she brings forth from inside the side opening of her cheongsam. Then she holds out her hand.

'You likee?' she asks me. 'I give you good time?'

'Fine,' I said, not wishing to appear too enthusiastic.

I take out fifty cents and hand it to her.

'No have got money,' she says to indicate that unless I have exactly thirty cents, which I haven't, then I'm going to pay over the odds.

'Jang-daw,' I say. It means robber.

She laughs cheekily and looks at me with appealing eyes.

'All right, keep it.' After all, you wouldn't get a 'gam' for seven pennies back in London – not even a quick hand-job behind the bushes in Hyde Park.

A little more expensive but less arduous on the legs was the 'Silver suck' provided by a Chinese-owned hire-car firm with an eye on what today we would call fringe-benefits.

There were three big taxi operators in Shanghai: the Ford company, the Johnson firm and the Silver Taxi Co.

The first two organisations got you there – and back if you wanted – and left it that. Not the Silver blokes.

You grabbed the phone, rang up a Silver garage, told a voice at the other end that you wanted a taxi – and added, if you felt horny, that you 'wanchee schoolgirl belong suckee'.

Within minutes a Silver car would be at the door, driven by a smiling Chinese gentleman who would proudly point to the back seats and indicate the presence there of a Chinese damsel.

A discussion with the driver. Did you want long ride, medium journey or a mad dash round the blocks – just enough to give the girl time to do her job and get you back behind the office desk bereft of concupiscent thoughts?

I usually took a long ride – up Nanking Road, into Bubbling Well Road, across St George's Square, up Great Western Road and back again to the Bund.

The girl kneels on the floor, gets her head in position over your flies, delicately undoes the buttons and brings it out – stiff as a frozen German blood sausage from Futterer, the butcher, but certainly not lifeless as its throbbing tumescence indicates.

'Ai yah,' she exclaims as she looks at it. This indicates surprise at the size of it, a good and well-used Chinese feminine ploy to fill you with manly pride.

'You belong English?' she asks and you wonder if there are characteristics about your John Thomas that denote racial background such as a Union Jack pattern of the veins or a bulldog droop of the glans.

Up Nanking Road you go – past Whiteaway, Laidlaw's department store; Macbeth, Gray, the tailors; Llewellyn's pharmacy; C. N. Gray, another tailor; the Chocolate Shop; out westward.

The girl has head well down, lips playing around the tip to get you ripe. You sit back in the taxi and appear to be completely alone to passers-by on the pavement as you stop for the traffic lights by the Sun Sun department store.

You spot old Paddy Duffy of the Shanghai Municipal Police in uniform up by the Sincere Company store. He sees you, waves and smiles. You wave back and look down at the mass of jet-black hair filling your lap. She's taking it all in now – but not making too hasty a job of it. There's a long way to go.

The driver has his eyes firmly fixed on the road ahead – not a glance in the rear-view mirror. Too well trained.

On you go up towards Jessfield Park. She's quickening up now – the tongue comes into play. Her lips move up and down and your hands are roaming all over the crouching figure as waves of excitement sweep through you.

Suddenly she goes all out. Her head moves rapidly. You feel the softness of the lips, the erotic touch of the tongue. You grip hard, sigh and prepare for the inevitable. Out it comes – in great big spurts. She takes it all.

You're on the way back. She takes out a cloth and wipes you off. She spits and you notice that there's a commode to your right on the floor. She wipes her mouth. The driver says something to her in Chinese and he slows down to halt the vehicle finally outside the Silver depot at St George's where the girl alights. As she leaves she bestows a charming smile on you and you notice that she has a large mole on the right side of her face. But she's pretty enough – and young, too.

Back on the Bund you pay off the driver – 50 cents for the journey, a dollar for the girl and 40 cents in tips to be shared. You wonder if the girl is going to be cheated. On second thoughts you know this is not possible. She is one of a legion of tarts owned by the gangster Tu Yueh-sen. She will be well protected by Tu's gun-toting minions who regularly collect the takings at the taxi depots. Woe betide any driver who falls foul of that cut-throat crew.

In English money the outing and fringe benefit have cost approximately two shillings and sixpence.

The Paris cinema in Avenue Joffre – a second-run house with cheaper admission charges than the first-run theatres – had a great reputation for sexual thrills. Look along any row as the show was proceeding and you'd be able to see some lucky male being jerked off by his girl-friend. Or a young chap playing with the exposed tits of some European girl – usually from the White Russian colony. The permutations were many and varied and the management, which was Chinese, encouraged the free-and-easy atmosphere as it meant full houses at the two night shows.

I was sucked off there by a Russian bar hostess I had picked up at the Joffre Bar and Restaurant, had bought out and had promised to take to see the film then showing at the Paris. 'Dianne', I think it was, with a young James Stewart playing the part of the blinded French soldier in search of his love – beautifully sentimental, a real tear-jerker.

For her it was not a chore. She was a penis-worshipper. Her phallic complex – and there are many females similarly enslaved – meant that she desired orgasmic relief through oral contact with the male organ, erect and throbbing with passion. She had to get it in her mouth and savour its fullness with lips, tongue and palate.

Thus in the Paris balcony, which provided double, arm-chair seating, she would open my flies and, for a start, play with my tool which had been erect long before her fingers had touched it. She stroked it, kneaded it, ran her fingers up and down its length, no doubt assessing its masculine potential.

She was a tall girl, black-haired, probably from the Georgia region of Russia. She had long legs which were encased in dark stockings but her main assets were two lovely breasts, big and bouncy, heavily nippled and constrained only by a button-down blouse. She wore no brassiere. She well knew that the sight of these two whoppers thrusting against the flimsy blouse material – visible but yet veiled – was enticement enough to any male bestowing his custom at the bar. Shanghai had more than its share of tit-men.

As she played with my rigid penis with her right hand, her other hand guided my left hand to her bosom. She was seated on my right. I had my right arm around her shoulders and we were pressed in close contact. I undid the blouse buttons and, cupping one of her breasts in my hand, brought it out and began to caress the nipple.

The erectile response was terrific. The nipple became hard and its length increased immensely. As I stroked it and, from time to time, cupped the soft mound, which yielded to my finger pressure, she sighed and squirmed in the throes of passion rapidly building up.

Her fingers were playing with my glans, touching the tip and sending spasms of delight through my frame. She urged me to increase my efforts on nipple receptivity. I reached and brought out the other breast. There they were in the half-light: two large emblems of feminine sex appeal, nipples thrusting forth, bouncy, easily responding to my movements as I cupped them in turn, lifted them, pressed them close together, savoured to the full their pliable elasticity.

Suddenly she leaned right over me, bending from the waist so that her head was over my lap. I could feel her tits hanging in my hand heavily. My right arm was now free. I moved it across her shoulders and around her body so that I could grasp her right breast. I now had both of them in my hands. I worked on the nipples, taut and responsive.

Her mouth closed over my tool. She was playing with the tip, lips encasing the sensitive glans. I could feel her tongue exploring its tumescence. By jerks of her body she encouraged me to increase the tempo of my nipple-caressing. I did so and she began to move her head rapidly so that her lips traversed the entire length of my enormous erection – then back to the tip. Up and down in quick, silky motions.

Her body was trembling furiously. My fingers played with two erect nipples. I was trying to restrain myself as long as I could, for this was a wonderful experience. On the screen the film was in mid-sequence. You could hear the voices of the stars – near but yet far-distant as the passion mounted. The screen was a dim blur of sets and human movements. Your senses were in a turmoil of lusty madness.

The head went up and down. The girl was moaning as she moved. My fingers gripped and released the hard nipple-lengths. I stroked them, lightly touched the tips. And then, the moment of frenzied release as my sperm gushed forth – right into the mouth that was holding my shaft, giving its all in convulsions of ejaculatory gratification.

She withdrew her head, shuddered and moaned, lay over me for about a minute and then gently withdrew my hands from her breasts. There was no doubt that she had had an orgasm. She did not speak as she sat up at the side of me, handled her breasts and placed them within her blouse, which she buttoned up.

We sat through the film, my arm around her.

The bizarre part of that episode was that the cinema was filled with people. Next to us – we had the aisle seats; I always chose end-seating – was a young Eurasian chap with his girl-friend, probably Portuguese. They had been cuddling each other, kissing and whispering sweet nothings. The chap, who sat next to me, must have seen everything that went on. His girl-friend, too, must have had a grandstand view. Not once, however, did they seem to evince any concupiscent interest though I have no doubt that voyeurism brought its reward in greater sensuality.

Just to stimulate audiences to greater sexual efforts, the Paris had its regular supply of 'hot pictures' which, in those days, would have been censored heavily in Britain and the other western countries, even France. They came from Tokyo, Korea, Harbin in what was then Japanese-occupied Manchuria, Saigon and Calcutta. All had English sub-titles but who cared about the dialogue when the action was, in uncensored reality, horny and self-explanatory!

At the Kavkas night club later, where we had dinner washed down by vodka, the girl, whose name was Tanya, frankly admitted her infatuation with the male penis. She traced the fetish back to her schooldays when, she confessed, a young male teacher at the Russian school in Harbin with whom she was madly in love at the time had coaxed her to indulge in fellatio with him. At first she had not liked it but she had discovered that, with the passage of time, the idea excited her tremendously and that if the teacher played with her breasts as she was performing the act a quick orgasm was always possible.

Normal intercourse, she said, repelled her – though, at times, she had had to satisfy male customers at the bar who wanted no variations from the standard method of copulation.

Tanya left Shanghai shortly after our trip to the Paris cinema. She married a pharmacist's mate in the U.S. Navy who fell head over heels in love with her and carried her off to California. My bet is that they've been divorced many years – that is if the sailor wanted normal sex.

The dream of every single White Russian woman in China was to acquire a passport. She was stateless, had no country, could go nowhere. She was not a Soviet citizen but a refugee from Communist rule. The best prospect, of course, was an American passport. Thus single American males became the chief prey – young, middle-aged, senile, handsome, ugly as sin, long, short, fat, thin . . . no matter. The goal was a passport. The British, the French, the Germans – anybody with a legal travel document – were secondary prey.

Unlike their womenfolk the White Russian males were doomed to suffer the stigma of statelessness unless, by some miracle, they could find their various ways to such countries as the United States, Australia, New Zealand or some British colony, there to reside long enough to apply for citizenship.

The lot of the Russian male in Shanghai was pitiful. The single man had little hope of marrying a girl of his own race – or any other. He had nothing to offer. Feminine eyes had in focus only those with a national status, with well-paid jobs, with homelands well up in the international league. What prospect, for instance, could be offered by a former officer in the Czarist army who was working as a caretaker in one of the Sassoon office blocks? Or a former Russian admiral eking out a precarious existence as a cemetery keeper?

For the young Russians, whose fathers had fled from the Bolshevik onslaught, absolute hopelessness, the omnipresent feeling of utter despair, thrust them into abject degradation. They became the victims of liquor and, much worse, drugs. A common sight in the French Concession, particularly in the vicinity of the Russian Orthodox Cathedral in Route Doumer, was the young Russian chap begging from passers-by – Europeans, Chinese, Eurasians, anybody. Or the degrading spectacle of young fellows, drunk or drugged to the point of absolute insensibility, lying on the pavements.

Typical of the debasement of the Russian male was the case of the vodka-swilling, near-impotent Nikolai Teslenko, fortyish, former officer of artillery, jobless refugee in single-roomed oblivion in one of the terraced houses in Route Vallon, sharer of communal kitchen facilities, dependent entirely on the earnings of his wife.

At least ten years younger than Nikolai was the wife, Natasha. She had been married in Harbin which was before the Japanese aggression of 1931 the 'Russian capital' of Manchuria. She stood five feet ten inches in height in sharp contrast to the short stockiness of her husband. She was a big woman, heavily busted, wide-shouldered, long-legged, strong as an ox, not pretty of face but nevertheless becoming in peasant homeliness, dark-haired and eminently desirable.

Natasha had married above her station. In Manchurian exile, young, strong and indefatigable in the homely pursuits of the peasantry, she had gained security in the home of Nikolai, who was at that time employed fairly lucratively as an officer of the guards on the Chinese Eastern Railway which had always been a Russian-operated transport system. The sensuality of her presence as housekeeper had inevitably inflamed the bachelor ex-officer into a state of rampant lustfulness which had developed into frequent visits to Natasha's bed and a bond of mutual affection. Marriage soon followed. The tall Natasha changed her name. The stocky Nikolai was proud of his bride though he had to admit that her education had been, to say the least, scant.

He spoke French fluently. He had a good knowledge of German and some English. His general demeanour was that of the officer and gentleman. Natasha, on the other hand, could only write with great difficulty. Her Russian was that of the illiterate peasant of Czarist times. Yet, in stateless exile with all the social divisions of happier times remembered only in the history books, the disparity in stations of life went unnoticed in the White Russian colony where desirable females all too often were the descendants of the serfs and, only a small step higher, the illiterate country farmer-peasants.

The Japanese occupation of Manchuria and the savage brutality of the Emperor's soldiery – a foretaste of the vicious outrages that were to be perpetrated in World War Two – forced the White Russians into wholesale flight to the security of foreign-controlled Shanghai where they arrived in their thousands. Nikolai and Natasha, almost penniless, set up home in the French Concession – rooming-house communality, cheap, uncomfortable, often squalid.

And then the inevitable degradation of the Russian male, unable to secure employment, penniless in a community of great foreign wealth, despised by the passport-holders of the western powers, assailed by the hopelessness of an irremediable situation. Vodka. Forgetfulness in the stupor of daily drunkenness.

Natasha became the breadwinner. Lacking education, unable to seek office employment, too poor of speech to seek shopgirl association with the rich females bestowing their haughty custom on the Rue Cardinal Mercier fashion houses, she joined the cabaret legion – dance-tickets, the sit-out gropings of lecherous males with money to spend, the job-keeping acquiescence of

107

submission to the lustfulness of those whose passions her large, robust physique had aroused.

Banished from single-room intimacy to a cot in the kitchen the besotted Nikolai slept in alcoholic stupor as Natasha catered on the double-bed for the sexual desires of clients.

Yet she was gentle with Nikolai. There was still affection for the sot who had once thrilled her – the former officer whose flamboyant worldliness had earned her undying admiration. She kept him supplied with the cash his craving made necessary. Strong arm around his shoulders she put him to bed when he had drunk himself into a state of insensibility. She fed him when he wanted to eat. She was sorry for him. She pitied him. In some inexplicable way his degradation had not killed her love.

In time Natasha discovered that her height, her muscular symmetry, her big-breasted femaleness, her long-legged lure attracted smallish fellows, mostly middle-aged, who desired her domination, who begged her to beat them, to humiliate them, to flog them, to chastise their genitals, to bind them. . . .

She left the cabaret. Advertisements in the English-language press, carefully constructed by Nikolai in a rare moment of mindfulness, produced the customers in Route Vallon: 'Attractive European woman gives massage, etcetera, at her home. Satisfaction guaranteed.' There was a phone number – few houses in Shanghai were without telephones. It was the 'etcetera' that interested middle-aged John Beck, an Englishman working in an import-export business, a close friend of mine.

John, at least twenty years my senior, was weedy, the product of squalid working-class life in the north of England but grammar-school educated and something of an expert on textiles. He had a good position. He also had a mamma-complex. He doted on his old mum who, from his accounts of life at home, must have been a domineering battle-axe, a virago who reduced her husband to cringing subjection but who, at the same time, showered protective affection all over little John – loved him, pampered him, kept him securely tied to her apron strings.

It must have been an awful wrench when John went out to China – no strong mother to depend on, no dominating female behind whom to shelter. So John got married – to an Englishwoman born in Shanghai, the daughter of a prominent business family, a horse-loving, big, stalwart piece of furniture. She was bigger than he was, weighed more, was certainly tougher – but she was no substitute for mum.

Little, weedy John – five foot six of frailness – desired a

motherly wife. He got one who wore riding breeches almost daily, took horses over fences with the best of the men, groomed her steeds with steely hand – and horse-whipped her husband when he failed to satisfy her violent sexual urges, gave him black eyes and abused him coarsely.

John was frank with me. He was desperately unhappy. He liked big, strong women – but to mother him, not knock him about. And then an amazing confession: mother had allowed him to cradle himself in her lap, to sink his head into her ample breasts, to get rampantly hard as she caressed him, crooned to him and, generally, dandled him as if he were still a baby. All this throughout his life in England – from childhood to middle-aged bachelorhood.

He was her baby. She had no use for husband who was a boozing nonentity. All her affection was poured on John whom she completely dominated. She became to him a sexual stimulus, which suited her for she wanted no other female to possess the product of her womb. So she patted him, petted him, let him get a mighty erection in her arms, watched his hand reach for it, bring it out and rub it – and not a word of reproach when the semen spat out and he fell back, panting, to be fondled as a small child.

The psychiatrist might know the cause of this mutual display of sensual affection. I haven't a clue – even today. Nevertheless, it happened. John was as honest as clear daylight. I didn't doubt him.

So he went to Natasha, whose English was permanently fractured, picked up by ear in the cabaret but who was made to understand what he wanted – a mother substitute, big and strong, a protective symbol for his manly childishness, his failure to emerge from the suckling stage of life.

So the strong Natasha sat on the edge of her bed, pulled him on to her lap, bared her breasts (which mother had never done), pushed his head into their yielding softness, clasped her arms arounds him and wondered at the imbecility of the little fellow as he got a rise, pulled it out and jacked himself off. But for this service she got ten dollars. That was good money, indeed. And it cost nothing in physical effort.

John got a divorce, became a regular caller at Route Vallon and perked up no end.

I was curious. Natasha intrigued me. I wondered what else she would do. I accompanied John one night to her room and waited outside while he got the mother-treatment. There was no sign of Nikolai.

John was shown out of the room by Natasha, who waited at

the door with dress on. In the hallway leading to the front door he told me that he'd be waiting for me at Tkachenko's, a Russian restaurant where the cakes were out of this world – and expensive too. I nodded my head and promised not to be too long.

Natasha ushered me in and looked me over. She was four inches taller than I in flat-heeled shoes. But I didn't want to be mothered. After all, I had wide shoulders and a sound, 40-inch chest developed through stretch-exercises – wire-pulling my low pals called it.

I came to the point. I wanted to be sucked off. We stood facing each other in the middle of the bedroom and I noticed that there was a picture of the late Czar Nicholas in scarlet uniform hanging over the head of the large double bed placed against the wall.

Niet! No. She didn't want to suck. Not nice. How about a massage? Or she could whip me. Make it nice. She could tie me up. She could do all sorts of things – but not suck.

I offered fifteen dollars. Still no.

Twenty. No – but only after long pause for some mental arithmetic.

Twenty-five. She was weakening. Only a shake of the head.

All right, thirty – but no more.

Thirty – in my money about thirty-eight shillings. In Shanghai a gift from Heaven, particularly in the Russian colony.

She agreed.

I made it known that I wanted to see her in stockings, suspender-belt and nothing else – tits bared.

She pulled off her dress and her big breasts bounced excitingly, big-nippled, two great handfuls decorating a wide, deep chest.

She wore brief panties, lace-trimmed, flimsy, pubic hair over the mound of Venus darkly visible.

She sat on an upright chair by a wash-basin in a corner of the room and pulled on stockings and suspender belt which she placed over her panties. Then she stood up – all five feet ten of her, magnificently built, athletic, fantastically long-legged – desirable enough to give even an Indian mystic the Himalaya of a horn, which was what I'd got as I gazed at those two outsize breasts and legs made even more enticingly touchable in their stockinged beauty.

I undressed quickly and soon stood naked by the door on a hook on which I had hung suit, shirt, underpants – the lot.

I turned to look at her. John Thomas was in rampant erection, thrusting forth in front of me, hard as a rock – pointing its bulbous head in her direction.

She looked at it and smiled, walked over to me and placed her hand around it. Then she gently pulled it, leading me to the bed.

I described the position I wanted her to adopt and she nodded her head in agreement.

I lay flat on the bed, head unsupported by the pillow under the Czar's picture.

Natasha clambered over me so that her head hung over my genitals. Her arms, on each side of me, stiffly supported her body, straight-backed over my stomach and chest. Two large, fleshy thighs straddled my head. Knees bent, long calves resting on the mattress, she manoeuvred herself into position so that, as I gazed upward I could see the entire expanse of her crotch over my face, thin strip of pantie material clinging silkily to vaginal entrance. Her breasts hung heavily and as she moved they brushed erotically over my upper stomach. In this 'four-legged' position, thighs touching my ears, arms in stiff 'front-legged' posture I could feel her body quivering, muscles flexing until I lifted up my head so that my face was pressed against the thin strip of material between her legs. I could feel the hair, thick and curly, the softness of lips, the hardness of bone. She became taut. I moved my arms outside the rigid thighs on both sides of my head. My fingers feverishly stroked the silkiness of her stockings and the firmness of white flesh above.

She lowered her head. Her breasts were pressed into my flesh. The pressure on my face increased – hard, exciting, satiny, carnal.

She sought my throbbing hardness with right hand, grasped the taut rod and lifted it upright. Her head came down, her lips closed over it. It was encased in her mouth. My hands ran up and down her large thighs, muscular, firm-fleshed. My fingers dug in. I rubbed my face in suffocating contact with her crotch, pushing my nose into the softness of lip-rimmed crevice.

Waves of voluptuous passion gripped me. My body shuddered in quick spasms as she moved her head up and down so that my shaft, thick, solid, intemperate, wallowed in the warm wetness of her mouth. I could feel her tongue. Her teeth closed on it at times, gently, making it kick wildly in delightful licentiousness.

It had to be a quick job. I was no ascetic, no tired, middle-aged businessman. I had enormous reserves of semen, ever-ready to be enticed from inner reservoir. I could feel her magnificent body stiffen as she sensed the swelling signal of imminent ejaculation conveyed to her lips. She moved more quickly.

The world heaved in luxurious wassail. Muscles contracted

111

and then expanded, shooting into that delightful mouth in huge, body-shaking thrusts great spurts of semen. She held her head still. Her body quivered. I sank, sated, breathing heavily, underneath her, heart pumping furiously.

Natasha quickly heaved herself on to the floor, made a rapid dash to the wash-basin, turned on the tap and began to gargle furiously. I watched her.

When she had finished she beckoned me over. She dipped a face-cloth in the water, caught hold of my now insignificant little chap and gave it a good going over. The water was cold and I got goose-flesh. She laughed.

I paid her, was thanked courteously and she saw me to the bedroom door.

As I entered the hall she closed the door and I heard footsteps behind me. I turned around and saw a fellow of about my own height and my build but fat and flabby about the belly and backside. He was shabbily dressed in a suit that had seen better times. He wore no collar and his shirt-neck was open to reveal part of a hairy chest.

He sidled up to me. He touched me. In cringing fashion and in wheedling tones he said in fairly good English, 'Can you let me have a dollar? My wife, she gave you good time.'

He wasn't drunk but he'd had enough. His eyes were weak and watery. His face, once handsome, I thought, was a mass of small red veins. His nose had that purplish tinge of the confirmed drunkard.

I reached into my pocket and pulled out a note which I handed to him. Without a word of thanks he brushed past me, quickly opened the front door and was gone.

That was Nikolai – off poste-haste to the vodka shop.

With John Beck, which isn't his real name – for all I know he may still be in the land of the living being mothered in his dotage – I became a regular client of Natasha – she added vigorous body-massage and a hand-job to the oral exercises – and she told me of the tragedy of Nikolai's decline.

It was the usual tale of the hopelessness of many of the Russian men. All I could do was to offer sympathy. She was not disgusted with him. She would certainly stick by him. He was no use to her sexually, though, sometimes, he made an effort and she tried to coax him along.

But we were a heartless, selfish crew in pre-war Shanghai. Our brains, for the most part, were in our balls. We were all right, Jack, and that was that.

112

Sudden Death

The telephone on my desk rang as I was typing a story about a fire aboard a river steamer which had roasted about a thousand pigs on their way from the Yangtse farmlands to the city abattoirs.

The voice at the other end was recognisable – that of 'Tiny' Pitts, a detective sergeant in the Shanghai Municipal Police who covered sporting functions for us.

'Tiny' he had to be for he was a full six feet five inches, broad and brawny, an English southerner whose high educational qualifications had quickly seen him transferred from the uniformed branch to the CID.

'Ralph,' he said, 'get on your bike and pedal like hell to the Broadway Mansions. You'll see an interesting sight.'

He rang off. I grabbed a notebook, hailed a rickshaw and set off along the Bund for the comparatively short journey over Garden Bridge to the skyscraper building which stood close to the Soochow Creek.

I saw a group of blue-clad SMP European officers clustered around a Johnson hire-car. Closely scrutinising the inside of the vehicle were several plain-clothes men among whom was 'Tiny'.

'How's your stomach?' he asked me as I flashed my police pass and walked up to him. 'Go on, take a look at that.' He pointed to the front seat of the taxi, blood spattered and severely gashed.

Staring at me from the steering wheel were a pair of eyes, wide open, terror-stricken – the eyes of a Chinese set in a head which had been completely severed from its body.

The head rested on the steering wheel, hideous and bloody. Of the remainder of the body there was no sign.

I got the facts as the police knew them. The man was the driver of the taxi. He had no criminal record. A call for a car had been received from Hongkew and the man had been sent there from the Johnson garage in the central district of the Settlement. His severed head had been found by an inquisitive Soochow

113

Creek coolie who had glanced inside the vehicle, parked on the wide road in front of the residential Broadway Mansions. No sign of robbery. No apparent motive.

Pitts had his own theory. It was that the Japanese, some way, had been involved. They had a hand in most of the crime in Hongkew, which was known as 'Little Tokyo' and which, if not *de jure*, was certainly *de facto* under their control.

Chinese gangsters, too, inflicted their own reign of terror on a population constantly assailed by violence.

They were well-armed, ruthless desperadoes, whose contempt for life often involved them in suicidal gun-fights with the police – street battles in which they fought to the end and, more often than not, in which they wreaked a heavy toll of the forces of law and order and of innocent citizens caught in the cross-fire.

There was yet another menace to add to the hazards faced by a population of more than four million – the underground war between the Japanese and their Chinese traitor-puppets and the loyal Chiang Kai-shek agents who carried on the fight in cloak-and dagger operations master-minded by the dreaded Kuomintang (Nationalist) secret police chief, Lin, who, it was said, often penetrated into the city in disguise from his forward base in Free China.

The removal by assassination of key figures in the puppet régime was the main assignment of what became known as the Chungking Underground which had its secret headquarters somewhere in the Shanghai foreign-controlled area and which employed a vast army of patriots sworn to fight to the death the traitors and their Japanese masters.

The patriots used an amazing variety of weapons to strike terror into the hearts of their enemies – revolvers, sub-machine-guns, hand-grenades, bombs, knives, strangling ropes, poison, acids and other lethal objects. They lived dangerously and often briefly. Once caught by the Japanese, violent death – sometimes after months of torture – was the only fate they could expect.

Pitts' theory that the Japanese were behind the severed-head mystery was proved to be correct after two more heads were found on the steering wheels of Ford and Silver hire-cars in Hongkew.

Again only the heads were found. The bodies had disappeared.

For a Chinese to lose part of his body in death was a terrifying prospect. It could only mean entry into the ancestral spirit world in dismembered form – a crippled ghost. Thus the removal of the bodies from the hire-cars pointed immediately to the motive behind the murders – intimidation, the striking of terror into the hearts of the taxi-drivers.

After the discovery of the third severed head not one driver would accept a fare into Hongkew and while the police had no positive proof, it was obvious that the new Japanese hire-car firm, which now had a monopoly of business in the district, had instigated the killings.

Of far greater significance to us in the newspaper business was the arrival in Nanking of Wang Ching-wei, one-time anti-imperialist revolutionary and close friend of Dr Sun Yat-sen, the founder of the Chinese Republic, to become the head of what was to be called by the Japanese 'the Reformed Government of the Republic of China'.

Wang, ranked only second to Chiang Kai-shek in the Nationalist hierarchy, had fled with Chiang to Chungking, the war-time capital in Szechwan, and his defection caused a world-wide sensation.

The Japanese were cock-a-hoop over their rich prize and they provided a spectacular welcome for Wang in Nanking.

Chiang called him 'the vilest of traitors' but told the world that his defection could never affect the determination of the Chinese government to fight the Japanese and their puppets until victory was achieved. It was a prospect that, at that time, seemed unlikely to be realised.

It soon became apparent that the Japanese and their puppets were bent on a campaign of harassing the Western nations in China, particularly Britain and the United States.

In Tientsin, British women and girls were being stripped and searched by Japanese soldiers at the barricades separating the Japanese-controlled area from the British Concession there. Protests were of no avail and British troops, who watched the degrading spectacle from their guard posts, were powerless to intervene.

It started after a group of Chinese, described by the Japanese as 'Chiang bandits', sought refuge in the British Concession in Tientsin. The Japanese demanded that they should be handed over 'for trial' which, as everyone knew, could only mean torture and death. The British authorities refused and the harassment commenced.

Finally, the British government gave in and handed the men over, a move which brought instant condemnation from Chungking and lost the Western powers much face among the loyal Chinese.

Worse still, a short time later the British government, which was supplying Chiang Kai-shek with much needed supplies over the Burma Road from Lashio to Kunming in Yunnan province, capitulated to Japanese demands to close the highway. This was a grave blow to Chiang Kai-shek but, thanks to American pressure, the route was re-opened several months later and it placed both London and Washington firmly on the side of what the Japanese called 'the Chungking bandit gang'.

Inevitably the foreign areas, more particularly the Settlement, were dragged into the test of strength between Japan and the treaty powers. First, the Greater Shanghai government, a puppet administration known officially as the Ta Tao, established police stations on their own territory bordering roads under the control of the Shanghai Municipal Council.

Then followed demands to the foreign authorities to hand over several roads which, claimed the Ta Tao government, were Chinese areas illegally occupied and policed by 'the uniformed and armed mercenaries' of the Settlement authorities.

Two major roads were involved – Edinburgh Road and Jessfield Road, both well-used highways which skirted the Settlement boundary.

A major confrontation between the Ta Tao authorities and the Settlement council developed when armed Chinese police patrols – never smaller than a party of seven or eight men – began to appear on both roads. Inevitably, dangerous situations occurred when S.M.P. officers were faced by a show of armed force by the Ta Tao men, most of whom had been recruited from village desperadoes.

Crisis point was reached when a Sikh constable on traffic duty in the centre of Edinburgh Road was shot dead by a Ta Tao party.

I was quickly out there with Mike Nenchew, who took shots of the dead Sikh, revolver still in holster, lying under the umbrella-shaped awning which shaded the post.

Armoured-car patrols now took the place of men on foot and any Ta Tao squads found in either highway were quickly confronted with an armada of mobile steel monsters, were summarily ordered back into their buildings or, in the event of belligerence, were fired on – and no nonsense about it either. 'Get off the road or we open fire,' was the order given by the British officers in charge of the armoured cars.

Up and down both roads the armoured cars patrolled day and night. Sikhs on traffic control were covered by a stationary armoured car as the uniformed mercenaries of the Ta Tao government watched from concrete guard-houses erected on the broad walls hiding the extensive grounds and mansions which accommodated various departments of the puppet administration.

The largest of these was 96 Jessfield Road, a Chinese-style residence containing several courtyards, deep cellars and a big garden which had been converted into a concreted base to support two lines of barrack buildings accommodating men of the Ta Tao police who guarded the high-ranking puppets using the place as headquarters.

The building struck fear into the hearts of the loyal Chinese. Behind its high walls it was known that, following the Japanese pattern of brutality in China, anti-Wang-Ching-wei elements were subjected to diabolical forms of torture and that it was unlikely that any man sent there for interrogation would emerge alive.

And while poor wretches languished in chains in the cellars, in first- and second-floor luxury top-rank traitors and their beautiful concubines lived off the fat of the land. Even Europeans passing the high walls and massive wooden doors of the mansion were afflicted by fearful tension as they felt unseen eyes from behind blockhouse slits watching their every move. Like the Japanese Bridge House in Hongkew 'Number ninety-six' was steeped in evil and from its grim structural facade there arose the miasma of death.

There arose yet another crisis when S.M.P. armoured cars were fired on from puppet buildings in the western district. The Settlement police returned the fire and four Ta Tao uniformed men at 96 Jessfield Road were killed in a hut built on the broad wall facing the road.

According to the S.M.P. version of the incident the Ta Tao men had opened fire first. There had been an immediate return of fire from one armoured car and an engagement lasting about thirty minutes had ensued. No S.M.P. men had been hit and it was not known if there had been casualties among the Ta Tao men.

The Japanese-supported puppet Chinese newspapers soon set the record right. Four officers of the Ta Tao police force, 'peacefully carrying out their duties of guarding Chinese property on Chinese soil', had been ruthlessly attacked by foreign members of the Shanghai Municipal Police and had been killed. There were demands for compensation, for immediate action to take over the roads by force and to end, once and for all times the 'illegal acts' of the treaty powers led by Britain.

Fabian Chow, our Chinese reporter, translated the reports for us and Peyt, who realised that the foreign areas faced a grave situation, called me into his office and asked me to try to get into the Jessfield Road headquarters of the puppets for an interview. 'Tell 'em,' he said, 'that the motto of the *North-China Daily News* is "Impartial but not neutral" and that we want to give full publicity to their side of the story.'

Fabian's face blanched when I told him to ring up number 96 and make a request for an interview for us. Poor Fabian was not at all certain that, once inside the building, he would ever emerge again.

And I wasn't at all happy when Fabian told me he had spoken to Tang Leang-li, Indonesian-born information minister of the puppet régime. We could go along the following day and they'd talk to us.

We told the taxi driver to take us to number 96. He went grey. I thought he was going to be sick. Did we want him to wait there? Of course we did. 'Tell him,' I said to Fabian, 'that he'll be all right. Nothing will happen to him.' Fabian rattled off in Shanghai dialect and looked at me with wide, frightened eyes. We were a trio of timid travellers but on we went.

The taxi drew up outside the massive wooden doors set into the wall. Fabian got out and pulled on a bell. We heard a muffled clanging inside the grounds and then the bolts were drawn back. The big doors swung inward and a face appeared in the gap. It was that of an officer of the Ta Tao police, khaki-clad, wearing a Sam Browne belt from which was suspended a holster holding a wicked-looking Mauser automatic. He looked at Fabian carefully, eyeing him up and down. Then he spotted me in the taxi. He smiled. Evidently he had been told to expect the foreigner from the press.

He barked an order and the doors swung open. He beckoned us to enter. Fabian came back, rejoined the driver in the front seat and we passed through the massive wall. The doors closed behind us. I noticed two Ta Tao uniformed men on the right. They were holding rifles. On the left there were three more, fully armed. The car stopped and the officer, politely, asked us to wait. He went inside a small hut just inside the entrance to the grounds, evidently to phone back to the house which stood some distance back up a long drive.

He returned, asked us to leave the car and, walking a pace or two in front of Fabian and me, beckoned us to follow him. We walked up a long driveway, past a large concrete patch on which were parked several trucks and two large Buick limousines, through a clump of high bushes by a small pathway and out into an expanse of lawn.

There was the large mansion facing us – Chinese-style roof, highly decorated wooden sliding screens instead of doors and two large concrete gargoyles at the base of the steps which we mounted to enter a large reception hall barely furnished with high-backed chairs and small blackwood tea tables. There we were asked to wait as the officer entered a room on our right.

A few moments later a Chinese, sleek-haired, smiling and wearing the traditional long gown advanced to greet us. This was Tang Leang-li, close personal friend of Wang Ching-wei, who had selected him to act as spokesman for the renegade régime. He shook hands with both of us, politely ushered us into the large room from which he had emerged and pointed to a large settee on which he bade us be seated. On a small table in front of us were three small bowls of green tea and from these we sipped the steaming liquid – the polite preliminary to any serious discussion in China.

Tang's English was good but Fabian translated my questions in Mandarin and the minister replied in that dialect. I got down to brass tacks immediately. The S.M.P., I said, had alleged that the Ta Tao men had opened fire first and had only returned the fire in self-defence.

Untrue, said Tang through Fabian. The foreigners had fired first and he would prove that it was a case of naked aggression.

He rose and walked briskly away to lead us again into the grounds and back to the main doors facing Jessfield Road. There we mounted stone steps to emerge on the wall, at least three yards in width, protected by a castellated barricade of concrete – a veritable miniature Great Wall of China. Just over the doors was a hut built of half logs, thick and heavy. An armed policemen, shoddily dressed, slovenly in appearance, came to attention facing Tang and opened the door for us.

There on camp beds were the bodies of four men in uniform. Each of them had been hit by bullets in the face and chest. The blood had been cleaned off but their faces were in a mess, gruesomely mutilated by the bullets.

Tang asked me to notice that not one of them was wearing boots. They were in their stockinged feet. I nodded. This was proof, said Tang, that they had been asleep at the time of the shooting. He explained that the S.M.P. had opened fire and that bullets had struck the log walls of the hut. The four men, who had been asleep on the camp beds, had been awakened, had rushed to the windows and there had been shot before they could do anything.

There were two windows overlooking the road. There was no glass in them. They were deep and provided a commanding view of Jessfield Road traffic, certainly good vantage points for marksmen. I didn't believe Tang but I was there to report the Ta Tao version of events so I took notes.

It was when Tang was escorting us back to the house that I got what I considered to be factual evidence to prove that the evil reputation of the place was well deserved.

We had just emerged from the bushes to face the mansion when, out of a side door some distance away, there emerged two big Chinese in uniform dragging between them a wretch whose face was a bloody mask. His head sagged forward. He appeared to be only partially conscious. His arms, well gripped by his two escorts, hung limply at his sides. His feet slurred over the ground to indicate clearly that had they relaxed their grip he would have collapsed.

The two men hesitated as they saw Tang. His face blanched and he barked out an order. Quickly they dragged the man inside.

I looked at Fabian. His face was chalk-white. I looked at Tang and he smiled in embarrassment. He was thinking quickly.

'There's been an accident,' he said in English: 'Most unfortunate.'

I said nothing but I knew that we had seen one victim of the Ta Tao torturers – a man who had been battered almost to the point of death.

Back in the mansion over the tea bowls it was apparent that Tang had lost his self-assurance. There was going to be a mighty row with the uniformed officer in charge of prisoners after we had departed. Like the Japanese, the puppets maintained a hypocritical facade of propriety which fooled nobody.

The Ta Tao administration got its version of events fully covered in the paper side by side with the police story. It did not end the confrontation.

Both the Settlement and French police forces, faced with an almost insuperable task to maintain law and order, erected barbed-wire barricades at the boundaries of the main roads. European officers and Asiatic constables, well armed, kept constant watch at the entry points, searching pedestrians, rickshaws, cars, trucks, hand-carts – anything likely to be used to carry arms or other offensive weapons into the foreign areas.

It was one of the beautiful women at number 96 Jessfield Road who caused the next serious incident between the Settlement police and the Ta Tao administration.

Sergeant 'Jock' Kinloch was in charge of the barricade search-party at the western edge of Bubbling Well Road when he flagged a large Buick saloon to slow down and stop on its way out of the central district.

Instead of obeying the order the driver of the car stepped on the accelerator and the vehicle made for the small gap between two sets of barbed-wire barricades. In the back seat was a young woman.

Kinloch did not hesitate. His orders were to open fire if anyone attempted to crash the barricades. His Mauser spat out bullets at the Buick. His Chinese constables also opened fire. But the car did not stop. It hit the barbed wire, pushed the wooden frames aside and sped through the widened gap on its way west-ward.

About half-an-hour later from 96 Jessfield Road came the news that the 'wife' of a high-ranking Ta Tao official had been shot and killed by a foreign officer of the S.M.P. From the puppet-controlled territory radio stations came the warning that vengeance would be taken – and taken quickly.

If any man in Shanghai had signed his own death warrant it was poor Kinloch. His days were numbered. No matter how long it took the puppets would hound him down.

I was standing on the waterfront a few days later when an army ambulance carrying sick members of the British forces drew up at the ferry point from where they would be taken to board a troopship bound for Hong Kong and Britain. There were a couple of men on stretchers and about five 'walking cases'. Among them was a tall fellow in the uniform of the Sea-forth Highlanders. He went quickly aboard the launch of the P. & O. Co. and disappeared below deck. I knew the man was Kinloch but I was sworn to secrecy. A few days later he was in Hong Kong, a British Crown colony, safe. Luckily, he survived the Japanese occupation of Hong Kong without his background in Shanghai being discovered – a fine policeman and undoubtedly a brave man.

Danger was always close in those days but many duties in-volved comical incidents which provided for us newspapermen accompanying police patrols belly laugh after belly laugh.

Opium raids provided the most fun. Raiding parties were usually made up of a British sergeant and about four Chinese constables, all carrying revolvers in their hands as they roamed about the hotel floors sniffing for the tell-tale aroma.

On the other hand, it was well known that, in some hotel rooms, nothing more dangerous than the popular pastime of female-mounting was in progress. Interruption of this form of exercise provided comedy for all of us.

The idea was to bash open a bedroom door, dash in shouting, point pistols at the bed on which, usually, a slender Chinese chap was thrusting excitedly into a Chinese female beneath him, pull back the blanket or sheet covering the couple and jerk the male forcibly off the nest so that he could be rushed at gun-point to a corner of the room. There, open-eyed, we would watch the almost instant descent of a rampant erection into terrified, drooping dejection.

Pat Kelly, a Yorkshireman of Irish descent, reckoned that his party held the record of three seconds in the 'Softening Stakes'.

On another occasion Kelly was too late. Natural processes had defeated him. As the Yorkshireman described the scene: 'We lugged t'bugger off t'girl and, bugger me, t'bed was all covered in coom.'

Opium raids merely touched the fringe of what was a wide-spread and immensely lucrative business. Dens ranged from squalid hovels serving the coolies to garishly decorated palaces frequented by the millionaires of which Shanghai had many. And there, too, lived Tu Yueh-sen, the King of the Underworld, the opium magnate, the gangster chief whose terrible power was wielded over an empire of crime that out-ranged in evil even that of Al Capone in Chicago.

Opium, the brothels, the trade unions, the hired killers, the slave-girl trade, the protection rackets, gold smuggling, gun-running and all kinds of crime were under the monopolistic control of Tu, the chief of the Ch'in Pang – the Green Circle Society – the Mafia of China.

It was in 1927 that Tu, twenty-two years before Chiang Kai-shek fled in defeat from Mao's armies, assured himself of a privileged existence under the protection of the Nationalists.

As Chiang advanced northward in his campaign to defeat the warlords, the trade unions and the Communists in the Chinese areas of the city staged an uprising and took control of Greater Shanghai. When Chiang arrived they declared their intention of handing over the city, excluding the foreign areas, to him. Fearful of the Communists with whom he had broken completely following the revolution against the Manchus he declared war on them and the unions. His principal ally was Tu. His thugs and Chiang's troops murdered 5,000 workers.

Tu's reward was an appointment to the Board of the Opium Suppression Bureau which enabled him freely to run the narcotics business with ever greater profits. He was also decorated with the Order of the Brilliant Jade. Thus the greatest criminal China ever produced was able in my time to demand – and to get – a constant French police guard on his mansion as the Communists and the workers, whom he had betrayed, forever looked for the opportunity to end his life.

Tu was too important a figure in the foreign areas to be affronted. The fact that he was the king of thugs, the chief supplier of opium, had to be overlooked in the cause of securing his cooperation to make life easier for the foreigners.

Woe betide the man who crossed Tu's path. Such a man was Superintendent Loh Lien-kwe of the S.M.P. Tu gave him information about a certain shipment of contraband coming to Shanghai that was not to be interfered with. Loh, seeking laurels, swooped on a river vessel with the cooperation of the River Police and the Customs and Tu lost many thousands of dollars.

Loh, poor chap, was shot dead as he emerged from his car at his home. It was no secret that he had fallen foul of Tu, but who could – or wanted to – prove where the guilt lay?

In any case, Tu led a charmed life, thanks, he believed, to the dried heads of monkeys that were always fixed to the back of his long gowns.

Like most Chinese, Tu was superstitious. He consulted the soothsayers regularly. Early in his life he had been told by one eminent fortune-teller that he would live to a ripe old age and would die peacefully in his bed only if constantly the head of a monkey reposed in the middle of his back. If Tu failed to follow the fortune-teller's advice then he could expect to die a violent death.

My friend, Charles Norman Gray, head of the tailoring firm of C. N. Gray and Co. in Nanking Road, was grateful to that soothsayer. Tu's belief in the omens meant regular trips for the tailor to Singapore in search of monkeys' heads – all expenses paid and much on the side. Tu would never trust a Chinese tailor. A knife in the back was more than a possibility during a measuring-up exercise. Thus Mr Gray, acknowledged to be the

123

city's best outfitter, became the gangster's personal tailor.

Always Tu was exceedingly polite to Gray, the Londoner who had really served his time in Savile Row, and who had gone out to China in 1912, there to start a business of his own some years later – a venture which flourished and gave C.N. several cars, a large houseboat, a cottage in Devon for holidays, a house filled with servants and such customers as the Duke of Kent, serving as a Royal Navy officer on the China Station, Charles Chaplin, paying a sightseeing trip to the city, ambassadors of several countries, consuls and such like.

The soothsayer's forecast was accurate. Tu died peacefully in his bed in Hong Kong, where I was working, in the early 1950s.

Tu was in his heyday of power in pre-war Shanghai. The pimps of the Szechuan Road brothels were working for him. Girl babies, sold by starving families, were being gruesomely mutilated by the leaders of his beggar gangs to be taken on the streets to arouse the sympathy of the soft-hearted foreigners. Many of them were deliberately blinded.

He exercised monopolistic control over the slave trade to fill the mills and factories with children in a city where more than 30,000 boys and girls – mostly girls – were abandoned by parents, who could not feed them, to be scavenged from the streets and the river in one year.

Boys and girls of eight and nine worked from six in the morning to late at night over boiling vats of cocoons in the silk mills or in the textile plants.

There was no shortage of prostitutes in Shanghai, where a handsome-looking girl could be changed into a skinny hag after endless toil in the factories. The most beautiful girls were sent to the brothels and if they demurred then all they could look forward to was the slavery of the mills and their bug-infested bed-boards.

All this was happening in the fat arrogance of foreign-controlled Shanghai where, on the Bund, gangs of starving peasants from the countryside, clad in rags, chased after lorries to slit open the sacks containing rice, millet or other grains. Grabbing handfuls of the contents as they poured forth from the cut sacks the wretches stuffed the grain in their rags and, often chased by Chinese or Sikh constables, ran madly into side-streets.

In winter, when frozen beggars were picked up in hundreds by the death-carts, armed with great hooks the peasants slashed into the bales of cotton-wool slowly being moved from the wharves by a starting lorry. This they stuffed into the rags they wore as padding against the bitter cold.

Caught by the police they were beaten mercilessly with truncheons or punched and kicked and then hauled off to the Central Station to be charged and imprisoned in Ward Road Jail, reputed to be the largest prison in the world with well over 1,000 inmates held in sections arranged for the different racial groups in the city.

In summer petty crime assumed more humorous proportions. There were always the pickpockets abroad on the streets, in the trams, in the buses – everywhere. Few of them were ever caught. Unless you travelled in your own car or rickshaw then you could reckon to lose at least three fountain-pens a year, a wallet or two, even your outside pockets carefully slit away by razor-blades.

But the most athletic performers were the hat-snatchers. Those were the days of panama hats, of straw boaters and similar light headgear. They were also days of steamy heat when the windows of trams and buses were pushed wide open to allow cooling breezes to make city travel a little more bearable.

It was a common sight to see a well-dressed Chinese gentleman, seated by a window, beautifully hatted, patiently waiting for the vehicle to start. Even more patient was the chap seemingly waiting for another tram or bus on the concrete of the terminus, his head just reaching the bottom edge of the opened window. No sooner had the vehicle started than the patient loiterer sprang to life. His arm went up, his grasping fingers reached for the hat, grabbed it, whipped it into the open air and he was off. Not a hope for the hatless passenger to take up the chase as the vehicle gathered speed and was soon a good quarter of a mile away.

What the thieves did with the hats they snatched I do not know. As they seemed to select the best headgear it would be a safe bet to assume that they trotted off to the nearest gentleman's clothiers and there sold the spoils. They never got me. I was worried about falling hair – I blamed the tight-fitting army head-gear for that – and I never wore a hat in Shanghai.

But the Chungking Underground nearly did get me one morning as I walked along the Bund to enter my office.

I had just passed the newly opened offices of the puppet-owned Central Reserve Bank, whose currency was circulating in the Japanese-occupied regions, when there was a terrific blast. I was lifted clean off my feet and hurled into the roadway, where, bleary-eyed and wobbly, I picked myself up and surveyed the scene.

Not far from me, just by the entrance to the bank, there were

125

about six bodies in the road. The front of the bank, as the smoke and spirals of rubble-dust cleared, looked as if a high-explosive shell had landed dead-centre in the hallway. Windows were shattered, heavy pieces of masonry had crashed to the pavement and where the two heavy wooden doors had been there was a smoking heap of twisted beams, masonry and glass.

We got the facts later. A bomb, placed in the entrance, had exploded just after I passed the building. Had I dawdled I would have been in the roadway with the half-a-dozen dead who had caught the full force of the blast.

Percy Finch, who had had a narrow escape when the Chinese planes dropped their bombs on the Settlement, took me along to the Shanghai Club, signed a chit for a double brandy and a whisky for himself, and we celebrated my escape.

That was one up to the Chungking agents. The bank was closed for more than a week and when it re-opened there was a tight security guard both inside and outside the building – Chinese and Sikh watchmen, armed with rifles, who stood on the pavement behind sandbags.

It also signalled the beginning of an intensive campaign against newspapermen and newspaper buildings by one side or the other. Randall Gould of the *Evening Post and Mercury* became the target of the puppets. So did the *China Press*, which made working conditions in that office somewhat hazardous as the pro-Japanese *Shanghai Times*, situated on a lower floor, was high on the list of the Chungking Underground for terrorist attention. And on the top floor of that block of offices on Avenue Edward VII was John B. Powell, whose *Weekly Review* had focused on him the combined hatred of both the puppets and the Japanese.

First of the buildings to get the sandbag war-time look was the *Evening Post*. A bomb was thrown at the main entrance and it caused a certain amount of damage though there were no casualties. From that time on armed police guards were placed on 24-hour duties outside the building and Randall Gould, uncowed, continued to write his outspoken criticisms of Japanese actions in China. In the interest of his own safety he was advised by the American insurance tycoon, Cornelius V. Starr, who had a major stake in the company, to hire a couple of bodyguards and, from that time onwards, Gould was never abroad without two tough-looking Russian gentlemen.

Powell, who was even more outspoken in his condemnation of the Japanese than Gould, realised that life could be dangerous when a Chinese hurled a hand grenade at him as he was leaving the American Club in Foochow Road one lunch-time. It exploded but it was wide of its mark and Powell escaped unhurt.

After being shot at twice by Chinese, who could not possibly have qualified as marksmen, Powell decided to make himself as scarce as possible in the hours of daylight, which meant that the almost one-man job of bringing out the Review became a nocturnal task.

I visited Powell in his office several times after the assassination attempts. It was like entering a citadel. On the ground floor armed police scrutinised everyone entering the building and searched all Chinese except the ones they knew were working there. As the lift reached the *Shanghai Times* floor armed bodyguards could be seen at the entrance to the editorial offices. Similarly the *China Press* was protected by gun-toting Chinese. Outside Powell's office at the top one had to pass a large Chinese from Shantung, who sat on a camp-bed outside the door with a Mauser automatic in his lap.

Powell was typical of the erudite, soft-spoken quiet American. Of medium build, approaching middle age, his general appearance revealed no sign of the indomitable courage that he possessed and that he displayed week by week without fail in his articles in the *Review*. Under the glare of electric lights he worked solidly until the early hours of the morning and then made his way homeward by changing routes – a hazardous foray into a hostile world that never seemed to quell his remarkable spirit and his determination to speak what he felt was the truth.

Threats of an untimely end could not intimidate another American, Carroll Alcott, Shanghai's most popular broadcaster.

Alcott was particularly vocal in his support of Britain then facing a test of strength from Hitler and Mussolini.

It was during the European war that his closing remarks after the lunch-time news broadcast caused a furore in the German community, all members of which, so it seemed, were fervent supporters of Adolf Hitler.

In the broadcast Alcott had quoted an agency report describing a Royal Air Force raid on Germany during which bombs had fallen on the home of Field Marshal Hermann Goering, the chief of the Nazi air force.

'It is with the fervent hope that Field Marshal Hermann Goering had a clean change of underclothing that Carroll Alcott is signing off his noon-day broadcast over Station XMHA,' said the ebullient newscaster.

Indicative of the strong American influence on day-to-day life in Shanghai was the popularity of Alcott's style of broadcasting which combined a fast-moving presentation and the sales-talk of commercialism.

Thus Alcott would always commence his midday broadcast with the greeting, 'Jello, Jello, Jello.' This signified that the newscast was being sponsored by the makers of a well-known jelly product being marketed under that trade name.

Similarly in choice of programmes the Shanghai radio stations provided a surfeit of American-made recordings – the big bands such as Duke Ellington, Rudy Vallee and his Connecticut Yankees, the Dorsey brothers, Guy Lombardo and his Royal Canadians and many others, the singers such as Bing Crosby, Dick Powell, Deanna Durbin or Louis Armstrong, and the sponsored radio shows.

But while Shanghailanders enjoyed to the full their pleasures in the theatres, in the night clubs and elsewhere the campaign of violence erupted with tragic results for many.

Charles Metzler, who was doing well in business in Shanghai and who had been elected chairman of the Russian Exiles' Association, was shot dead as he left his car to enter the association's headquarters in Avenue Edward VII.

His assailant escaped and there was no clue to the motive behind the assassination. It was well known that the Chungking Underground had warned the White Russians not to cooperate with the Japanese but, as many members of the community were employed by Japanese firms and lived in Japanese-controlled areas, this placed Metzler and his committee in a precarious position.

There was also the likelihood that the Soviets could have been responsible. There was a small Soviet community in the city, which had been subject to some harassment by the Japanese, probably helped by White Russians. The hatred of the Whites for the Bolsheviks had not been dissipated by years in exile and the Russian Ex-Officers' Club was known to be the headquarters of royalist supporters deeply involved in plots and intrigues destined to pave the way for their return to power in 'Mother Russia'.

Metzler's successor, a former Czarist officer, Colonel Ivanoff, was shot down and killed in practically the same spot a few months later and there was little doubt in the minds of the police that the Chungking Underground had to be the prime suspect.

While most of the papers were filled by reports of political violence the gangsters were as active as ever and when a group of British Royal Marines from a cruiser in the river were injured in Ma Jackson's popular tavern in Bubbling Well Road it soon became evident that Tu Yueh-sen was pressing home his claim to extort protection money from such establishments.

The marines were having a darts game in the tavern when, from a car slowly passing the bar, there came a hail of bottle-bombs which smashed the windows and set fire to the front of the building. Most of the marines were injured by flying glass though none seriously. The Eurasian lady who kept the bar and who traded under the name of Ma Jackson quickly came to heel and sought protection.

Occasionally we had assassination attempts involving high-ranking Japanese, particularly those in the service of the Shanghai Municipal Council.

Charlie Tombs, small though he was, showed that he had a remarkable amount of courage when at a public meeting on the Racecourse he flung himself on a Chinese gunman who had tried to shoot one of the Japanese. The man was captured and little Tombs was acclaimed a hero. Nobody was shot although the Japanese raised a commotion over what they alleged had been a singularly deficient security system at the meeting.

But when Mayor Fu Siao-en met his end, the blame rested squarely on the shoulders of the Japanese and puppet intelligence services who should have done their homework more thoroughly.

Fu, as befitted his exalted rank, kept a remarkably large establishment which included several excellent chefs. He was particularly proud of one cook whose expertise earned the praise of the hundreds of guests who were regularly entertained to lavish banquets at the Kiangwan mayoral mansion. The cook's speciality was choice Yunnan ham which melted in the mouth. That and a delicious dish of sauted garupa fish.

The cook regularly took Fu his breakfast in the mayoral bed-room. It was after one of these early-morning visits that the chef arrived back in the kitchen and told his colleagues that his master had told him to go out to buy something special for a banquet. He went out and never returned.

Some hours later the body of Fu was discovered on a blood-soaked bed. Not only had he been killed by a razor-sharp knife but someone with an expert knowledge of anatomy had done a carving job that would have done credit to a surgeon.

There was no doubt that the cook had been the murderer. He simply disappeared into thin air. It was after the Japanese sur_ render in 1945 that I met a Colonel Lincoln Y. Wang of the Chinese army in the home of Chiang Kai-shek up in the hills outside the war-time capital. He told me the story of Fu's untimely end in vivid detail. The chap who had done the job was a member of the Nationalist secret service – a man who really could cook and who was proud of his prowess over the kitchen stove. He had bribed his way – this was the only certain method of securing a job in China in those days – into the Mayor's service and, over a period of several months, had established himself as an excellent and reliable servant. The rest was easy.

The first Briton to become a victim of the terrorists was 'Tug' Wilson, a former sea-going character who had established himself as a co-partner of a bar in Blood Alley.

He was entering the *Shanghai Times-China Press* building late one night on his way to get one of the first editions of the *Times* when a gang of armed desperadoes came flying down the hallway and filled him full of lead as he stood silhouetted in the moonlight and looked as if he was barring the way out of the doorway into the street. Poor Wilson was killed instantaneously.

The gang had shot up the editorial floor of the *Shanghai Times* but, luckily, had hit no one there. Reactions were quick in the newspaper fraternity and no sooner had the killers burst in through the lavatory entrance than every man-jack behind a typewriter was flat on the floor. There were a lot of holes in the walls but nothing else.

Life could be hazardous every day in Shanghai and a newspaperman could depend on an average of ten murders a day to keep him, if not particularly happy, at least busily employed.

But Shanghai's bloodthirsty record could never dampen the ardour of its multi-racial inhabitants for a taste of the artistic life or the multifarious entertainments that the small foreign enclave offered. War or no war, danger or no danger, in life or in death the lights burned brilliantly at night and the unceasing round of enjoyment continued unabated.

Culture

The British community in Shanghai, or, rather, its members who belonged to the Shanghai Amateur Dramatic Society, owned the only theatre in the city offering live entertainment. But it was a sad fact that, apart from the purely amateur productions of such men as Peyton-Griffin, who fancied they were transplanted Henry Irvings, the cultural flag was kept flying by the nationals of other nations, particularly the Russians and the Austrian Jews.

It meant profit for the S.A.D.S. because, in the Lyceum in Rue Cardinal Mercier, they had the only theatre readily available for such spectaculars as the Russian Ballet, the Russian Opera, the Russian Light Opera or a full appearance of the Shanghai Symphony Orchestra under its Italian conductor, Maestro Mario Paci.

The Russians with their long tradition of cultural pursuits were pre-eminent in making Shanghai one of the best-known artistic centres in the Far East. Flight from the Bolsheviks had bestowed on the city the presence of ballerinas from Moscow and St Petersburg, first-class opera singers and, most popular of all, musical comedy stars such as Sophie Bitner, Rosen and Valin who became in exile almost as great an attraction as they had been in Moscow.

But in the puppet-controlled regions there was plenty of entertainment for fellows like me, whose minds rarely rose above belt-level. One of the best areas was the 'Badlands'. What went on there in a variety of establishments embraced practically every erotic delight, but the trouble was that for a foreigner to venture without invitation into the territory exposed him to various dangers, not the least of which was the risk of being robbed and shot by gangs of thugs who roamed freely in the maze of alleyways that bordered the narrow mud-roads of the district.

Luckily Cal Hirsh received an invitation by ticket to attend the opening of a new night-life establishment in the Badlands and asked me if I would like to go along. I accepted knowing full well that the underworld would have been informed of our status as guests and that we had nothing to fear.

So we went by taxi to the boundary road and there entered Ta Tao land soon to find the place – a huge stone-fronted mansion, brilliantly lit by illuminated Chinese characters over the wide entrance and guarded by several shoddily dressed Chinese carrying shotguns in their arms with loaded bandoliers slung belt-fashion around their waists.

We were met by a luscious, long-legged beauty in a cheongsam who led us through the spacious entrance hall to a large room, dimly lit with tables and chairs set around a small dancing space. She took us over to a table where a Chinese in European suit sat alone. With a bow she informed us that this was Mr Ma, the owner of the establishment.

Ma, who was excessively polite, welcomed us to his 'humble place' and assured us that he would be at our beck and call so long as we desired to sample its services, which would, he cooed, include a Western-style dinner – or a Chinese repast, if we so desired. That and drinks on the house, cigarettes, cigars, anything we fancied.

The chief attraction was opium. In a garishly decorated room on the ground floor, low ceilinged and luxuriously carpeted, we saw several rows of velvet-covered divans on which lay Chinese males, young, middle-aged and old, some with long opium-pipes held in their mouths and the others eagerly awaiting the offer of prepared pipes from one of the twenty beautiful girls busily engaged at tables between the rows.

On the tables was the apparatus which transformed a small blob of opium – the sap from the pod of the opium poppy (*Papaver somniferum*) – into a bubbling, fume-exhaling lump for insertion into the end of the pipe: a lamp with a small flame, a long needle to hold the opium over the flame, twirled expertly by the girls: and the long pipes quickly carried with their bubbling, smouldering lump and placed in the hands of the addicts lying on the divans.

The addicts noisily sucked in the pain-killing fumes and soon lapsed into the blissful state of half-sleep, eyes narrowed to slits, minds taken over by dreams of beauty or eroticism, depending on age or magnitude of addiction.

There were no women smokers in the room. The customers were all male – well-to-do patrons who could afford to pay for the comfortable surroundings provided by Mr Ma, who, no doubt, was closely allied with gangster suppliers, the puppets and their Japanese masters. Women, of course, did smoke opium – the old Dowager Empress could not have lived without the drug – but the pipes were taken in the privacy of their homes.

Another part of the mansion upstairs was devoted to gambling – both Chinese and Western. There was a fan-tan, cricket-fighting and dice alongside such games of chance as roulette, chemin de fer and various card-backing pastimes. The Chinese were inveterate gamblers and huge sums of money were involved at every table as young hostesses, moving among the gamblers, handed out the steaming-hot towels, eau de cologne, and other aids to personal comfort in the hot, exciting, smoke-laden atmosphere.

But by far the greatest attractions of the new night club were the erotic shows staged in an annexe off the gambling hall where on the walls in vivid and colourful relief men and women – and even animals – were shown indulging in such delights as those described in the *Kama Sutra* or the ancient and sexually, revealing Chinese classics.

The appetite of the patrons, who included some women – both Chinese and foreign – was stimulated by the appearance shortly after midnight of a dancing team of Chinese girls, everyone of them naked apart from tap-shoes.

But Cal was not impressed. Whisky in hand, eyes wearily bleary, he looked at me and said, 'Shorty, they couldn't raise a beat in a state penitentiary.'

But more exciting acts were to follow and even Cal was forced to sit up straight and take some interest.

A dusky, well-formed Indian girl – described by an announcer as Princess Somebody-or-other – literally tied herself in knots and in a posture that revealed her genital opening, shaved and tinted with henna, invited a male member of the audience to thrust fully home a beer bottle. A man got up carrying a bottle – I fancied that he was in the act – and putting on all the diffidence of one who was embarrassed pushed it right up.

There was tumultuous applause as the girl performed several acrobatic acts which fully revealed the base of the bottle held captive within her. Then with a flourish of drums she pulled out the object and held it aloft in triumph.

Cal eyed the bottle and drawled: 'She'd make a good living in the Horse and Hound (a Shanghai replica of a British pub). You Britishers like your beer hot.'

The woman, doelike eyes flashing, sculpturesque bosom heaving as if in great passion, clapped her hands and four Chinese wheeled on to the floor a life-size golden idol, seated in contemplative fashion, cross-legged, hands clasped over navel, lifelike, naked. The Chinese lifted the statue on its wooden dais and placed it on the floor facing the Indian girl.

We were told by the master of ceremonies that the Princess was going to give us a glimpse into Hindu history when the famed Temple of Juggernaut at Pooree was staffed by a thousand priestesses whose duty it was to entertain their god-idol.

Accompanied by seductive Eastern music, the girl writhed in spasmodic fervour, moaned in simulated demoniac passion and with hot, moist hands commenced to caress the golden idol, starting at the head and sinuously working down the body to finish at the feet. As she jerked in passionate spasms, her breasts quivered voluptuously. She thrust her mound forward, almost touching the face of the idol with her pubic hair.

Suddenly Cal nudged me. 'Jeepers,' he said, 'look at that statue. He's stiff.'

I took my eyes off the girl and looked at the god-idol. Sure enough there was a tremendous erection thrusting forth.

I was more than surprised. While the statue was human-like in its appearance I had had no idea that it was a living being. On its dais it had squatted motionless, expressionless, gleaming in golden paint. Now the 'god' had come to life.

I had another look at the 'god'. He was large, muscular and from the contours of his face I judged him to be an Anglo-Indian.

Slowly the idol stirred. A tremor ran through his body, his hands slowly moved down from their navel position and grasped the stiffness that was thrusting upward. He was certainly well endowed, a massive organ that brought gasps from the audience. As if gathering strength from the electric responses of the naked female who moaned and sinuously moved snakelike ever closer to him he shuddered violently and then thrust himself erect on his dais. He stood about six feet in height, broad-shouldered, slim-waisted but heavily thighed. His entire genitalia, fully exposed, revealed him as the possessor of an enormous virile limb, taut and throbbing as he grasped it in two-handed embrace.

Then came a performance that not only left us gasping but, as far as I was concerned, excited me to the point of a wet erection. Probably Cal was unaffected. After all, he was much older than I and at that stage was in an alcoholic stupor.

I once read that Indian experts in erotica knew of no less than 700-odd coital positions. While the Indian girl and her 'god' fell far short of matching the Indian experts' grand slam they certainly demonstrated a variety of positions that would be contortionally impossible for most of us watching.

The theme of the act was that the girl was the devotee of the god, had to rouse him sexually and had to offer herself to him in sacred prostitution.

Thus she toyed with him, touching his testicles and out-thrust yard with sensual strokes of her long fingers, placing her lips at its tip and darting tongue forward to caress the glans. As mighty shudders swept through the body of the golden-painted Adonis – for the man was exceedingly handsome – the girl roused him to further heights of eroticism by intermingling boldness with coyness – winking, cooing, pouting and giggling, pinching and clawing and then darting away with the speed of a doe.

As the man moaned with simulated feverish desire – for he must have performed the act hundreds of times before excited audiences – the woman embraced him lovingly, murmuring and gently touching warm, moist lips to his forehead.

When he gripped her shoulders she clung about his neck and moaned in ecstasy. She writhed in spasmodic fervour and slowly twined her churning thighs around him, crawling up his body like some sinuous snake.

The real performance then began. The man placed his muscular arms under her buttocks and lifted her firmly upward so that her mound, her opening, was directly in front of his erect member. Gradually he eased forward so that, in full view of the audience, the act of penetration could be seen. But this was not the end. He held her squirming body as she sank on to his shaft and then withdrew, still erect, still unrequited.

The man then lowered the woman to the floor, drew her body against his and rotated the head of his shaft against her vulva, an action which drew from her lascivious moans, exciting, utterly sensual.

For another twenty minutes or so we were given demonstrations of various coital postures: the man supine on his back and the female squatting over his length; penetration of the woman from the rear; a squatting position in which the man lowered himself between the girl's thighs and gently eased her forward and upward to encase him; both sitting at the squat with the woman's limbs gripping the man's waist . . . and several more which revealed the athletic prowess of both entertainers as they entwined limbs and twisted their bodies into grotesque shapes to reveal what we all wanted to see – the massive male organ entering the receptive vagina of the supple female.

135

My admiration for the man knew no bounds. How he managed to prevent an ejaculation I never knew. Had I been in his position I would have blotted my copy-book within the first few minutes.

An ejaculation he did have – but it was not in coition. The idea was further to excite all of us watching the performance by allowing us to see his sperm burst forth. So when various coital positions had been demonstrated and the man's penis, stiff and throbbing, had been fully exposed, the girl came close to her partner, seized his shaft and placed it between her palms. Then moving her hands in a churning motion she quickly brought him off. The spermatozoa shot forth, splashed on to her body and slowly descended over her smooth skin. And then total darkness for several seconds. When the lights came on again the centre of the floor was empty. The show was over. There was tumultuous applause in which I joined but the couple did not reappear and the next act was announced.

This involved a woman performing erotic acts with a large dog which appeared to be mostly Great Dane. But I failed to see the end of the performance as Cal, who was filled to the gills, started a slow descent from his chair and ended up on the floor.

I could not leave him alone. Supporting him – and he was terribly heavy – I managed to get him out of the building and into a rickshaw.

Dawn was breaking by the time I got Cal home. I paid off his rickshaw coolie after much argument about the amount due and left my American colleague by his front door. I was not going to risk a confrontation with his wife.

Cal, as large as life and as ebullient as ever, was at his desk in the editorial room before noon. I suggested another visit to the Badlands establishment and he said he would arrange for a trip the following week.

It never came off. A few hours after Cal and I had left the establishment was razed to the ground by fire. It was all part of the gangster scene in Shanghai. The instant popularity of the place had roused jealousy on the part of other owners of similar night spots and no sooner had it closed down after the first-night opening than thugs broke in, sprayed the inside with kerosene and set fire to it.

Physical culture in many forms was popular in Shanghai and the interior of the Racecourse was the place to see the foreigners engaged in athletic exercise.

Soccer was the most popular pastime and the Chinese teams. semi-professional in amateur guise, were the best. Tung Wah and

Lido were the most successful. But the British regiments, the police and the Italian forces from time to time produced worthy opponents and the local stars gained prominence in type among the newspaper headlines.

Softball was also popular. There was a local league for men and the girls' games attracted such lechers as me.

Basketball had a large following and offered the prospect of seeing several women's teams in action. Big girls they were, too – tall and busty, muscular and tough. They showed their power on one occasion when the journalists got up a scratch team to play a squad of Portuguese-Eurasians at the Foreign YMCA.

We were well and truly trounced by the girls who, on occasions, showed some unsporting tendencies when they found their bottoms were being grabbed instead of the ball.

After the game we entertained the girls to dinner at the Sun Ya restaurant in Nanking Road. I took one of them home in a taxi. No sooner had I begun to embrace her, to try to stroke her long legs and to caress her ample bosom than she told me to control myself and to behave like a gentleman. I had a mighty erection. I was in the grip of intense sexual excitement. I pleaded with her. Wouldn't she please allow me to kiss her, to caress her body. I assured her that I did not desire to possess her body, to have intercourse – only to attain satisfaction through heavy petting.

'You men are funny creatures,' she said. 'Wait until we leave the taxi.'

At her home in the French Concession – or, at least, within yards of the front door – she asked me what I wanted her to do. I did not reply. I reached down, opened my flies and drew out my rod. I placed her hand on it. The girl laughed out loud but did not attempt to withdraw contact and quickly brought me off.

I felt extremely foolish as the girl said: 'You could have done that yourself, you know.'

Boxing, so far as I was concerned, was the most exciting of Shanghai's sporting offerings. The Russian Regiment gave us 'Iron Man' Andre Shelaeff, Paul Lojnikoff, his brother, Peter Lojnikoff, another fighter named Levchenko and one or two more. The American marines, under their boxing mentor, Sergeant 'Slug' Marvin, produced Chuck Haines and a lot more big fellows who appeared regularly on the Canidrome bills. The U.S. Navy when in port could always be relied on to send a real flattener into the ring. So could the Royal Navy and the British regiments. I remember the prowess of such British fighters as Royal Marine Duncan and Fusilier Llewellyn of the

137

Royal Welch Fusiliers – great scrappers who usually emerged triumphant.

Shelaeff was the best of the lot. He had a wicked punch that signified a count of ten, or longer, for any opponent foolish enough to allow it to be delivered on the point of chin. One of the Lojnikoff brothers was out for several minutes after Shelaeff had set about him in a championship fight.

Joe Morang, sports editor of the *Evening Post and Mercury*, a former marine, took Shelaeff under his wing and prophesied for him world prominence could he be removed from the Shanghai scene to the rough and tough American circuit. This was accomplished and Shelaeff found himself in California.

He didn't do too badly and it looked as if Morang's prophecy might come true when disaster struck. It was after a tough battle in San Francisco that Shelaeff collapsed in the dressing room and died from a brain injury.

Quite a lot of Shanghai women attended the boxing shows. One regular was Joy Lacks, wife of the photographer, George Lacks. She was young, good looking and, like her husband, a professional picture-taker. When she climbed into the ring and displayed her panties to a cheering audience of males prior to taking a picture of the victor then the authorities stepped in. They banned her from entering the ring. They said it was unseemly. To clamber through the ropes meant that she displayed too much of her charms. But she still stayed at the ringside to take excellent photographs.

The comedian was 'Charlie Chase' Collaco, whose antics were likened to those of the Hollywood film funny man after whom he had been nicknamed. His punches came up from the floor. He did tap dances before a bout and sang a song after a victory. Strangely enough Collaco was a good scrapper. Despite his laugh-raising grimaces, his weird variety of punches and his corner-buffoonery he rarely lost a fight.

Nor did Marine Duncan. Sadly this magnificent scrapper lost a hand during the war which effectively prevented his reaching the top rank of British boxers. He effectively disposed of the best that the Americans could offer and, on his return home, it was expected that he would leave the service and take up the fight game professionally.

Similarly Fusilier Llewellyn was a thorn in the flesh of the Americans, who, as on the world scene, reigned supreme in the Canidrome ring. British service fighters were severely handicapped by the rules of army boxing which restricted bouts to three rounds, made compulsory the wearing of vests and prohibited any vocal encouragement from spectators – real gentlemanly stuff compared with the bare-chested, rough-and-tumble aggression of the Americans who could easily last ten rounds or more. Nevertheless, in Llewellyn they found one Limey – if you could place a Welshman in that category – who could hand it out like an old-time boxing-booth champion.

Sadly for the British troops who were flat broke by Monday, Llewellyn's victories were earned at the Canidrome on Thursdays, one day before the weekly pay was handed out, and the challenge of the American sailors and marines to 'put yer cash down, bud' could not be faced. But those who did manage to back their British fancy had no cause for regret. Llewellyn was ever-victorious.

Foreign Devils

Percy Finch, who was a staunch supporter of the Shanghai Club, often used to tell me that two Wongs never made a White. My predilection for oriental females had alarmed him and though he was no racial bigot he made it plain that lasting – and legal – alliances with Chinese or Eurasian women could only result in a rapid descent down Shanghai's social ladder.

'If you fancy a bit of oriental tail, Ralph,' he would say, 'then follow the old empire-builder's dictum: "Screw 'em and leave 'em".'

When I arrived on the Shanghai scene it was clear that the white-supremacy lobby had lost the battle against the lure of oriental women who had much to commend them.

Shanghai's Eurasian community embraced people of many nationalities – British subjects, born of legal liaisons with the 'natives'; Chinese subjects not similarly blessed; Portuguese passport-holders, 98 per cent Chinese and tracing ancestry back to Macao, the oldest of the colonies; French citizens; Germans; Danes; Norwegians; Swedes and many more.

One thing was certain: their antecedents precluded elbow-bending with the exalted tipplers lined up sometimes three-deep at the Shanghai Club bar. The club was exclusively white. So it was that a former sergeant of artillery, successful in the textile trade but almost illiterate, a school-leaver at fourteen, as blunt of speech as any raucous drill-square martinet but born of pure-white parents in some terraced hovel in Keighley, could pay his monthly dues and enter the sanctum sanctorum.

Not so the product of Haileybury and Oxford, possessor of an M.A. degree, partner in a highly profitable import-export enterprise – but born, unfortunately, in a large mansion in Avenue Haig of a union between the descendants of a pukka sahib and a Chinese female, nice and all that, but certainly not pukka.

There were those who still referred to the Eurasians as chee-

chees, a derogatory term from India. They were said to have a touch of the 'tar-brush' which, so far as China was concerned, was untrue in that I never could see the 'yellow' in the 'yellow race' nor, for that matter, the 'white' in the ruddy hues of the Europeans.

To the Chinese it was also obvious that whites were not white but red. Thus they were known as 'red-skinned devils', 'red-haired devils', 'long-nosed devils', 'foreign devils', or just 'devils'. They were also known as 'long-nosed barbarians', 'outer barbarians', 'cow-smelling barbarians'.

Even today in Hong Kong and other places where there are sizable Chinese communities we are still the 'hung moh gwai' – 'red-haired devils' – or just 'gwai loh' ('foreign devils'). The terms, invented by supercilious Mandarins, have lost their acid content and are now accepted colloquialisms for the white races.

Certainly 'devils' we were in Shanghai.

As the British were the most important element in Shanghai and the other concessions elsewhere and wielded the greatest influence on patterns of behaviour, it had to be admitted that the infliction of indignity on the cultured Chinese race – and others not of pure European stock – was, largely, a British crime.

Strangely enough the French, whose policy at times in China was as harsh as that of Japan, inflexible on maintenance of treaty rights, were on remarkably good terms with the Chinese.

The Portuguese, the Belgians, the Dutch, the Spaniards and the Scandinavians treated the Chinese on an equal footing and the Americans, whose record on race relations at home was a deplorable one, accorded the Chinese much more dignity than most Britons.

The American Club in Foochow Road was open to Chinese who had studied in the United States or to those with close American connections. Nevertheless, I never saw a black man there and there were many black Americans in Shanghai.

British racial policy was extremely short-sighted. I saw at the time it was going to leave a legacy of hate everywhere and when I saw the scurrilous treatment meted out by many of my compatriots to the Chinese I felt ashamed, so much so that I decided I would never join the Shanghai Club. During my ten years in China I never did.

It was well known that, on one occasion, an important minister of the Chinese government calling on an English friend in a British-owned apartment building in Seymour Road had been curtly told by the Russian watchman there to use the back lift as

Chinese were not permitted to use the front entrance.

Once when Gordon Morriss decided to entertain Mayor Fu Siao-en of Greater Shanghai to lunch at the Shanghai Club, there was a committee meeting called to debate the proposition that he should be blackballed. Had the committee warned him of the danger of entertaining a hated puppet of the Japanese then one could have seen reason in their decision.

The complaint, however, was that Morriss had introduced a Chinese guest into the club and this was almost tantamount to high treason. Morriss was reprimanded but he had too much money and influence to be thrown out of the establishment.

Few Britons ever thought of trying to learn Chinese. If the 'natives' did not speak English then it was their tragedy. There was no job in a British firm for any Chinese who could not let the pidgin flow. English was the language of Shanghai and, by God, the Chinese would learn it or starve.

On the other hand, the Chinese kept some forms of entertainment free of foreign encroachment. There were the cabarets where only Chinese was spoken and where the girls blanched at the thought of being held by the ruddy, big-boned, cow-smelling Europeans. The Paramount at St George's was one. There were also the Metropol Gardens, Ciro's, the Lido and several more.

Not that Europeans were barred from entering. The Chinese were far too polite for that. So a foreigner might enter and find not a soul speaking English, which usually left him in total isolation, unable even to order a beer or the green tea which most Chinese males drank in vast quantities. More often than not the 'barbarian' left pretty quickly for a place where he would feel more at home.

Unlike most other Europeans I was always welcomed at the Paramount or at the Metropol Gardens, the two places I favoured. The reason was that I had previously taken the precaution of endearing myself to the girl-managers there – a cumshaw, a present or two, a worming-in process that had convinced them I was different from the remainder of the barbarians, politer, more Chinese.

And, on the floor with a long-legged Soochow beauty to guide in some quick-step variations, nary a dirty thought, not a tremor below the belt, only an overriding desire to impress with steps that would have done credit to Victor Sylvester himself.

A little pat on the shoulder from my partner to acknowledge that she had enjoyed my company, a polite bow, and the 'little gentleman' – that was me – walked back to table and ordered, of

all bloody drinks, a Coca-Cola, which, alas, had the propensity to make me fart. So, occasionally, I did spoil myself, by failing to keep the wind back in some particularly energetic jig. Not that it worried the girls, too much. After all, nice as they were, they farted, too. Who didn't? And they were frank in speech – not like the prim hypocrites of my race who never would mention such things in polite conversation as farting, or peeing, or burping . . .

They were, however, much to polite to tell us that we smelt like the cattle which we ate and which they did not – or, at least, rarely and, certainly, never in the poorer families.

But one Chinese friend of mine, a lady, with whom I was on intimate terms, did let me know that we were generally regarded as 'cows on two legs'. Unlike her own race, she said, we stoked up with butter, animal fats and too much beef. This not only caused European females to sprout hair where there should have been an unblemished and smooth surface for stroking – the legs, for instance – but nearly all of us to exude the aroma of the cattle-pen.

While the Europeans, or most of them, in Shanghai stayed socially aloof from the 'natives' I found several good Chinese friends, including the playwright Yao Hsing-nun, who wrote in Chinese such historical masterpieces as *The Sorrows of the Forbidden City*, later to be made into a Chinese film in Homg Kong.

Yao, who spoke excellent English after studies in the United States, alternated between European clothes and the traditional Chinese gown. He had a great fund of witticisms and his knowledge of Chinese erotica was profound – all based on studies of ancient literature in Soochow University, where he studied, in Peking and elsewhere.

There were still eunuchs in China when I arrived in Shanghai. These were the people – mostly Manchus – who had served in the imperial household. They had lost their 'precious parts' willingly in order to obtain lucrative careers in the royal household and, as proof of their emasculation, they carried their testicles with them in sealed jars. The jars and their contents, like season tickets on the buses, had to be produced as proof of their bona fides when they applied for such posts as servitors of the concubines of the Emperor or the princes.

But, as Yao explained, loss of 'eggs', which is how the Chinese referred to testicles, could not dampen erotic excitement unless castration had been carried out before puberty. Then in adult.

143

hood the eunuchs had a feminine appearance with shrill voices, sloping shoulders and rolls of fat – womanly apart from the 'tea-pot spout'. After puberty, however, the desire was still there and erections possible.

He said it was well known that the Emperor's concubines, who were constantly frustrated when he found it physically impossible to serve them all on a regular rota system, gained some solace in erecting the impotent yards of the eunuchs and, most secretly, of vastly enjoying the fantastic delight of the seemingly never-ending tumescence of which they were capable.

Other eunuchs not so favourably placed, according to Hsin-nung, used to clasp each other around the waist and, with stomachs close together, jump up and down to cause friction to the sensitive glans. Thus the term 'jigging eunuchs' came into being and caused girlish giggles among the female servants of the imperial household who were called on to repair the frayed fronts of the eunuchs' underwear.

In fact, said Yao, who had picked up enough American slang to qualify as a bar-room raconteur during his Chicago days, while in the west it was the clerks who got shiny arses, in the old Forbidden City the perennial problem was shiny flies.

A not uncommon sight in Shanghai in the pre-war years was the woman, usually middle-aged or elderly, tottering unsteadily on tiny feet which had been bound in childhood.

Bound feet, tiny, satin-slippered, aroused Chinese men to heights of passion, particularly among the upper classes whose womenfolk for three score generations or more had been subjected to the torture of foot-binding in childhood.

The feet were encased in long, narrow bandages which compressed the toes and heels. The torture of the pain as the bandages were pulled tighter and tighter produced many tears and sleepless nights but, at the end, when the arch of each foot had been totally destroyed and a Chinese woman's foot measured no more than four-and-a-half inches there came the realisation that the mutilation had bestowed on the sufferers great erotic advantage over the peasant girls, whose usefulness on the land precluded foot-binding.

The practice effectively tied most women to the house. They were destined to hobble throughout their lives – chattels of their menfolk but powerful in possession of two tiny feet which bestowed on them the power sexually to arouse their lords and masters.

So great was the fetish in China over bound feet that in several establishments all that a woman needed to do to arouse males was to stand or sit behind a thick curtain and to thrust her slippered feet under the curtain for them to be admired. This aroused great excitement among the men, who had paid for the privilege of gazing at the feet, and the usual result was masturbation.

Many times a day in Shanghai and, later, in Peking, Chungking and elsewhere in China I saw those tiny grandmas hobbling almost precariously among the busy crowds on their bound feet. Usually clad in long, padded trousers, long-sleeved jackets and wearing their jet-black hair twisted round at the back of the head they signified the end of an era in China – the finale of the age of male supremacy.

The daughters of these grandmas and their female grand-children walked on natural feet. Like the queue – or the pigtail as it was called in the West – the Nationalists considered bound feet to be a sign of China's previous backwardness. With the end of the Manchu dynasty edicts were issued ordering all Chinese males to cut off their queues and the practice of foot-binding was forbidden.

Similarly the practice of chest-binding died out and Chinese girls were allowed to develop natural breasts though they rarely attained the proportions of those of Western women.

My friend Yao was a fount of knowledge on the amatory arts of ancient China. As he made clear, kissing on the foreign pattern was considered to be degrading, a barbaric custom. What the Chinese male desired to rouse him in intimate contact with a woman was to smell her, to run his nose closely over her smooth skin, to explore every part of her body. He was in no hurry – unlike the impatient foreign lover. Sometimes the process of love-play could proceed for more than an hour, a gradual build-up of erotic fervour that could erupt, at last, in the heavenly joy of copulation.

And it was not only the 'missionary' position that the Chinese couple adopted. Old classics, outspoken and in many instances well illustrated, revealed a knowledge of amatory postures that had been ingeniously contrived – for instance, the threesome which involved two males, one of them obviously a homosexual, and one female. While the lady is penetrated from the rear position by one of the men, he, in turn, is mounted by the other chap. It was all shown in a picture the caption under which delicately explained that here was a method of satisfying both the normal urge for the female and the not-so-normal predilection for the manly bottom.

Another old classic showed a variety of positions some of which involved a garden swing, a boat on a canal, the turret on a castle wall and other unlikely objects all introduced to add spice and variety.

I had another Chinese friend, C. C. Wong, who spoke excellent 'Oxford English' although he had never been outside China in his life.

Wong managed two cinemas – the Golden Gate, a second-run house in French town, and the Metropole, a first-run theatre in the Settlement. He seemed to spend most of his time in running in a sort of shuttle service between the two houses and in giving me free tickets for shows at both.

He was typically Chinese. He always wore the traditional gown, ate only Chinese food, followed Confucian ways – and yet, on the screen, spoke a brand of English that was impeccably pukka.

Not that he appeared in films. The Golden Gate ran at every performance a series of slides advertising this, that or the other commodity on sale in the city. There was with each slide a spoken commentary in English eulogising that particular product. That was Wong. He spoke 'live' into a microphone placed in the projection room and I must admit that, at first, I believed the Golden Gate voice to be that of a well-educated Englishman. It was only after I had met Wong by chance in the foyer of the cinema that I discovered he was giving a 'live' performance every day before rushing off to the Metropole to see how things were progressing there.

Wong was the epitome of diligence. I was surprised to learn that he had picked up English himself and had acquired his 'Oxford' accent simply by listening to British actors on the screen. He loved to talk to me just to give him the conversational practice that he lacked. From time to time he visited me at my apartment and we worked away at commercial blurbs which he had prepared for the Golden Gate slides.

As I look back on my China days, C. C. Wong typifies the Chinese zest for hard work, for supreme diligence in providing for family and total dedication to educational enlightenment.

Hard work on a pattern that was never seen in the Western world – even in those days of exploited labour – was omnipresent in China. A man worked for his family – all hours that God sent. It was his duty. Not only had he a wife and family to support but usually aged parents or uncles or aunts. Old age was respected in China. Any Chinese who spurned his parents or grandparents, or

146

any members of his family, when they reached old age would have been branded as a savage. Very few Chinese died in loneliness in old age. Such a fate was unthinkable. No matter how poor a family was it was a son's duty – usually the eldest – to care for the father and mother, to whom he owed filial devotion, when old age overtook them. And if there were still grandparents alive or a widowed grandmother then decency demanded that they should be accorded a place of honour in his home.

Now China has a stable government in effective control and the shameful exploitation of the peasantry has been ended.

The Chinese seem to have decided to bury the bitter memories of past exploitation in a new spirit of universal forgiveness. When one remembers the atrocious brutality of the Japanese in China it can only stand to their credit that the word 'revenge' appears not to exist in the Han language.

The 'Saints'

Missionaries – known to journalists as 'God botherers' – were considered by most businessmen in China to be meddlesome and futile. They belonged to a great diversity of Christian sects who showed much un-Christian-like hostility to one another and it could not be denied that a total of about two million Chinese Christians, won over by the missionaries after almost a century of endeavour in the field, was not exactly a success story. These converted Chinese – known universally as 'Rice Christians' because it was said that they had been tempted to forsake China's many gods by lavish hand-outs of the country's staple food – exerted little influence on the 400 million or so 'pagan' Chinese who continued to kowtow before the gods in the temples.

Nevertheless it had to be admitted that the missionaries and the Chinese Christians, for the most part, were not only selflessly dedicated to the spiritual and temporal improvement of the masses throughout the country but were possessed of remarkable courage in the face of almost omnipresent danger.

Unlike the foreigners living securely under the protection of the foreign powers in Shanghai, Tientsin, Peking and the other large centres many of the Christian missionaries in China chose to work in rural areas, often isolated by the lack of roads, telephone or telegram facilities and, in many instances, by the violence of the times which in some regions resulted in warlord rule, Communist invasion, bandit depredations and the open hostility of anti-foreign populations.

From time to time missionaries were murdered, kidnapped, assaulted, imprisoned, raped and generally ill-treated in districts where the rule of the gun held sway. Nevertheless, they displayed remarkable courage in refusing to leave their Chinese converts.

The Japanese aggression against China in 1937 and the spread of hostilities inland had exposed many of the foreign missionaries to great danger. The Japanese were violently anti-Western and the presence of foreign Christians in regions under their occupation or under attack by their military forces provided them with heaven-sent opportunities to involve them in the reign of terror which they had unleashed. Many missionaries were 'accidentally' killed or wounded in bombing raids. Others were injured when victorious Japanese soldiers entered a captured town and brutally assaulted them or when in vain attempts to protect Chinese girls from being raped they were shot or bayoneted. And the women foreign missionaries, often alone in districts overrun by the Japanese, forever faced the danger of being sexually assaulted.

It had long been decided by the Western powers that to avoid embarrassing incidents with the Japanese as many missionaries as possible, particularly women and children, should be removed to the safety of the foreign concessions in Shanghai, Tientsin and Peking.

The hair-raising stories brought back by the missionaries from the interior aroused great interest in editorial conferences on the *North-China Daily News* and it was suggested that I should go to some danger spot and sample the sort of perils they were facing.

It was also suggested that I might be able to 'do a piece or two' on piracy 'up the Yangtse'. Naval guards were being provided for British merchant ships which had been attacked by gangs of pirates. The usual mode of attack was for a pirate gang to embark on a vessel as deck passengers and then when the ship reached a pre-arranged rendezvous to produce a variety of weapons from their baggage and to open fire at officers and crew while junks loaded with shore-based accomplices drew alongside and joined in.

On several occasions British naval guards aboard the ships had been in action with considerable success. Valuable cargoes had been saved and the bodies of many bandits, dumped ashore in Shanghai, bore solid testimony to their efficiency.

Eventually I set sail aboard a Jardine river steamer for Hankow – a cargo vessel with limited, but excellent, accommodation for a small number of passengers. The food was good. So was the liquor. The service, by Chinese stewards, made me feel like an old-time aristocrat in feudal times. And my fellow passengers were a congenial lot who found comfort in the presence aboard of some British naval ratings under the command of a petty officer.

There was a great difference between the old *Dilwara* and the Jardine 'tub' which was the description given to the vessel by its master, a middle-aged Merchant Navy salt who knew every nook and cranny of the tortuous and treacherous Yangtse. For one thing, I was addressed as 'sir' by the Royal Navy petty officer whenever we met. It was also pleasant to dine with the ship's officers and to be served by white-coated attendants rather than have the *Dilwara* sludge heaved at you by a massive, foul-mouthed Scandiwegian.

My musical education was further enhanced by a British lawyer from Hankow, a former member of the Honourable Artillery Company in London, with whom I shared table.

As was the custom among Britons at that time we established contact via the old-school approach and I learned that he had been at Rossall, which is a Lancashire public school. My Rugby bona fides satisfied him and, nightly after dinner, we smoked and drank in an atmosphere of ever warmer friendship.

As the liquor warmed us up and unloosed inhibitions we found that we were both instant gigglers, ready to double up in paroxysms of mirth as, alternately, we went through our respective repertoires of dirty jokes and reminiscences of humorous occasions back home.

Later, to the delectation of our all-male, non-missionary passenger-list, my friend, who had a nice tenor voice, regaled us with some marching songs of the HAC. Three of them I shall never forget. The first was called 'My Wife, My Maid and I'. I cannot set down the music but the words are imperishable:

'My wife, my maid and I, my wife, my maid and I went out for a shite on a moonlight night and the maid shat more than I.

'My wife was peeved at this, my wife was peeved at this. She said to me if you'll agree we'll challenge the bugger to piss.

'Three pisspots came at call, three pisspots came at call. She lay on her back and opened her crack and bloody nigh filled 'em all.

'My wife was peeved at this. It nearly broke her heart. She said to me if you'll agree we'll challenge the bugger to fart.

'My wife and I went (loud raspberry). My wife and I went (loud raspberry).

'But the girl with a bum like a musical drum went (extra loud raspberry, extra loud raspberry, extra loud raspberry).'

There was another song which started: 'I gave her inches one, inches one, inches one.'

Then came: 'I gave her inches one: she said "George, you're sure to come. Put your belly close to mine and waggle your bum".'

150

And so it went on to 'inches two' – 'George you're nearly through. Put your belly close to mine . . . '

'Inches three' – 'George I want to pee. Put your . . . '

'Inches four' – 'George, I want some more.'

'Inches five' – 'George, your prick's alive.'

'Inches six' – 'George, we're in a fix.'

'Inches seven' – 'George, this is heaven.'

'Inches eight' – 'You've come too late.'

'Inches nine' – 'This is divine.'

'Inches ten' – 'Let's start again.'

And then the final chorus:

'So I gave her inches all, inches all, inches all. Yes I gave her inches all, inches all, Yes, I gave her inches all – and she took my balls an' all. Put your belly close to mine and waggle yer bum.'

The third song, 'The Lady of the Mansion' told of an aristocratic woman, returning to the hall, who saw 'a bloody great tinker pissin' up against a wall'. He was well endowed and the lady preferred him to her old man. So he did valiant deeds up at the mansion culminating in his 'buggerin' the butler which was the dirtiest trick of all'.

And so we reached Nanking, the new capital of China on the south bank of the Yangtse, midway between Hankow and Shanghai.

The Japanese were in supreme control although the Wang Ching-wei puppets nominally constituted the government in power. Japanese soldiers swaggered everywhere and the city still bore the scars of their savage brutality in burnt-out buildings, half-demolished shops, bullet and shell marks on walls and, in the wide river, the masts of sunken vessels.

I noticed that there were few women about. The sexual inhumanity of the Japanese, who raped and then killed in cold blood, had struck fear into the hearts of any females who had been spared death during the occupation of the city and the bestiality which had ensued. Practically the only Chinese to be seen on the streets were men, either slovenly dressed puppet soldiers or policemen and civilians whose livelihood forced an unwilling appearance out of doors during the daylight hours.

At night the city seemed deserted. Groups of Japanese soldiers were still roaming here, there and everywhere, usually inflamed by drink, in search of women who cowered in terror in their homes as soon as the sun had set and the tramp of marching feet on the roads and sidewalks signalled yet another barbaric assault on a population which had undergone with amazing fortitude and stoical calm a period of fiendish torture.

In the foreign quarter, where most of the mission compounds were located and where many Chinese women still sheltered under the protection of the American, British and other Western flags, I met a young American missionary teacher who told me how she had rescued one Chinese girl she found lying terrified under the body of a Japanese private about to ravish her.

The girl was about fifteen. She had been seized by the soldier, thrown on her back in the road and her silk, samfoo trousers roughly torn away. The soldier was on top of her when the teacher, a tall, well-built woman, came on the scene.

Without thought of the risk to herself she ran forward, grabbed the soldier by the neck and pushed him off the hysterical girl. Before he could fathom what had happened she had shouted to the girl in Chinese to follow her and had led the way to a mission clinic where the poor girl found safety.

There was no doubt in my mind that had the Westerners been in the same defenceless position as the Chinese they would have suffered similar torment.

This, of course, was proved after the outbreak of the Pacific War. During the fighting in Hong Kong, Japanese troops entered St Stephen's College at Stanley which had been converted into a hospital for wounded British and Canadain soldiers. There were about 160 patients and seven nurses in the hospital, all of them entitled to be treated as prisoners of war.

Instead the Japanese killed men in bed by bayoneting them and then mutilated them by cutting off their ears, tongues and noses and gouging out their eyes.

The nurses were raped and murdered. One nurse, who managed to escape, told of how she was made to lie on top of two corpses and was raped several times by a Japanese soldier. Other nurses were found beheaded in the hospital grounds. All had been raped.

When the Japanese captured Singapore their troops went through the first floor of the Alexandra Hospital and bayoneted every person there. In the operating theatre, where a soldier was undergoing an operation, they bayoneted the patient, the anaesthetist and the surgeon.

From Nanking we sailed up the Yangtse to Hankow, brilliantly lighted at night and with the Union Jack on the funnel held in focus in the glaring beam of a spotlight. There was fighting still proceeding on both banks of the river as the Japanese pressed inland from Nanking and Hankow, which had recently fallen. Overhead in the daytime we saw squadrons of Japanese aircraft on bombing and strafing missions and in the river several Japanese troop transports, crowded with steel-helmeted soldiers and escorted by small naval craft, moved northward.

From time to time we spotted British and American gunboats at anchor in the river. Their duty was to protect the lives of Western citizens living in up-country areas that had been engulfed in the titanic struggle between Dai Nippon and the government of Chiang Kai-shek.

There had been terrible events at Hankow. From Nanking the Chinese government had retreated to the city and had made it the temporary war-time capital until the inexorable advance of the Japanese had forced yet another retreat upriver to Ichang.

I met British residents who had seen Chinese men being tied to trees and bayoneted by the Japanese. In another village near the city all the women had been raped and twenty-four of the inhabitants murdered before the entire neighbourhood was burned to the ground.

These Westerners were, for the most part, missionaries who had sheltered Chinese converts in their compounds over which flew the Stars and Stripes, the Union Jack and the flags of the other treaty powers. Thanks to the presence in the river of a fairly large force of British and American gunboats there had been few attempts to interfere with the missions but, as the Japanese raped, murdered and pillaged, the danger of grave international incidents was omnipresent, particularly as many of the foreign Christians were women who, courageously ignoring the record of the invaders as sexual maniacs, braved the wrath of the Emperor's warriors by going abroad in the streets to gather in hundreds of hysterically terrified Chinese women.

The city had been taken by a force under the command of General Hata and many Chinese prisoners had been captured. They suffered a terrible fate.

An American, Albert Dorrance, who was manager of the Standard Oil Company's Hankow operations, told later how from the deck of one of the four American gunboats on the river he witnessed the atrocious behaviour of the Japanese.

He saw several hundred Chinese soldiers marched by the Japanese to the Customs Wharf. They were herded along gang-planks running about half a mile into the river and, in groups of three or four, hurled into the Yangtse. As their heads appeared above water they were shot by Japanese soldiers on the gang-planks.

Dorrance and a large number of American sailors on the gunboat watched in horror. When the Japanese saw the Americans they changed their plans and embarked their Chinese prisoners in small motor launches, taking them downstream until they were out of sight of the American gunboats. There they threw them into the water and shot them.

In other parts of the city hundreds of Chinese soldiers were lined up and shot merely to give the Japanese practice in machine-gun traversing fire.

I heard the story of a Chinese family whose home was entered by the Japanese. The daughter was stripped and raped and when her parents insisted that she should be returned to them and not taken away they were shot and killed. The soldiers returned to finish their ravishing of the daughter whom they shot and killed before they left.

It was impossible to walk about in Hankow without seeing the horror that 'benign Japan' had inflicted on the Chinese – ravished women everywhere, a river laden with the murdered bodies of Chinese soldiers and civilians, sorrowing parents whose daughters had been taken away from them to be thrust into the brothels run for the army, orphaned babies whose parents had been murdered in a bestial orgy of sadistic slaughter, burned-out homes, groups of men, women and children, hands tied behind their backs, being taken for torture and inevitable death . . . all this and hundreds more gruesome sights.

And yet the Chinese Christians, who had survived the Japanese holocaust, were rarely deterred in their dedication to the Christian ideals.

I managed to send a few features down to Shanghai from Hankow. It was easy enough by one of the regular steamers. Telephones or telegrams were out of the question. The city and the countryside had not yet returned to normality and communications were extremely difficult. In Changsha – if I could get there – I realised that I would really have a problem in getting any news out.

I was lucky. The British gunboat *Sandpiper* was in the vicinity. This was the shallowest of the small warships on the river and it was on its way to Changsha where the water was extremely low and where an imminent Japanese attack was expected following the collapse of Hankow.

The passage of the warship meant that a flotilla of small craft, British-chartered, could sail under its protection with supplies for the missions and for the representatives of British concerns in the region.

So I found myself aboard a motorised junk, Chinese-owned but flying the British flag, proceeding choppily and uncomfortably alongside the half-speed gunboat.

There were many deck passengers, all Chinese. I was the only European. There were no cabins and no services. Most of the passengers cooked on charcoal burners at the poop end of the massive, unwieldy craft. And as they used unpurified oil extracted from nuts the smell was atrocious. I shall never forget the power of that sang yao oil. It assailed me from the stalls of the street food vendors in Shanghai making me heave and choke as I passed by. On the junk it almost clubbed me into unconsciousness as the crew and passengers heated it to smoking intensity and then threw into it pork, greens, ginger, herbs and a host of other ingredients for a quick-fry session. The smell of the oil is indescribable. It has in its smoky ebullience the astringent odour of tram-driver's socks discarded unwashed after months of midsummer use. The aroma from a glue factory or a leather-tanning emporium is sweet in contrast. I can still smell it in what has now become nostalgic imagery of the China that I knew and loved so much.

It took us several days to reach Changsha and we were not troubled by the Japanese. Shortly after leaving Hankow we passed out of the territorial limits of Japanese conquest and though I did not know it at the time entered a wild but beautiful region of small hills and flatlands, riverine estuaries and picturesque villages occupied by the Chinese Communists who had been engaged in operations against the Chiang Kai-shek government for many years but who, in time of national crisis, had united with the Nationalists to form a patriotic front dedicated to the defeat of the 'island dwarfs'.

I did not suffer too badly aboard the junk. I had taken the precaution in Hankow of laying in a small store of canned foods – mostly the products of the Hazelwood factories in Shanghai owned and operated by genial American Anker B. Henningsen, whom I was destined to meet later as a prisoner of the Japanese. I had several varieties of packed meats, beans, fruits, vegetables and sweetmeats and though the diet became monotonous it kept body and soul together.

My greatest difficulty was not the inner man but the outer shell. This was assailed by two of the greatest afflictions of rural China – the flea and the bug. I was bitten everywhere. I scratched

155

and I scratched. I took off most garments daily and instituted intense searches which resulted in the mass slaughter of at least the bed-bugs, which I could see, but the elusive fleas eluded me to torment me every minute. So it was with great joy that I saw the outlines of the city of Changsha.

I managed to get a room in one of the city's best Chinese-style hotels. I was an object of curiosity to hordes of small Chinese children, who gathered, giggling and wide-eyed in wonder, as I went out to see the sights. The kids followed me in packs. I wasn't annoyed. Every time I stopped they halted – at a safe distance. I knew nothing of the dialect of this central China region and I hadn't the faintest idea of how to find some English-speaking person to lead me to the missionaries whom I sought. There were Chinese soldiers everywhere, the remnants of the retreating Nationalist forces, armed to the teeth and seemingly wandering aimlessly about.

It was on one excursion that I met a plump little Chinese woman, black-gowned, bespectacled and rosy cheeked. She had watched me for some time. She approached me and in excellent English asked me if I needed any help. She was a godsend. She told me that her name was Wang, that she was working with a foreign mission, was a Christian and had only recently escaped from Nanking.

She became my guide and mentor in Changsha, a wonderful encyclopaedia of local knowledge, an interpreter supreme, the best companion a stranger could wish.

I had seen signs of devastation on the riverside and several ruined buildings closer to the town. This damage, I learned from Miss Wang, had been inflicted by Japanese aeroplanes in terror raids on the town. There had been fires and serious loss of life but she assured me that the spirit of the Chinese people had not been broken. They were brave and ready to endure to the end. There had been a flood of refugees into the town fleeing from the Japanese terror and many of the casualties had been among them in their riverside hovels.

The missionaries, foreign and Chinese, were facing the danger like the rest of the population – with great courage and devotion. Classes had been organised to make clothes for wounded soldiers. Many of the missionaries had become quite clever tailors and were meeting regularly in groups with all sectarian differences banished for the common good.

Many foodstuffs had become scarce. Butter was unobtainable. Milk and sugar were luxuries that few could afford. Prices were soaring at an alarming rate. But the missionaries were determined to stay on and face the worst. I admired their fortitude and their calm acceptance of times that had become hard to bear.

The Japanese, probably occupied elsewhere, did not bestow their attention on Changsha during my first week there and for this I was grateful as I did not relish the thought of being quartered slap in the middle of a dropping zone.

With Miss Wang and a tall Englishwoman missionary with a northern accent, long-legged and angular, we went by bus to stay at a Chinese preacher's home in a small village. His busy little wife cooked our meal of rice and did her best to make us comfortable. Miss Wang waited on us hand and foot. She could not bear to see us, two Europeans, in such poor surroundings. She got us extra eggs and produced hot water for us to wash with.

Then after a night's rest we set off for a farm on a hill some five or six miles away where there was a Christian family. The family wanted to know all about the war and its progress. Miss Wang translated fluently and with great fervour as I told of the terrible atrocities of the Japanese everywhere.

Soon the wife and daughters of the farmer were sweeping the mud floor and dusting the chairs for us to sit on. We unrolled our bedding and laid ourselves down in a large room with a screen separating me from the women which was just as well for I was feeling severely frustrated without the outlets provided by the Blood Alley cabarets or the suckee-suck girls back in the Silver taxis. But I behaved myself admirably and, as a male, became the object of much attention from the farmer's females.

Back in the town I visited one mission where I saw the women were busy making padded waistcoats for wounded Chinese soldiers.

Also among the visitors that day was a Mr Wu, one of the town's wealthiest businessmen, who voiced his faith in God.

He told me, 'God has heard our prayers for China before and He will again. We've prayed about the Communist problem and now they've all gone. We prayed for Chiang Kai-shek and I am certain that, no matter how we suffer, China will triumph in the end.'

Prophetic words but, at that moment, there were few who believed that mighty Japan could be defeated by the Chinese alone.

A few days later I got my first taste of the war in Chinese-held territory. I had gone some way out of the town to climb a hill and to enjoy the sunshine on a lovely day. There were planes hovering

157

overhead as I crossed the river. I thought they were Chinese. As I walked towards Hunan University I looked back and saw a huge fire raging in Changsha.

At the university I found staff and students literally running in circles, excited and aimless. The planes were Japanese, I was told – three of them and they had been machine-gunning the ground on their run-in over the city.

As we talked one of the raiders flew over the university. It circled round and round but there was no firing and, eventually, it flew off, much to my relief.

Back in Changsha bombs had been dropped and there had been a great influx of citizens into the mission compounds where they thought they would be safe. In one centre alone there were more than 400 people hiding in the cellars under the main houses. Many of them were women with babies in their arms.

I had a look at the damage done by the raiders. Several houses had been destroyed and hundreds of men were groping frantically in the ruins to bring out the dead, the dying and the badly injured inhabitants.

Many folk were flocking to the hospital run by the missionaries to help the wounded and to carry them in for treatment.

I saw a little Chinese boy who had been eating a bowl of noodles on the street. When the first bomb dropped he had been blown up to a roof on which he perched precariously, screaming for people to help him. He was brought down and, miraculously, had only superficial injuries.

A young couple were being married Chinese-style in a hotel and there was nothing left of them or their guests when a direct hit blasted the building to rubble.

I watched a team of six men digging out a Chinese woman, a very pretty girl, from a pile of debris. She was unconscious and looked to be badly injured. A missionary told me that she was a Biblewoman, a helper who spread the gospel among the Chinese in the rural areas.

Members of the Young Men's Christian Association and the Young Women's Christian Association, armed with gauze and cotton, were working until near midnight digging out people and removing them to hospital if they were still alive. As they worked they sang patriotic songs, filthy, sweat-streaked, tired but filled with indomitable courage.

They were returning home when the police called them back to dig in a huge pile of rubble that had been a one-storey house. As they heaved away clearing the mass of twisted beams and bricks a boy's head emerged. Frantically they pushed in their spades and their bare hands to free him. He was a little fellow, no more than six or seven. And he was alive. That was certain. In wide-eyed terror, speechless from shock, he watched the team working until hours later he was gently lifted from the ruins, placed on a stretcher and taken to hospital. His father and mother were later found dead in the ruins that once had been their home.

Despite the carnage I was amazed to find among local inhabitants an extraordinary friendly feeling towards Japan. They expressed sorrow for the retribution that would fall on that country and its people. They were certain that Japan would have to suffer for its misdeeds but, in true Confucian compassion, they felt very deeply for the ordinary Japanese people, who, they were at pains to point out, could not be associated with the militarists.

On top of the air raids another problem for the city was the flood of wounded soldiers coming in from the war front. They just streamed into Changsha and were scattered about in cinemas, temples, bath-houses – anywhere they could find to lie down, exhausted, many of them with suppurating wounds and in agony.

The missions rose to the occasion. They visited the soldiers wherever they could find them, taking small comforts along to be handed out. The women changed some of the men's dressings on wounds which had not been touched for five or six days. The stench was terrible. Wounds were turning gangrenous. Men were screaming as medicaments were applied. There was little hope for many of the soldiers who lay cheek by jowl on straw on mud floors.

What medical services the Chinese army possessed had broken down completely in the headlong flight from Japanese superiority in arms and training. Once a soldier's usefulness as a fighting machine had vanished he had to fend for himself. For many of them death came as a relief from indescribable suffering. Others, often limbless or blind, could only hope to spend the remainder of their lives as beggars on the streets. And yet all of them were imbued with the will to live in a land which had discarded them. They did not want to die. They fought with courage to live and their patriotism, despite their rejection by the government, still burned brightly.

There was no doubt that the Japanese threatened Changsha. About ten thousand of the inhabitants had left the city but thousands more, refugees and soldiers, were arriving to take their place.

I attended a meeting of the missionaries called to discuss future moves. On the agenda was a suggestion that the Fu Siang school should be moved to a safer place in the country.

No decision was taken but the school was doomed whether or not the Japanese arrived.

I was talking to Miss Wang a day or two later when we told by an excited policeman that planes were on the way. People were pouring out of their homes and making for the missions. Missionaries wearing yellow armlets were directing them to the cellars under the houses when the first bombs dropped.

I heard several deafening crumps and the crack of the anti-aircraft guns. Everyone started running madly. I wanted to join them, but remained where I was trying to look as calm and collected as the women with their yellow armbands.

I looked up and my heart sank. There were twelve Japanese planes roaring overhead. I could see the bombs dropping as they flew, miraculously, it seemed, unscathed between the puffs of bursting anti-aircraft shells. Frightened folk came streaming in. And then amid a series of deafening explosions not far away which made the ground shake I saw six of the planes, engines roaring, head away eastward.

And then silence. The missionaries quickly organised rescue parties and I accompanied them with a medical team from Java consisting of overseas Chinese who had come to the homeland to help the war effort.

I saw two Chinese women Christians carrying a stretcher and Miss Wang took medicines. We were delighted to find that there had only been five casualties and that these were not serious. The bombs had dropped on the outskirts and the damage had been negligible. We returned to the mission and drank tea. My admiration for the coolness of these women and their steadfast belief in their faith knew no bounds. Nothing ever seemed to shake them out of their purposeful calm.

Even more remarkable was the phlegmatic stoicism of the Chinese Christian refugees who had flocked into Changsha from places around Shanghai and Nanking.

At the China Inland Mission compound in the city I found seven Chinese women refugees from Shanghai. They had all lost good jobs. Indeed, they had lost everything. They told me that their beautiful new church had been razed to the ground and their homes as well. Some of them had seen their families slaughtered. They were without news of the friends they had left behind. They had had a ghastly time getting to Changsha and some of them had

160

walked. And yet they did not want to talk about their own sufferings but were pleading with the foreign missionaries to send them as preachers into the countryside.

Nobody was ever turned away from the missions. One day eleven rickshaws turned up at the C.I.M. compound bearing refugees from Kiangsi and their luggage. The place was bulging at the seams but the missionaries, harassed by accommodation and severe feeding problems, would not say 'No'. The result was about forty people were placed in six small rooms not much bigger than a European kitchen.

With Miss Wang I visited a Chinese theatre accommodating about 150 wounded soldiers. She drew my attention to one man who showed us a shattered leg, all bent and shrivelled. He was very thin and pale.

He spoke in a country dialect which Miss Wang understood and translated for me.

'They killed my father; he had a beard,' he said and began to sob.

'They've killed my mother, an old lady. They've taken my children to ... '

He broke down and wept uncontrollably. He tried to pull himself together and went on:

'They've taken them . . . they were only little children, just little ones. My two big brothers I think they have killed them, too.'

In great, body-shaking sobs he rambled on repetitively:

'They've killed my father; he had a beard. They've killed my mother, an old lady. My children. My brothers . . . '

The tears rolled down his face and fell on the hard pillow on which his head rested.

Looking at me he said imploringly, 'Why doesn't England help us? The Japanese are going to take my country. Oh, why don't you help?'

I was hearing the heart of China cry out for succour. I comforted him as best I could with Miss Wang, brave heart that she was, holding back a flood of tears.

And as we left he moaned: 'I can't run away from the bombs now.'

Later a group of the missionaries prayed for him and his fellow wounded soldiers. A doctor told us that he had little hope of recovery.

I had seen enough. There was enough material in Changsha for a book and I began to look around for ways to get back to

Hankow and from there to book a berth on a steamer for the Shanghai run.

Here the missionaries were of great assistance. They made what I expected to be a difficult operation easy – with the Chinese owner of a river launch, who regularly ran a service from the city upriver to a point where passengers were transferred to a second launch, which covered another fifty miles or so and then anchored for the turn-around. At the third point, I was told, there were regular sailings to and from Hankow. There would be no trouble. I was not so certain. But I had to take the risk.

All was settled and my supply of dollars dwindled considerably. The charge was high for a foreigner and though the missionaries haggled on my behalf I was taken for a ride, which was nothing unusual in China.

Before I left we had the worst air raid the city had experienced. It was a Sunday, quiet and peaceful with hundreds of children attending scripture classes in the missions. Suddenly the roar of aero engines and, in an instant, the streets were a seething mass of fleeing humanity, most of the people running for the missions over which flew the flags of the treaty powers.

The planes roared overhead – how many I do not know. There must have been twenty at least. I saw the Indonesian Chinese medical team members running to prepare their ambulance. The fire brigade, sirens screaming American style, tore down the main street on an antiquated Dennis appliance. Their brass helmets glinted in the sun. Soldiers joined in the rush. Men poured out of the police station. As the bombs fell women screamed and clasped their babies to their breasts. All around was pandemonium.

But once again I was lucky. The town intself was not the target. As the planes circled overhead, we could see the Rising Sun emblem on their wings. Amid the puffs of bursting anti-aircraft shells they manoeuvred in echelons of three or four and screamed away towards the river, circling again in the distance and then roaring in to drop their load of death on the other bank.

I ran towards the river. The scene was one of absolute chaos. Members of the fire brigade were trying to get across in small sampans. The Indonesian Chinese had got their ambulance aboard the ferry which was making for the opposite bank. By this time we could see huge fires roaring into the sky from buildings on the hillside facing us. The missionaries, men and women, with their yellow armlets were being rowed across with the firemen. There were hundreds of craft in mid-stream. I joined a party of police and we piled into a small sampan which literally sank down to the gunwales. But eventually we got across without mishap.

We ran like people possessed towards the fires on the hillside. The planes had gone and there was nothing to be seen in a cloudless sky except great spirals of black smoke rising from flaming infernos on the ground. Hurrying past us were the stretcher parties carrying the victims of the attack to the river to be rowed across for hospital admission. From the hillside we heard cries of 'Help! Help!'

Finally we reached the scene of devastation. It was the university, singled out by the Japanese for a concentrated attack. It was well known that the Chinese universities were the centres of patriotism and of anti-Japanese propaganda. This was a terror raid to cow the Chinese people, particularly the intelligentsia. Like every Japanese act of savagery it failed in its objective and only fanned to ever greater heights the flame of resistance in the hearts of the people.

We stumbled over fallen telegraph wires. There were broken trees everywhere. We saw mutilated bodies being loaded on stretchers into the Indonesia ambulance. Hundreds of people were digging in the rubble to bring out the dead and the dying. Finally we reached the science block, which was in ruins. How many bodies were buried underneath the mass of masonry there I shuddered to think. Firemen, police and soldiers were digging and bringing out bodies.

I ran round the corner and saw a woman wailing over the bits and pieces that were all that was left of her husband.

We saw a ruined house and a young student with bandaged head told us, 'There are six people in there.'

A high wall without support tottered visibly over the ruins. Heavy furniture was thrown here, there and everywhere. The fire brigade gingerly raked the debris as the wall could have collapsed on them every minute.

The destruction and the loss of life at the university were appalling and yet within twenty-four hours classes had been started in wooden huts hastily assembled on the campus and the students and professors, many of them bandaged and several of them bereaved, were poring over their books and scanning blackboards as if nothing had happened.

I set off back for Shanghai after saying fond farewells to the missionaries and, particularly, Miss Wang, who assured me that China would never be vanquished and that, some day, we might meet again in happier circumstances. We never did. I am sure that she survived the holocaust and returned to her native heath after the war there to work for a few years until the great Communist tide swept over China. As a Christian and a friend of the 'imperialists' she would certainly have been included in the Communist blacklist of 'imperialist lackeys'. This inevitably would have meant arrest and 're-education' in a labour camp unless with thousands of other Christian Chinese she managed to make the long journey into exile in Taiwan.

The journey up to Hankow was uneventful. I boarded the passenger launch in Changsha and we chugged merrily up-river past the gunboat *Sandpiper*, which had just arrived after a trip to some out-stations where there were British interests. It cheered my heart – and no doubt those of the missionaries I was leaving behind – to see burly British jack tars hard at work on the deck of the little vessel. But they were as vulnerable to Japanese savagery as the defenceless people to whom they were showing the flag.

The launch was not half so bad as the motorised junk. Nor did its cargo seem to consist of any insects apart from the ubiquitous cockroach, which did not bite. I had a stock of food provided by the missionaries, a good supply of Golden Rat cigarettes and I was continually supplied with copious quantities of green tea by the skipper, who spoke pidgin English and, as a waterman, was full of admiration for the maritime British.

I left him with hearty handshakes to board the second launch which would take me nearer to Hankow. The vessel was bigger and had a more powerful engine. We made good speed until we reached the boundary of the war zone and then we anchored to wait for nightfall. The fear was that the Japanese in daylight would bomb the craft. There was no sign of the Japanese army which was pretty far inland and, as dusk fell, we set off on the final stage of the trip to a small village where the launch was due to pick up a cargo of big bristles.

There those of us bound for Hankow were transferred to a long, shallow-draught motor-boat which, the skipper told me, had been built in England. There were more than thirty of us aboard and the old tub – for she must have been built a good forty years previously – wallowed down deep and sluggishly in the muddy brown water. We set sail at night, a dark, murky cloud-filled sky blotting out the moon.

The danger was that we might run into Japanese naval craft on the river – launches carrying troops, small armed patrol boats or

164

sampans forced into military service and carrying two or three soldiers. But, as the skipper explained to me through an interpreter, a student going to Hankow to see how his family had fared after the occupation of city, there was rarely any trouble if his passenger-list was 'clean' and he was not carrying contraband cargoes. Nevertheless he preferred to run at night rather than risk a brush with the Japanese, whose actions were unpredictable.

From time to time we heard the chug-chug of other vessels on the wide river. None of them carried lights. This was not unusual in the less-used reaches of the Yangtse where piracies were frequent, but how we managed to avoid head-on collisions I'll never be able to explain. At times the motors sounded so near that I jumped up from my seat of packed straw on the deck ready to swim for it when the crash came. Miraculously we hit nothing and nothing hit us.

We crept into Hankow shortly after midnight, unchallenged, and we tied up amid hundreds of junks and sampans along the busy waterfront. The old boat was completely lost in the welter of craft bobbing and scraping against the wooden wharf. It would have taken a good pair of eyes to have singled out the vessel as a new arrival or as a suspect from a region not then occupied by the Japanese.

I disembarked after paying the skipper and made my way in the darkness to the old concession quarter which was brilliantly lighted and where, it seemed, some of the old gaiety was creeping back. At least, I found a bar, owned and operated by a German, still open and inhabited by several officers from a British steamer who were downing vast quantities of Scotch. I ordered a beer and asked the proprietor if he could fix me a meal. In guttural English he told me that he could. What did I want?

'Ham and eggs and French fries with lashings of bread.'

'Can do.'

A stentorian shout through a hole in the wall and I could hear sounds of activity in what must have been the kitchen beyond.

My scruffy appearance – I certainly needed a shave – attracted the attention of the officers and we were soon in conversation. They were impressed when I told them that I was just up from Changsha and when I graphically described what was happening there. For them China meant the bright lights of Shanghai and the security of treaty-power status in Nanking and Hankow. They listened intently to my story, bought me several drinks and watched intently as I tore into the first European meal I had had for a long time.

165

I stayed there until daylight and then visited the offices of the Great Northern Telegraph Company from where I sent a wire to Percy Finch to advise him that I was on the way back with 'good material'. Then to Jardines, who had no steamer in port. They advised me to try rivals Butterfield and Wire, who had two ships in the river port. I did and within an hour was aboard a 5,000-tonner ready for the voyage home.

I reached Shanghai after a fairly long stop-over in Nanking, where we took aboard a cargo of pigs bound for the abattoirs in the Whangpoo delta. Never have I seen animals so cruelly treated. Each pig was tied securely inside a cane basket. They were piled on top of one another on the foredeck without food, without drink – without attention of any kind. Those at the bottom of the enormous pile of baskets were almost at the point of suffocation. They could not move an inch. The pain they must have been in was not hard to imagine. Some of the animals were bleeding from their snouts or mouths after they had been cut by the razor-sharp edges of their cane prisons in frantic efforts to get air. When we reached Shanghai many of them were dead. Nobody seemed to care and when I spoke to one officer about the enormous cruelty of the operation he only laughed and said, 'What the hell, they'll be pork in a few hours. You should see 'em being killed, mate, and then you'd have something to write about.'

There were more pigs below deck roasted alive! They had placed the animals in their cages right against the ship's steam pipes. They were literally burned to death by the tremendous heat of the pipes, their flesh scarred and shrivelled. But, again, nobody seemed to care.

At the office Percy, with a twinkle in his eye, asked me if I had enjoyed my 'holiday'. While I had been gallivanting on 'a Cook's tour' my colleagues had been working their fingers to the bone and suffering cruelly from writer's cramp. Perhaps, he cynically suggested, the priceless prose that I was about to commit to posterity would recompense poor old Harry Morriss for the 'fortune' it has cost to send me swanning around in luxury. And, almost as an afterthought, had I heard that in the Palace Hotel bar there was a new Polish Jewess barmaid who had a pair of tits the size of two prize-winning garden marrows?

I took his banter in good part. Percy, fine newspaperman that he was, realised that Changsha was no picnic. I produced a series of graphic eye-witness accounts of the bombing raids on the city, of the courage and selfless devotion of the missionaries and of the terrible sufferings of the Chinese people. They were printed and I have an idea that they scored me a black mark in the Japanese security section across the Soochow Creek in Hongkew.

Alas, poor Changsha was doomed. Almost the entire city was destroyed – not by the Japanese but by the Chinese army which burned down the arsenal, hospitals, schools, food stores, anything that could be of value to the advancing Japanese in pursuance of Chiang Kai-shek's scorched-earth policy. Before the Chinese retreated from the city the place was a raging inferno and thousands of its citizens were fleeing by any form of transport available into the far interior, often penniless, starving, sick and dying.

As for the missionaries, most of the foreigners were evacuated by the gunboat *Sandpiper*, when the fall of the city was imminent. They were loathe to leave their Chinese colleagues and their flock of converts. Some of them refused to leave their charges. Others joined the trek into the interior. 'God-botherers' they might have been but the word 'courage' was indelibly stamped on their stout hearts.

Night Beat

I had arrived in Shanghai full of good intentions, determined to follow the example of the missionaries and to set aside for the good of my soul my predilection for carnal gratification. Like any New Year resolution it flourished for a week or so and then gradually gave ground to the insidious advance of lascivious legions of impure thoughts induced by the sight of leggy Chinese girls, the bounteous bosoms of the Russians and the 'Come hither' call of the brightly lighted cabarets and night clubs. I gave up the fight and banished purity to where it rightly belonged – in the mission compounds.

My little amah started the rot by scrubbing my back with carbolic to rid me, once and for all, I hoped, of the suspected presence of Changsha fleas. Inevitably her presence and the silkiness of her touch conquered good intentions and I developed a great erection which begged for deflation in the manner to which it had become accustomed – the application by hand of a great deal of lather and gentle finger-tip titillation of the sensitive part.

There was, also, the new arrival at the Palace Hotel bar who Percy had told me about.

She had, indeed, an enormous pair of boobs, certainly as big as prize marrows only more enticingly shaped.

Black-haired, bright-eyed and ruby-lipped she sat on a high bar-stool facing the customers, all of them European males pretending not to have noticed the enormous up-thrust of two over-sized mounds revealed almost down to nipple level by a low-cut dress.

I had no scruples. I did not believe in hypocrisy. I was at the bar to gaze at a pair of tits the like of which the staid old Palace had not seen for many a year. I ordered a beer from one of the white-coated boys and I watched the Jewess shaking dice with a goggle-eyed chap from Jardines.

When he left I managed to dart in quickly, beating six or seven other men in the rush to get a grandstand seat. I was not a dice-player but I had to conform to custom if I wanted to catch her eye.

She shook and I shook. I kept my eyes on her tits, never taking them off the target except to call out what I had rolled out from the leather shaker. She looked embarrassed and her eyes, from time to time, strayed down to see what her dress was permitting me to look at.

'What are you staring at?' she asked.

'As if you don't know,' I replied, nodding my head in the direction of her chest.

She laughed.

'Cheeky man,' she said, not at all displeased. 'You like them' eh?'

'Lovely handful,' I said. 'Just the thing to raise my spirits.'

The point was not lost. A girlish giggle and she leaned forward so that all – or nearly all – was revealed.

I was blunt.

'You've given me the jack,' I said. 'I'm as stiff as a board.'

'Well, keep it to yourself,' she replied, playing hard to get. 'I can't do anything about it.' And this meant that she could – at a more opportune moment.

I had to get back to the office. She was obviously going to be an expensive handful which meant a night out at the Kavkas, the Hungaria or the Tower night club at the Cathay Hotel. I had some expenses to draw which would cover the cost and if they didn't there was always the good old pencil to sign my forth-coming salary away.

I fixed a date two days hence. She said she would like to be taken to the Park Hotel night club.

'If you wear a high-necked dress I'll scream the place down,' I said. 'Can't stand shocks like that.'

She made no reply – just smiled.

I told Percy that I'd managed to get a date with the young lady at the Palace, 'you know, the one with the big tits'.

'Well,' said my news editor, lapsing into broad Yorkshire, 'tha'd 'ad dun as weel if tha'd gone up ter t'Scotch Dairies and grabbed thissen an 'andful of udder. And it ud cost thee nowt.'

I called for her in a Ford taxi. She wore a long gown covered with a fur stole, form fitting and silky. It was not until we reached the Park Hotel and she removed the stole that I saw what she was nearly dressed in. Apart from two straps at the back, crossed in the middle and fastened at the waist, she was fully exposed in the rear. No brassiere, either. The front of the dress was high-necked but it didn't really matter because every time she bent down the material sagged forward to leave large gaps at the sides and an unimpeded view of two of the biggest beauties ever to rest their weight on a bar counter.

We sat in an alcove on imitation-leather wall seats, well padded and yielding. In front of us the table, long and narrow and most tastefully arrayed with imitation candles softly glowing from small electric-light bulbs over an expanse of immaculately laid-out cutlery, crockery, napkins and wine glasses.

Directly facing us across the small dancing space, highly polished and reflecting the light of ceiling chandeliers in shimmering beams of silvery incandescence, the Filipino band led by a dusky man from Manila impeccably dressed in white tuxedo, purple cummerbund and frilly evening dress shirt.

I realised that the meal was going to be a costly affair, particularly as my partner decided to go for the à la carte dishes rather than the cheaper all-in dinner, but when she leaned forward to spoon up the soup the sight of an enormous breast thrusting forth banished all miserly thoughts.

I delayed tackling my own soup in order to savour the wondrous exposure. This girl, surely, was the answer to any tit-man's prayer.

We ate well and drank a lot and all the time she knew that from my position on her left I was gawping goggle-eyed most of the time. She knew, too, that I was hard as the Rock of Gibraltar with fly buttons exerting full power to keep the monster respectably at bay.

I commenced the preliminaries when we started to dance. The floor was small, the music was soft, slow and sentimental and, in the crush, there wasn't much room to manoeuvre so I banished all thoughts of showing off a tricky step or two and settled for a lascivious belly rub.

I pulled her even more closely to me. I could feel her pelvic mound pressing into my groin region. Her legs swished against mine. She wore stockings and I got the erotic message of hose-top connection with suspender belt. But most exciting of all was the wobbly, bouncy, softly yielding pressure of two un-brassiered breasts.

Gradually I worked my arm closer and closer to gap at the side.

'I'm not a wrestler,' said the girl, but there was no trace of rancour in her voice. She knew what the goal was. I wasn't the first bear-hug groper she'd met.

I made it. My fingers touched the soft, satiny sheen of the right bosom and the flesh yielded in a most tantalising way. It moved when I pushed it. I thrust it sideways so that it touched the other one. I played my fingertips up and down and didn't give a damn if the whole world watched me caressing that mighty protuberance.

'Naughty, naughty,' said the girl but she wasn't referring to my exploratory efforts. As she spoke, she was pressing into me harder and harder. I was in full bloom – steel-like stalk, thick and soft-tipped, caressing in masculine fever the top of her mound of Venus. And she liked it – pulled me in closer, swished her belly against mine and moaned.

I kissed her behind the ear – silkily. My right hand caressed her breast though I could not reach the nipple. I could see the flush on her face, the parted lips and the glassy stare of eyes miles away in the dreamland of erotic experience. I had no doubt that she was wet. So was I. I knew that any more dances like this one and, hey presto, the floodgates would open. I was glad when the music ended and we sat down. It gave me time to re-cover.

In the alcove she allowed me to put my arm around her and to pull her into my chest so that penetration of the gap was easily accomplished. In the dim light of the dancing session it didn't really matter what we did. I moved my left hand across her chest and through the silkiness of her gown caressed her nipple which was stiff and long. She liked it. I bent over and kissed her on the lips, thrusting my tongue in and out. She responded passionately so that our tongues were working in febrile contact. She moaned. I gasped. I felt the onrush of spasms that betokened the opening of the seminal locks. I broke away rather hurriedly.

She knew the reason. She gazed down at my lap and her hand came down to rest there but it did not move. She had my hardness under her palm. Any caressing, as she well knew at that stage, would have the steam pressure blown sky high. As it was I had enough engine power down there to drive the old *Queen Mary* across the Atlantic and back with the full Cunard fleet in tow.

So I calmed down gradually, ordered more drinks and we listened to the music. I did not take long to regain my composure and we were ready to dance again. Cheek to cheek we danced on until the early hours.

Shortly after two a.m. I took her by taxi to my place. The old liftman, whom I roused from slumber on a cot in the hallway, opened his eyes wide when he saw the girl but with typical

Chinese politeness he feigned no attention at all during the ride up to the fifth floor. Once inside my living room I seized her in my arms and kissed her passionately. There was immediate response and as we pressed together in close embrace her hand descended to my fly front and explored in swift movements the throbbing jerkiness of an organ raring to go.

But we didn't start right away. I brewed some coffee from a Chase and Sanborn tin of grounds and as we drank she sat on my lap in the big easy chair. She allowed my hand to roam underneath the long evening gown so that I was able without restraint to raise it to thigh level where my finger trickled to the inside of her thighs and slowly moved to feel the sticky wetness of two large lips, easily opening to my thrust. She heaved deep sighs and with parted lips pulled me into a long, passionate kiss in which our tongues darted in and out in ever quickening movements.

Our coffee forgotten on the floor beside us, we rose from the chair and stood facing each other. I placed my hands at her back and pulled the press-studs at her waist. The crossed straps flew loose to expose her entire back in lissom nakedness. I raised my right hand to her neck and fumbled with the clasp securing the collar which was now the only piece of material keeping the front of the gown from falling away completely. In a moment the entire front had dropped to dangle from her waist and, with a great gasp, I saw naked in front of me what I had longed to see for days and days.

I stepped back and gazed enraptured at the immense beauty of her curves. Her breasts were statuesque in their eye-catching magnitude and yet, huge as they were, they were lovely to look at – held firm by youthful muscles, thrust from chest in dimensions that were amazingly unreal, long nippled . . . delicious.

I moved towards her and placed a hand under each breast. I tested their weight and then lifted them, slowly, silkily, feeling the soft skin. Up and up I lifted. And then, suddenly, I let go and watched them flop back to bounce and shake as their weight found the solidity of the chest which supported them.

I moved my face into them and pushed hard. Seizing each breast by hand I pushed the two enormous globes into my face, smothering it completely in mountains of resilient softness.

And then, lightly, I drew back, advanced again and placed my lips over the right nipple, letting my tongue ride up and down the softness that was there. I felt the nipple tighten. I sensed a shudder in the girl. As my tongue trickled quickly in feathery touches the swelling increased until, like a miniature phallus, the nipple stood out, stiff, bloated with passion.

I placed my arm around her and guided her towards the bed and I watched her step out of her dress. I looked at her stockinged legs and at the expanse of bare thigh riding up to lace-frilled, brief cami-knickers.

'Keep your stockings on?' I pleaded. 'I want to feel them.'

The girl took off her high-heeled shoes and lay on her back.

So I mounted her, determined to postpone the explosion for as long as my will-power was in control. I had stripped naked. No sooner had flesh touched flesh and the girl, in great excitement, had pulled me down fiercely so that she could entwine her legs around my backside, than I realised that I was about to give a repeat performance of the premature-ejaculation fiasco with the Korean, Anna.

Not that I expected the girl to emulate Anna's assessment of my performance with the same words: 'Shaw, you're a bum fuck!' Nevertheless she would certainly be frustrated and not pleased.

How many minutes I lasted I do not know. It was a remarkably speedy orgasm that followed actual penetration – gallons and gallons, or so it seemed, exploding, unchecked, well inside.

The girl had moved passionately with me. Had she kept her pelvic region static then there was a chance that I could have lasted longer. And had I not let my hands roam wildly over those enormous mounds and, from time to time, slipped one hand down to feel the tautness of thighs in their silky encasement of hose the gods would have been with me, perhaps. It was when we kissed passionately and fiercely, crushing our lips together, tongues meeting in frantic ebullition, that the signal turned to green and I gave her all I'd got. Nothing on earth could have stopped me. She took it all. It was up to her whether or not she was protected. I wasn't.

I could still feel her muscles gripping my rod, jerking, squeezing, relaxing and tightening in passion. But even that sort of titillation is helpless in the face of a man's orgasm. It went soft and slipped out.

'I'm sorry,' I said. 'I couldn't wait. You excited me too much. It had to come out.'

She took it better than I expected.

'Never mind,' she replied. 'You're only young. We can't all be perfect.'

Her English was impeccably Shanghai – evidently born in the city and educated there.

'Help me,' she said after a few seconds. 'Kiss me here' pointing to her nipples. 'Put them in your mouth,'

I leaned over her and did so, watching her legs jerk furiously as my tongue tip tightened them, tickled them. I moved from one to the other and used my hand to excite the nipple not in my mouth. It was hard work but I could see she was going for an orgasm and I continued my exertions.

Finally the girl brought herself off by energetic employment of her pelvic muscles. Not once did she use her hand to stimulate clitoral excitement. All she required was my oral caressing of nipples and, as a further stimulant, a rapid stroking of my body with hands that gripped my buttocks fiercely when pelvic wildness signalled the coming of the relief I had been unable to give her.

To this day I have no idea what that girl's name was. I never asked her. In Shanghai it was not important to know such things. Women were merely sexual objects, most of them desperately anxious to secure the favours of the male in order to keep body and soul together.

I didn't go with her again. The truth was that I was ashamed of my performance. I knew that she considered me to be sexually inexperienced in a city containing many experts. I gave the Palace a wide berth and did my drinking elsewhere.

On the news front I found there was much to do after my return from Changsha.

For the first time in my life I saw a British judge don the traditional black cap and sentence a man to death by hanging, an emotional experience which affected me much more, it seemed, than the man in the dock on whom it was passed.

He was a private in the Seaforth Highlanders named Eckford. He was charged with shooting a lance-corporal in his regiment, a Yorkshireman called Davies.

The murder had been committed in a blockhouse on the Settlement perimeter and all the evidence pointed to a long period of persecution by Davies on Eckford, who had, finally, killed the NCO with a .303 bullet from his rifle.

It was late in the evening when the jury in the British Supreme Court found Eckford guilty with a recommendation to mercy. Sir Alan Mossop, who obviously did not relish the task he had to perform, turned to face Eckford in the dock and, almost apologetically, informed him that, under the law, there was only one sentence he could pass – death by hanging.

I watched Eckford, dressed in best khaki uniform. He stood

straight as a ramrod, not a flicker of emotion on his face, staring fixedly ahead as the judge uttered the words that signalled his imminent death on the scaffold.

The case aroused enormous interest and a petition was organised by the British community asking for commutation of the death sentence to one of life imprisonment.

I signed the petition myself and I believe that the British Ambassador, Sir Archibald Clark Kerr, as the King's representative in China, did finally commute the sentence.

Then there was an exciting occasion at Kiaichow Park. I was in the office when a call from a police contact told me that there was a 'bloody big riot' at the camp of the Chinese Lone Battalion at the park.

I got hold of Mike Nenchew, who armed himself with a couple of cameras, and we set off in a Ford taxi. We stopped outside the high walls of the camp where we were greeted by photographer Joy Lacks in a remarkably short skirt for that day and age.

There was pandemonium inside the camp where the Chinese soldiers had attacked their guards from the Russian Regiment and were still on the rampage. Several of the guards had been seriously injured and there were casualties among the Chinese.

Outside the camp about 100 members of the Russian Regiment, steel-helmeted and carrying clubs and shields, were drawn up in two lines facing the main gates. While some of the detainees had managed to escape, the Russian guards inside had managed to prevent a mass break-out but they were under exceptionally heavy pressure and badly needed reinforcements.

These had arrived under the command of a Russian officer who had fought in the Imperial army against the Bolsheviks but who in his British uniform as an SVC member had that pukka Sandhurst look.

He barked out orders and his men raised their shields and clubs, turned and in pairs entered the camp with the officer at their head. The carnage started.

Nenchew, who was pretty agile, climbed the high wall and from a precarious perch there took several shots of the battle. Joy Lacks, dainty and utterly feminine, clambered up the wall, not to be outdone by a mere male. I watched her closely. She was struggling magnificently up the stonework, camera slung around her pretty neck. And what an expanse of stocking-clad limbs she was showing us who were gathered on the road below.

As she struggled upward, feet in high-heeled shoes gingerly

testing for a secure foothold, I had an unimpeded view of green-coloured cami-knickers clinging voluptuously to her rounded buttocks. A thrill went through me, lecherous sod that I was. I could see the entire expanse of her slim legs encased in sheer hose and above stocking tops pure white flesh. Nor could she hide the narrow strip between her legs which while it did not reveal bare flesh and pubic hair nevertheless advertised the shapeliness of the mound it guarded.

Finally Joy made it and joined Nenchew as the noise from inside the camp grew in intensity. I should have been up on that wall myself but I wasn't fool enough to discard a position that permitted me to indulge in such erotic contemplation of the female figure!

When the Russians started to bring out battered Chinese soldiers in blood-stained blankets I had to come down to earth and take some interest in the proceedings. Some of the poor chaps I saw looked well beyond hope of recovery – bloodied and broken. There was no doubt that the Russian Regiment had gone in determined to restore order by the use of the utmost force. They were big, strong young fellows, more than a match for the smaller Chinese.

It was all over soon enough and, from Nenchew's description of what he had seen from the wall, I was able to write a good colour story.

'Why didn't you come up?' he asked me.

'Too stiff,' I replied and left him to chew that one over.

The Chinese government protested vigorously to the Shanghai Municipal Council over the action taken and demanded that the men should be released. With the Japanese watching the foreign areas so closely and with Japanese serving on the council and in various departments of that body, including the police, such a move would have created a tense situation and the possibility of Japanese action to seize the men. So the unfortunate men of the Lone Battalion were doomed to remain in captivity until such time as there was peace between Japan and China.

That day, of course, did not arrive until 1945 and, prior to that – in 1941 – the Japanese seized the International Settlement. What happened to the Lone Battalion I do not know. Whether or not they had time to escape from Kiaichow Park before the Japanese army reached that perimeter spot I cannot say. I hope they did.

In the office there was considerable uneasiness over the steady fall in the value of the Chinese dollar as the war continued and as the drain on China's reserves mounted week by week. Prices of essential commodities had risen, rents were going up and there was gloom over the future which, according to Percy Finch, was going to be bleak unless the Morriss family could be induced to match the higher cost of living.

We did not have a union to represent us and as the journalistic staff contained members of several nations we did not have the united approach needed to press for more money.

Percy conducted his own campaign with Gordon Morriss at the bar of the Shanghai Club, aided by Hoste. And a lot of bad blood it created between employer and employee. Hot words were exchanged as the liquor loosened inhibitions and the niceties of social behaviour fell by the wayside.

As for me, I was signing my life away with the pencil in various night spots and it was essential that I should get a rise.

Finally, I wrote a letter to Harry Morriss asking for an increase in 'stipend' in view of the rapid increase in the cost of living in Shanghai. I thought 'stipend' had a Dickensian flavour that would associate my financial plight with that, say, of a struggling, under-paid curate, probably dying of consumption in some mouldy garret at the time when debtors were hurled into Newgate prison.

There was no response from the management.

I wrote another letter, this time omitting the word 'stipend'.

Not a word from the boss's office on the second floor.

I waited a week or two and sent Mr Morriss another pleading missive.

I was surprised one morning when Harry Morriss walked into the editorial department, came over to me at my desk and asked me, somewhat bluntly, why I was showering him with so many letters asking for more money.

'Do you think I grab money out of the air?' he said angrily, raising his right hand over his head to sweep through the tobacco fumes in a scooping motion.

I had to act quickly and effectively. I rose to my feet and extending my right hand above my head I imitated Morriss's scooping action.

'Do you think I grab food out of the air?' I replied, in high dudgeon.

Morriss gave me one hard look, turned on his heel and walked away.

To say that I was a worried man would be an under-statement. I was in a blue funk. Histrionically my performance had been perfect – too good. It was evident that Harry had been taken aback by my display of righteous indignation and that he had not expected such rebellious sentiments. I prepared myself for the letter of dismissal that would surely arrive on my desk the following day.

Old Dooley Dunne did little to dispel the gloom.

'Well, old man,' he said cheerfully, 'it was nice knowing you. See that you get a first-class fare back home. There's always the Army. They'll have you back.'

The next day I waited apprehensively either for another appearance by my millionaire employer or for a missive from his office. I got neither.

Instead, at about 11 a.m., in walked a young Chinese messenger from the second floor. He was carrying a large wicker basket. He spoke to Jim at the entrance and our number-one pointed at me. Within seconds the young fellow had deposited the basket on my desk with the words, 'Mr Morriss he say I pay you' which meant that the basket was intended for me.

The contents were covered with thin tissue paper. I tore it off and saw what I thought were plums – hundreds of them, small, yellow, oval in shape. Then I saw the note. It read: 'With the compliments of Harry Morriss. Golden pippin tomatoes from my garden. Hope you like them.'

I was speechless. While there was a certain amount of relief that I had obviously avoided the chopper this was soon displaced by seething anger when I realised that instead of cash all I had got was a load of tomatoes which looked as if they were suffering from yellow jaundice.

'He can stuff 'em up his bloody arse,' I exclaimed.

'Stuff what?'

The question came from Dooley Dunne over in the corner doing the court stories for the *North-China Herald*.

'These bloody yellow perils – from Harry Morriss,' I replied.

Dooley came over, peered at the tomatoes and then the note and dissolved into screaming hysterics of such violence that his bottom plate was dislodged and protruded from his mouth in tobacco-stained unloveliness.

Finally, he recovered and said, 'Bugger me, does this mean that in future we are to be paid a high cost of living allowance in fruit and veg?'

In a jiffy half the staff were around my desk gazing spellbound at the boss's reply to my letters asking for a better financial deal.

'You can always get a stall licence and sell 'em in Nanking Road,' said Sapajou.

'Probably make a fortune, too.'

'Bollocks,' I said.

'Come now,' said Sapajou, 'in Russia serfs like you who were rude to their masters wouldn't be rewarded with tomatoes but with the lash.'

'What we need here is another bloody revolution but you're all too yellow-livered,' I retorted.

'So will you be when you've eaten that lot,' exclaimed Dooley.

And so, gradually, the wonder of it all dissipated as the call to work drew the crowd back to their desks and dear old Sapajou to his drawing board.

I must say that the tomatoes were excellent – sharp, juicy and delicious in a salad. But I'd rather have had the money.

Events in Europe at that time were moving nearer and nearer to war. Chamberlain had been to Munich and secured what he called 'peace in our time' but it was evident that Hitler had merely played for more time to annex by force the European nations on which he had set his sights.

It was evident, too, that Japan in the Orient was ranged solidly on the side of the Axis powers, Germany and Italy, and that the militarists in power in Tokyo, despite the opposition of the Emperor, were preparing for a showdown with Britain and the United States.

A crisis was also developing on the newspaper. Finch, exasperated by the failure of the management to increase salaries at a time when the value of the Chinese dollar was dropping daily, had words with Gordon Morriss in the Shanghai Club.

He called Gordon an 'apostate Jew' and resigned his post, giving R. W. Davis, as general manager of the concern, one month's notice.

Gordon stopped his daily visits to the editorial floor for the regular drinking session with Finch and Hoste at the club along the Bund and it was evident that a state of enmity existed between management and senior staff.

As for me the resignation of Finch, who was to remain in Shanghai as the *Daily Telegraph* representative came as an event which gave me furiously to think.

The opportunist within me advocated instant action to apply for his job. I was still young – only in my twenties – but I knew that I was considered to be the best reporter on the paper, that I had the confidence of Peyton-Griffin and of Hoste, the night editor. Logical successor to Finch would be, of course, Hoste and if Hoste was to be promoted then Cal Hirsh seemed to be the man who would take over the night job – or Charlie Bruce, then doing the world cables at night as number two to the night editor.

Thinking things over I came to the conclusion that Hoste would move up to take Finch's job in the day-time and that I might as well apply for the position of night editor. I typed out a long missive to Peyton-Griffin in which I stressed that I had been trained on a British newspaper and that I had an all-round knowledge of newspaper production

To the consternation of many members of the staff I got the job and, as Peyton-Griffin explained, one fact which stood in my favour was that, of all possible contenders for the post of night editor, I was the only one who had had the sense to apply for the job.

So I took over the paper at night – the man in complete charge of choice of front-page stories, of lay-out, of the entire staff. And I got an increase in salary which eased, to some extent, the problem of expenditure on the lascivious entertainments provided by a city almost entirely dedicated to satisfying the sexual needs of the European male.

I initiated several innovations to liven up the monotony of night work such as smearing the ear-piece of the main office telephone with printer's ink so that anyone using the contraption was sure to walk around for hours with a decidedly muckily embellished flapper and give us great amusement by so doing.

That act had to cease when Peyton-Griffin came in one night and clapped the phone to his ear. I was called in to his sanctum the following day and told that his pillow-slip was one unholy mess of printer's ink and that he was going to fire the 'the bloody idiot' who perpetrated such asinine tricks.

I said that I would keep my eyes open and try to catch the blighter who was responsible. Later I made it known to the night gang that we would have to think of other methods of amusing ourselves.

So we started to pin on to the backs of the unsuspecting pieces of paper bearing such messages as 'Kick my arse' or 'I'm good for a feel' – schoolboy antics which proved just how young we really were.

But the greatest amusement of all was the nightly aeroplane contest. Break-time was at about ten o'clock when all the news was with the composing staff of Chinese and we were waiting for the final proofs on the galleys. It was then that, from quarto-sized pieces of copy-paper, we made model aeroplanes and from a position behind the counter sent them soaring over the desks on the editorial floor. The longest flight won the award of the day – a bottle of beer.

We became expert in the design of our 'planes', weighting them carefully with a paper clip or carefully trimming the wings to produce a replica of a Messerschmitt or a Fokker of that time. And the more we played the more dear old Jim smiled.

Jim was rich. Of that there was no doubt. We knew that he owned a block of houses in Hongkew. Number-one boy he might be but, outside the office, he was a person of rank, a Chinese grandee to be respected.

As was the custom throughout China, squeeze had to be paid to the provider of a job. On the editorial floor Jim was in sole charge of the Chinese staff serving the journalistic operation – the messengers, the coolies, the sweepers, the lowly toilet washers. From each and every one of them Jim had taken his cut as the 'employer', the godfather who had selected them to serve him as benefactor. It was the custom. There was no use railing against the iniquity of the system. It was prevalent in every foreign firm where the Chinese compradore – the go-between employed by the foreigners – quickly rose to a position of immense wealth.

And Jim also provided the alcoholic refreshment for a staff of journalists ever desirous of slaking the mightiest of thirsts. Drinking where the work was actually performed was frowned upon and so Mike Nenchew's office, way down the corridor, was chosen as the bar where, nightly, we sat and guzzled UB or Ewo and signed chits to be handed to Jim in the morning by his Chinese night representative.

Jim, too, was good for a loan. Of course he charged interest but it was only small. He saved my bacon on one occasion when Mr Koo of the Palais cabaret seemed over-anxious that I should settle chits amounting to nearly six hundred dollars. I paid off – had to – Jim over a period of several months and it only cost me about five dollars for every hundred loaned.

We finished work at about one o'clock in the morning. Apart from Charlie Bruce, who was a clean-living specimen, we all had carnal urges and this meant a pre-finish conference on choice of night spot to visit in search of liquor and lechery.

Jock's Bar up near Jessfield Park in the western district was a favourite haunt. The Seaforths were good customers until midnight when they had to be in barracks. Thus it was called Jock's Bar. It had been Taffy's Bar when the Royal Welch Fusiliers were on garrison duty in the city. Earlier it had been called the

Red Rose when the East Lancashires had done Shanghai duty. Old Jock knew his titles and the custom they attracted. He looked as much like a Scotsman as an orang utan. Not that he resembled the Borneo ape but it was a definite fact that outside the Chinese restaurants in Glasgow nobody had ever been born with such mongoloid features as Jock or, for that matter, with such a chopstick-English accent. The nearest he had ever been to Scotland was Woosung but so long as the Seaforths were his best customers Jock he would be.

And so we of the N.C.D.N. gave Jock our custom until eight o'clock in the morning or thereabouts.

The main attraction at his bar was the bevy of girls he kept there to render various services to the customers, the most important of which was to mount a steep flight of stairs to the first floor where were situated about a dozen cubicles, partitioned off by wooden boards which left a gap of a foot or so from the ceiling, and there to strip off and offer themselves to customers.

The cubicles were furnished with single beds. Underneath every one was a bowl containing a solution of potassium permanganate. Once finished one was supposed to dip one's rapidly sagging member in the purple stuff and so avoid contamination. The trouble was that the stuff usually spilled over and stained vest or other under-garments so that anyone with a wife waiting at home for return from 'office duty' would, to say the least, be at a loss to explain the presence on pants of a decorative, Picasso-like daub.

But Jock's was renowned for its willingness to provide cheaper services for the poor of the community who were, without doubt, the underpaid British Tommies.

The bar was made of a series of alcoves, all partitioned off on two sides. Inside each alcove were two long seats and a table. On the seats sat the girls and the drinking customers. The idea was to rouse the lustfulness of the patrons so that an ejaculation of semen became imperative.

This semen could be received by the girls during the act of intercourse which was the method usually favoured on a Friday, pay-day for the soldier. But intercourse upstairs in one of the cubicled rooms cost more money than was usually available from Monday to Thursday and so Jock, who took as much care of the cents as he did of the paper dollars, let it be known that he was not opposed to his girls giving hand jobs in the alcoves providing he received the twenty cents a time.

One could enter Jock's Bar during the day and see the great

hamptons of British soldiers being delicately handled by the bar girls in the alcoves. And when the time for ejaculation arrived the girls would urge their customers to edge forward on the seats so that the drops spattered on to the floor rather than on uniforms.

Inevitably it came to pass that Jock's polished wooden floor of which he was inordinately proud became stained with the seminal offerings of the soldiery. The sticky stuff just dried and left ugly-looking patches. Poor Jock was upset. He pondered long over the problem. While he was loath to forego twenty cents from a dozen or so soldiers each day he had no desire to see his floor ruined.

Then he came up with a solution.

He issued the paper-bag edict. Every one of his girls would use one to catch the stuff before it could reach the floor. Successful it was too.

So the customer entering Jock's would be stirred by the sight of a taut rod, a small feminine hand grasping its stiffness, being steered delicately towards a large brown paper bag held open by another delicate feminine hand underneath the table. Not a mark on the floor. Not a drop on a good khaki uniform. The bag had saved the day – worth every cent of the extra outlay to ensure preservation of polished purity.

I was popular with the girls at Jock's because I was always acting the fool. In fact I was known as 'Gondoo' which, I suppose, could be translated as 'Crazy' or 'Crackers' or 'One Screw Loose'.

Some of the girls were very attractive. They were country wenches who had probably been sold by poor parents to the Tu Yueh-sen organisation which had then either sold them to the bars and brothels or hired them out.

One of them I liked very much. She was a tall, strapping girl. I always had her at my table during the early-morning hours and I loved to feel her long and shapely legs. Her skin, like that of other oriental girls, was satiny smooth and the touch of her thighs was delightfully erotic.

From time to time I took her upstairs ignoring the basin of potassium permanganate. There she undressed completely so that I could gaze at her supple youthfulness – broad, sturdy shoulders, well muscled arms, a flat stomach, and, by far the best of her assets, a pair of legs which were worth insuring for a considerable sum.

Her breasts were not large but there was enough of them to make a nice handful.

She wanted to be penetrated normally and had refused to suck me or to adopt any other position than that which was considered to be decent. So she lay on her back and I mounted her and thrust my rod into her while she pretended that my actions were exciting her which they were not. So as I pushed and panted on top of her she would moan and whisper in deep throatiness, 'Darling, darling, darling.' She knew I was a leg man and she guided my hands to her thighs so that I could stroke them and hasten the end of the session. I always came quickly enough, had a quick wash-off at the sink – but not in the potassium bowl – and we would go downstairs to join my friends and to continue the drinking session until dawn.

It was the custom of the girls to encourage quick finishes by the lads they took upstairs. More money could be gained from cadging 'drinks' from the customers and by urging them to knock back their own drinks quickly and to order more and more from a smiling Jock behind the bar counter.

The girls were thrifty and could save the cash they earned. They lived on the premises and though they paid for their food it was possible for many of them within a few years to buy their freedom.

My tall girl from Jock's did just that. I saw her after the war in Hong Kong, beautifully made up and expensively dressed, entering the dress circle at the Queen's Theatre on the arm of a middle-aged Chinese who was obviously a wealthy man.

She saw me and recognised me but she did not greet me. I was a reminder, I suppose, of the slavery to which she had been subjected in Shanghai.

I once gave an exhibition of intercourse with her at Jock's. At least, two of my colleagues on the paper saw to it that my penetration of the girl was made public.

It happened when I went after night duty up to the bar with Brown and Bothello. I had gone upstairs to 'tear a piece off' and had left the couple downstairs quaffing large glasses of U.B. beer.

I was thrusting energetically into the girl when, suddenly, she let out a yell and lost all interest in the proceedings. Her eyes were glued on the top of the partition by the door. I looked round and saw there the grinning faces of Brown and Bothello. They had found some steps and were intent on watching my performance.

'Carry on Private Shaw,' said Brown from the partition top in the approved Sandhurst manner.

'No can,' screamed the girl. 'No belong ploper.'

'Piss off you two,' I said. 'You've spoiled my action.'

'Oh, go on Shortie,' said Bothello. 'You've got a lovely arse when it's in motion.'

It was obvious I wasn't going to get rid of those two leeches who were determined to remain in their balcony seats until I had completed my chore – and chore it was beginning to be as the girl had frozen all over, all chaste and virginal in her reaction to the four prying eyes.

'Come on,' I said to her. 'Let's get on with it.'

'No can.'

'Why no can?'

'No belong ploper.'

'Oh bugger off, you two,' I implored.

They didn't move.

I seized the girl roughly, thrust her back on the bed and held her there while I regained my steam and pushed it inside again.

As I moved in great jerks I heard Brown's voice:

'In-out, in-out, in-out. One-two, three-four, five-six.'

He had been to a rowing school in England and was giving a fair imitation of John Snagge broadcasting on the boat race.

'You rotten sods,' I shouted.

'Lovely stroke,' said Brown, 'but I think you caught a couple of crabs.'

The girl was having no more of it. She jumped up from the bed, naked, dashed to the door and vanished through it to some other cubicle along the corridor.

'Now that's a silly thing to do,' said Brown. 'Most unsporting, definitely not cricket.'

I took it all in good part – I had to.

We went downstairs and drank the night away. The girl never appeared on the scene, too embarrassed to show her face. Strange that a lass who had received more standing cocks than good dinners should be so coy when her performance was being watched. Perhaps it was her oriental upbringing that taught her that the female could only be passionate in privacy but definitely not in public.

Jock's, of course, was only a glorified brothel. So were most bars in Shanghai. The girls would have been mortally insulted had they been called prostitutes and yet that was what they were. Once a client had suggested a spot of bed exercise then they didn't refuse – not unless he was suffering from leprosy or looked like the hunchback of Notre Dame. At least, unlike the women in the normal brothel, they could be selective – but it was in their interest to keep their jobs and too many refusals would not please a boss who wanted to keep his clients.

Brothels were everywhere in Shanghai and a sleazy lot most of them were – back-alley dives, dirty, squalid, odiferous, abysmally dingy.

I visited one which I found in a labyrinth of alley-ways off Szechuen Road. I mounted a steep staircase and came to a landing on which I could see several partitioned cubicles on the pattern of Jock's Bar.

I looked around and saw a door on the right of the landing which was closed. I advanced towards it and nearly fell over a low tub which I saw contained the evacuations of the inmates. The light was dim and did little to banish the sinister aura which the darkened corridor and the silence of the place presented to the newcomer literally groping his way forward in the gloom.

I gingerly opened the door and saw in front of me a large room, sparsely furnished with a few upright chairs and one table by the wall at which sat a very fat Chinese in long gown. There was dirt everywhere, a heap of washing in one corner and cobwebs on the ceiling corners.

The gentleman rose as I entered, smiled and bade me sit down.

'You wanchee long time or short time?' he asked me in fairly good pidgin.

'Short time, ' I replied.

I was beginning to regret that my carnal desires had landed me in such a dismal dump. I wanted to turn tail and flee but I decided to stick it out and see what happened.

'Five dollar,' he said.

'No can,' said I.

'Four dollar.'

'I pay two dollar for short time,' I said firmly.

'Can do,' he said, knowing well that five dollars was the usual charge for a full night's session.

'You waitee, I fix,' he grunted as he rose heavily from his seat. 'You look-see.'

He waddled out and returned about half-a-minute later at the head of a line of seven girls, all of them gazing at me curiously. As I sat there they paraded before me. They walked slowly in line round the room, each one of them wearing a cheong-sam which showed leg development. Their faces were highly painted but even the heavy application of cosmetics could not disguise the fact that each one of them bore the facial signs of the rigours they had undergone. They were an unprepossessing bunch and though one or two of them had nice figures I couldn't see myself being roused by any of them. Nor did I fancy that much attention had been paid by their master to their internal cleanliness.

Still they paraded slowly before me like slaves in an oriental market. Had they been chained together with big black eunuchs cracking whips to keep them moving in servile subjection then I wouldn't have been surprised. It was like a scene from the Arabian Nights set in squalid surroundings. And then my heart went out to the poor females whose degradation I was witnessing – girls sold into slavery, thrust at the onset of puberty into prostitution, destined to rot – which many of them did – from venereal disease, prisoners for life of some bloated brothel-keeper.

I could take no more. Abruptly I rose, fled past the parading girls and hurried down the stairs into the fresh air.

The position of women in China, despite the advent of the Nationalists with their various reform movements, was still deplorable in the 1930s. In Chaotung, for example, plague and famine only a few years back had forced starving families there to sell 3,000 children, most of them girls, to slave dealers. They were carried off in baskets like poultry. In other regions there were reports of dead and of living infants, again mostly girls, being thrown away to be gnawed by dogs.

A girl of fourteen was worth about £4 in English money. Later she could be sold for more than twice as much as a concubine or, if she was only plain, for about the same amount to a brothel-keeper, who would force her to live in squalor, treat her brutally and throw her on the streets when her usefulness as a money-earner was over. Many of the wizened old female beggars who daily importuned us in Shanghai were cast-offs from the brothels.

The rich Chinese – and there were many millionaires in Shanghai – often had 'harems' containing as many as 24 concubines, all of them subservient to and often badly treated by the number-one and legal wife.

There were, of course, the high-class brothels and in the Settlement they were, appropriately enough, located in a small street called Love Lane leading off Bubbling Well Road.

The most famous establishment there was that of Margaret Kennedy, an ebullient female who had been in the business for years and who occupied an exalted position in the social world, knowing as she did most of the sexual weaknesses of the influential foreign taipans who could afford to pay her exorbitant fees.

Margaret kept only European girls, whom she treated almost

like her own daughters. Her establishment was located in a large mansion in Love Lane and the interior decor was luxurious. It included a large sitting room equipped with expensive settees and arm-chairs on which clients sat and downed their drinks before selecting a girl for intimate attention in one of the bedrooms downstairs and upstairs.

At one time, so C. N. Gray told me, Margaret believed in the 'Never on Sunday' routine. This was a day of rest for her girls, who came from Britain, France, the United States, anywhere in the Caucasian world. On Sundays she would hire a large carriage pulled by two magnificent horses, seat herself and her beauty chorus in the coach and undertake a leisurely tour of the city.

This Sunday drive by Margaret and the girls often was a source of embarrassment to some of the local gentry out for a Sunday walk with their wives. It was a well-known fact that, married or not, most of the Europeans in the city were not infrequent visitors at the Love Lane bordello. Margaret valued their custom and she was a firm believer in rigid maintenance of the rules of etiquette. Thus, spotting a lavish spender at her house, she had no qualms about waving a greeting to him with her parasol – a polite custom in which all the girls joined. And it did not matter whether or not the gentleman had with him a female. It was left to the embarrassed gentleman to explain to his better half how in heaven's name he had been singled out for such attention by 'that wicked woman'.

I visited Margaret's only once, going in at about ten o'clock at night. In the sitting room I fancied a well-built Russian girl and bought drinks for her as a preliminary to bedding down for the night. She was well stacked which suited me fine and very soon she led me out into the spacious hallway of the house and into a ground-floor room, heavily carpeted and luxuriously fitted with heavy drapes and antique furniture which included a fair-sized bed.

There was only a dim light in the room. Indeed it was in semi-darkness and I had to grope my way around. I was about to undress by the bed when the girl halted me and asked me to open my flies. 'Gawd, she's in a bloody hurry,' I thought to myself. 'Ralph, you're going to be squeezed dry by this one.'

I undid the buttons and plonked it out, half-hard. Instead of the lascivious feminine assault that I expected the girl walked over to the dressing table, took from it a long battery torch, flicked it on and returned to me. She took my rod in hand, pulled the foreskin back expertly and shone the light directly on the glans which she squeezed and squeezed in an effort to produce some signs of gonorrhoea or even worse. There were none. I got her certificate of approval but, by that time, the clinical coldness of the entire operation had reduced me to Antarctic frigidity and all desire had fled.

'Get stuffed,' I said impolitely, buttoning up. 'And you know what to do with that bloody torch. It should be big enough.'

I walked out in high dudgeon. Margaret's never saw me again.

In the office following the departure of Percy Finch there came yet another change on the editorial floor when Charlie Bruce and Peyton-Griffin did not see eye to eye over certain matters of policy and Charlie departed for other fields. In his place on the cables desk came little Charlie Tombs, plus the usual bottle of whisky he always carried around with him for 'medicinal purposes'. And into the reporting team there arrived a Shanghai-born young Englishman, Julian Bates.

In Europe events had deteriorated rapidly. Despite Chamberlain's pledge of 'peace in our time' Hitler had betrayed the trust of the British Prime Minister and Poland had been invaded. On September 3rd, 1939. I tuned into the large radio set we possessed and, in an atmosphere charged with patriotic emotion, heard the sad, tired voice of the British leader tell us that we were at war with Nazi Germany. A few hundred yards from the *NCDN* journalists in the office of the local German weekly newspaper, supported by Nazi party funds, were listening to the recorded voice of Der Fuehrer bellowing his tirade of hate against England and France. We were enemies on friendly territory.

War in Europe provided a bizarre situation in Shanghai. There were two British battalions in the Settlement, the French had their garrison in the Concession, the Italian Savoia Grenadiers, now cut off absolutely from their homeland or the Italian colonies by the strength of the British Far Eastern fleet, were still legally part-guardians of the international inviolability of the foreign area, the American marines, still not involved in the hostilities though patently anti-Axis, remained in their western sector and the Japanese continued their so-called defence role in Hongkew.

The advent of war affected many of us in Shanghai who had served in the British forces. Peyton-Griffin called me in and asked if I was likely to be called up for the duration. I did not know. Nor did a large group of ex-servicemen in the police force, at Ward Road Jail or in any other field of endeavour in Shanghai. Then the order came from the British Consulate-General that, for the moment, we were to remain in our posts, that we could be more useful to the British war effort by continuing our employment in China and that, if there was to be a change in policy, we would all be notified promptly.

I breathed a sigh of relief. It was not that I felt afraid of becoming a combatant – even the bravest man, which I wasn't, could not relish the thought of facing the grave perils of the battlefield – but, having only recently achieved the miracle of freeing myself from the purgatory of military service, I was loathe to return.

Tombs was made of different metal. He was a belligerent little sod. What he lacked in stature he made up for in possession of guts. He had been a Merchant Navy officer and nothing was going to stop him from doing his bit in the Royal Navy. Day after day he visited the Consulate and pestered the officials there to get him his Royal Naval Reserve commission. He finally succeeded and was posted to Singapore where, in the end, he made the supreme sacrifice.

But, for many weeks before he donned uniform again, Tombs stayed with us and, from time to time, posed problems which threatened to disrupt our nightly schedules. There was the time when we found him fast asleep at his desk, an empty bottle of grog by his side. This was not unusual but the fact that he had made a pillow for his head of the entire output of the news agencies made it imperative that we should disturb his slumber. So, as Julian Bates grabbed him by the hair and hoisted his head aloft, I slipped in my hand and withdrew the stack of paper without which we should have had no major headlines.

While the firm had finally realised that the Chinese dollar was pretty valueless as coin of the realm and had provided each employee with a high cost of living allowance there were occasions nearing the end of the month when our early-morning excursions in search of entertainment found us in the humiliating position of being without the ready cash for a sortie to some spot where we were not known by name and, therefore, could not sign the ubiquitous chit. Such a place was the Majestic cabaret.

It was Tombs one night who guided us in the direction of the Majestic after assuring us, bombastically, 'Don't shit yourselves, you bloody landlubber scum (he loved the nautical form of expression), I've paid enough there to buy the fuckin' joint.'

'Ah, but do they know that? Can you sign there? That's the main point,' said Bates, very dubious indeed.

'Fuck me,' replied Tombs. 'Do they know me? The sun shines out of my arse there, mateys. They'd let me sign for a million.'

190

Before we called the Johnson taxi for the trip we made certain that Tombs knew he was in the chair and that his pencil – and no one else's – would be our guarantee of drinks and girls at the table. We'd settle accounts later when the chit was delivered to the office for payment.

There were five of us – Tombs, Bates, Brown, Bothello and me. And a right royal time we had as Tombs, our guardian angel, ordered round after round and we waxed lecherously merry feeling the tits and the legs of the taxi-dancers whose attendance on us was going to add up to an eye-goggling amount.

When it became apparent that we had well exceeded the century in doller expenditure I suggested to Tombs that, surely, it was time to make certain that the chit would be offered for his signature.

'Bollocks,' said the little fellow, whose hand was busy exploring the inside of a Russian girl's skirt. 'I've bought this fuckin' joint a hundred times. Pipe down and get on with the drinkin'.'

We did.

It was only a short time later that the floor captain, who had been eyeing us warily from the back of the dance hall for some time, ventured up and proffered, most apologetically, the bill. It was for an amount near enough two hundred dollars. Tombs took it, gulped, blanched, and then with a great show of bravado pulled out his pencil and said, 'I sign. Belong good customer here. The manager he know me. Can do?'

'I look see,' said the captain, taking the chit and hurrying away.

'Well, that's it, you pierhead bastards,' said Tombs. 'Full speed ahead now.'

A few minutes later I saw a fat Chinese gentleman take a stance at the door with the captain. He looked at us and then said a few words to his minion.

The captain returned.

'Manager he say no can.'

We all looked at Tombs. It was up to him to save the day.

'Call the manager,' said Tombs, assuming all the authority he could.

The fat gentleman arrived. He had a worried look. And he gave no sign of recognition as Tombs addressed him.

Tombs explained that they were old friends. The manager excused himself and added that while this might be so he could not recall having met the old salt from Australia before.

'Bugger me,' said Bothello. 'We're in the dung.'

He used such terms as a follower of the horses.

And then Tombs assumed his best quarter-deck manner and gave a sterling imitation of Captain Bligh of *Bounty* fame, fulminating furiously in a full frontal assault directed against the rotund manager.

It was all to no avail. Cash was needed. There would be no chit signing. The girls left the table and our eyes were fixed on the man who was our guarantor of pay-later pleasure.

Tombs spoke. His voice had a whining tone.

'Can we have a whip round, chaps?' Nautical language evidently forgotten. 'I'm sure we can make it if we all dip in.'

'Not on your bloody life,' I said. 'You've bought the joint, haven't you? The sun shines out of your arse here.'

'It's in eclipse at the moment,' remarked Bates.

'Come on, fellows,' pleaded Tombs. 'Help me out.'

'Fuck off,' said four voices in unison.

The truth was that we all possessed cash of varying amounts and might have raised enough to satisfy the manager with a down payment of half and a chit for the remainder. But old Charlie's bullshit had got us on the raw. We were determined to teach him a lesson.

He pleaded and pleaded but all he got was the cold stares of four colleagues.

Finally he and the manager left the table for a discussion in some office cubby-hole at the back of the hall.

It was a grey-faced Tombs who returned, tight-lipped, very angry.

'I've had to leave me fuckin' watch as security,' he said. 'It's a master mariner's chronometer. You're a lot of shits.'

'Balls,' I said, rubbing it in. 'You've bought the fuckin' joint.'

Tombs walked off. His parting shot: 'You can never trust pommy bastards – wet-arsed bilge scum.'

As Tombs left we sorted out what cash we possessed and continued our session, recalling four of the girls and paying cash for each round.

'That'll teach him to lay off the bullshit in the future,' said Brown.

'Amen,' said Bates solemnly.

War

The outbreak of war in Europe set in motion in Shanghai a gigantic propaganda contest. On the British side there was the *North-China Daily News* which became the mouthpiece of the British information agency in the city. The *Shanghai Times*, though it was, of necessity, pro-Japanese, was still a British-registered journal and as such followed the patriotic line of the *N.C.D.N.* In the French Concession the community newspaper, *Le Journal de Shanghai*, was staunchly anti-Axis. The American-owned *Evening Post and Mercury*, still neutral in the conflict, adopted a strong, pro-British stance and its radio station joined with XMHA – again American-owned – in backing the Allies.

Carroll Alcott, who was the city's most popular broadcaster, increased the ferocity of his tirades against Hitler and Mussolini and, as a result, was publicly threatened by the Italians with large doses of castor oil which, at that time, appeared to be Il Duce's drastic method of flushing out from his enemies the animosity they preserved within their democratic bowels.

Not that Alcott worried unduly over the Italians. He had a car. With him always were two stalwart Russian bodyguards – a match for any 'goddammed wop' he told me once when I visited him at XMHA.

I played my part, too, on the Alcott pattern. Every evening I prepared a news broadcast, strongly pro-Allied, for the newsreader on station XCDN in Sassoon House. I enjoyed the work which brought me extra cash and a nightly meeting with a most attractive young woman named Kitty Sharp who was the reader at that time.

Kitty Sharp was a shapely red-head. She had earned some fame locally as an actress in the Shanghai Amateur Dramatic Company and was in the full bloom of lovely womanhood. What I liked about her was her habit in the confined space of the broadcasting studio of lifting one leg high as she leaned against the table to read over the script I had handed to her.

As she stood there, eyes closely following the printed word, I

193

was able to work myself into a lather of lechery by leering at the magnificent expanse of thigh which her posture revealed. It was entirely an involuntary action on her part. When she was concentrating up came one leg or the other. Sometimes she clasped a knee with her hands. At other times the leg was left alone as hands clutched the sheaf of papers which I had prepared.

Later, her place was taken by my friend, Frank Fearon, who had been educated at Monkton Combe school in England and had a good microphone voice.

Another friend of the Allies was J. B. Powell whose *Weekly Review*, still published behind locked doors and the protecting Mauser of his bodyguard, joined in the crusade against the German-Italian Axis.

And yet British army teams were still playing football with the Italian Savoia Grenadiers on the Racecourse.

I attended a British Legion rally in the Shanghai Race Club when the guests were members of the local American Legion. There was wild cheering when the American Legion chairman declared with passion and fervour, 'We were with you in the last war and, by God, in this one we shall make it our duty to see that you are victorious.'

Almost every American in Shanghai, even those of German origin who, had they been back home, would have been wooed by the pro-Hitler German Bund under Fritz Kuhn, was solidly on the British side.

Possibly the reason why the French failed to stir the Americans into a real love relationship was the language barrier. While the Americans spoke English I must say that there was a great gulf between us and them and, often, phrases common to both countries conveyed to one or the other entirely different meanings, sometimes with embarrassing consequences.

When an American spoke of the great Louis Armstrong as 'the man with the horn' who could blame an English listener conjuring up a picture of the trumpet maestro sporting an enormous erection.

There was the young second lieutenant of a British regiment at a cocktail party who told a dispirited young American female to keep her pecker up. She replied, 'I can't; I haven't got one.'

As any British public schoolboy will tell you to keep one's pecker up is to be of good cheer, to be of good courage. As any American will tell you the old pecker is the John Thomas of the male. If it is up, they'll be at pains to point out that courage is not the inflating agent.

The Americans would often tell us that they 'tossed off' a remark or two. To the Briton this could only mean the act of masturbation and how in the hell did you masturbate words? 'Queer buggers, the Yanks,' said the average British Tommy.

English girls giggled when an American, of either sex, would glibly say of someone that he (or she) was full of spunk. Spunk, colloquially admittedly, could only mean the stuff that was ejaculated by a male during a sexual climax. To the American spunk was courage, the intangible possession of the brave-hearted.

We went to the bog. The American visited the John. We knew that only girls possessed fannies. When the American sat on his fanny then the indication was that his backside was taking his weight. In those days boobs could only mean in the British mind blunders. A chap boobed – made a mistake. Now, as we all know following America's verbal conquest of the world, boobs equal tits, possessed by females, much loved as erotic objects by males.

From time to time, powerful friends of China and of the Allies in Europe paid visits to Shanghai. Among them was Henry R. Luce, who died in 1967 at the age of 68.

Luce, who had been born in China of Presbyterian missionary parents, owned a magazine empire in the United States of which it was said that every third American read one or the other of its publications, the most important of which were *Time* and *Life*.

Luce was a devout Christian, a devout capitalist, a devout American, a devout anti-Communist, a passionate lover of China – a figure of awe.

We welcomed him in the *N.C.D.N.* with open arms for he quickly came to see the cataclysmic dangers of Hitler and Mussolini and he used his magazines to make the urgent case for U.S. preparedness.

Luce, throughout his long and successful career, backed Chiang Kai-shek and played an important part in guiding American policy in the Far East.

I met Luce once – at the American Club. He was then young and vigorous and to me was a reflection of all that was good in America – the possessor of dynamic drive, of a vital energy that seemed to be lacking in the peoples of the Old World, of a far-sightedness in business and politics that had placed him in the forefront of the many successful men the American scene had produced.

I spoke to Luce about the war. He was brutally frank. He told me that Britain and France were unprepared, had failed to build up a modern economy, had lamentably lagged far behind the disciplined and hard-working Germans and that, sooner or later as in World War I, the Americans would be called on to pull our chestnuts out of the fire.

It was hard stuff to swallow but it was not long before I had to admit that he was a true prophet of future events and an objective and fair critic of the Old World Blues which seem still to afflict us.

When the German juggernaut finally started rolling, by-passing the Maginot Line and rolling back the French and British armies across Holland and Belgium, it soon became clear that we were getting a clobbering.

Alcott was not dismayed. He finished off one broadcast with a denial that Field Marshal Goering had been shot down over Britain. Further investigation had revealed that what was believed to have been the plump Goering had turned out to be a barrage balloon.

In the Japanese press anti-British sentiment was growing stronger and the tension between Japan and Britain and the United States, particularly over the China issue, continued undiminished.

Then came the bitter blow of Dunkirk. We knew that the French army had virtually collapsed and the British forces were fighting their bloody way to the sea at Dunkirk.

German propaganda poured in. The British were trapped. They had no line of escape. It was only a matter of days before the entire army would be annihilated or captured.

And then came the miracle of Dunkirk when the courageous resilience of the British people shone like a blazing beacon in a darkened world and the flotillas of little boats took off from the beaches their cargoes of soldiers, wounded, exhausted, shocked, but still a fighting force.

Dunkirk was my personal triumph. From Reuter and the American agencies there was little on which to build up a story except that the British retreat to the sea was still proceeding in disciplined fashion.

Then the messenger from Domei, the Japanese agency, arrived with a flash. I read it with disbelief.

It said: 'The larger part of the British expeditionary force in France has successfully evacuated Dunkirk.'

I was wildly excited. Here was the news we were all waiting for. And yet the sobering thought flashed through my mind that not one other agency had carried the news.

I rang Reuter and the other friendly agencies. It was news to them. They were inclined to disbelieve the Domei story. They promised to make urgent enquiries.

It was about 10 p.m. and I had time to wait for results from Reuter. I badly wanted to use the Domei flash but I needed more proof than a report unattributed to any source.

And then, panting, the Domei messenger arrived again. He carried another flash:

'Many units of the British army have landed at various ports in the south of England. The evacuation is proceeding. Losses have been sustained but most of the army has left Dunkirk.'

I seized the phone and rang up Peyton-Griffin. I had a hunch that Domei, with typical Japanese opportunism, had broken some way – probably through diplomatic communication channels – a top-secret embargo on the evacuation until it had finally been successfully completed.

Peyt was very excited. I pointed out that there was no substantiation of the report from any other source but I felt that such a world-shattering event would not be reported by any of the news media unless it was true.

I remember saying, 'Domei'll look like bloody fools forever if they're wrong.'

'You're right,' said Peyt. 'Let me think.'

After about 15 seconds he came on again:

'All right, run the Domei flashes at the top as they come in but stress that the reports, so far, have not been confirmed. Be guarded – but run it and run it big.'

I did just that – banner headline across page one: a lead-in line – 'Dunkirk Successfully Evacuated – Report' and then the big letters – 'British Army Safe'. This was followed as then was the style by a two-bank heading and the Domei flashes. I built up the remainder of the story from other agency messages and made it clear that, so far, there was no official confirmation of the Japanese report.

The next morning we were alone. I was worried. Not one paper had used Domei – except us.

Then, in the late afternoon, the flashes came flooding in – from Reuter, from the Associated Press, from United Press, the International News Service, Havas and, once again, Domei, that the British army, almost intact, had successfully evacuated Dunkirk.

Peyt jumped for joy. So did I. There were handshakes all round.

'Well done, Shaw,' he said. 'We've beaten the bloody lot of 'em. They're 24 hours behind us.'

And then another bitter blow – the surrender of the French and the disgrace of Hitler's insistence on the signing of the surrender documents in the railway coach at Compiegne where in 1918 the defeated German army had been forced to beg for peace.

In Shanghai it soon became evident that the Concession authorities were going to give their allegiance to Marshal Petain and the Vichy government. Similarly, in Indo-China full support was given to the Vichy government and it became clear to the British government that former allies in war had to be regarded, if not as enemies, then as a new hostile force.

For the Japanese, Dunkirk and the collapse of France were seen as a great historic moment. Britain, France and the Netherlands had, in their estimation, been defeated. It was plain that the three countries were in no position to defend their possessions in Southeast Asia and it was well known to us on the *North-China Daily News* that plans were afoot to transfer the British forces in Shanghai and the other treaty ports to Hong Kong and Singapore.

While it was obvious that neither the two British battalions in the city nor the American marines would be a match for the Japanese and their puppet forces in the event of an attack on the Settlement, their presence acted as a reassurance to us all. We were, in effect, isolated in hostile territory. All around Shanghai and far into the coastal plains the Japanese were in control. The French were already collaborating with the Japanese in their concession and the systematic arrests of many patriotic Chinese in residence there were being carried out by the Kempetai often in the company of members of the French police whose sense of guilt transformed their former friendly co-operation with the Shanghai Municipal Police into cold and isolated enmity.

In September, 1940, Germany, Italy and Japan concluded the tripartite alliance which effectively made Japan an Axis power.

The American marines began packing up. The small force in North China was brought down to Shanghai, leaving only a few legation guards in Peking.

I watched on the Racecourse the last parade of the Fourth Marines, whose long history in China had forged bonds of friendship with many British regiments.

Finally the Leathernecks marched out of the city and boarded a transport for the Philippines. I didn't know it at the time but one of the marching men was Carroll Alcott, much threatened, heavily abused but still with us behind the microphone.

Alcott had been warned. If he stayed then he faced peril. War with Japan seemed to be on the way. So far as the Germans and

Italians were concerned he was the most hated man in the city. They would have killed him without compunction had they been able to lay hands on him. The Japanese, not one whit less hostile, had him marked for 'special treatment' in the future.

So Alcott donned marine uniform and, hidden in the ranks, marched his way out of Shanghai to the waiting transport. It was a sensible move for had he decided to quit the city the normal way by ocean liner then there was the chance that Axis agents – and there were many in Shanghai – would have tracked him down and closed his mouth for ever.

I met Alcott many years later – in 1961 – in Los Angeles where he was broadcasting on the CBS network. We in Britain owe much to his unstinted support of our cause in China at a time when our fortunes were at their lowest ebb. He never wavered – despite threats and omnipresent danger – from his dedication to the democratic cause.

His successor on XMHA was another American, Elroy Healey. When he had completed his first broadcast which, in the Alcott pattern, had been courageously pro-British and anti-Axis, his fate was sealed. He had signed his own death warrant.

In his 'fortress' office at the *China Weekly Review* J. B. Powell, warned by the American authorities of the danger he faced by remaining in Shanghai, refused all pleas to get out.

Within a few months the British forces, apart from naval vessels, including the gunboat, *Petrel*, had evacuated the city and we were left forlorn and fearful in a Settlement which had been written off by the world's major powers.

I took the opportunity, before the last of the British details had departed, to visit the old military hospital in Central Road where some of my army friends were still in residence. We said our farewells over pint mugs of British-brewed beer in the canteen and I wondered if I would ever see any of them again.

I have no idea what fate had in store for them. If their destination was Hong Kong or Singapore then I have my doubts whether many of them survived the barbarity of the Japanese, particularly any men caught in the Malayan peninsula, the prison camps of which provided the thousands of victims of the infamous Siam 'Death Railway'.

We still had the Italians of the Savoia Grenadiers and the gunboats but they were a joke, unwilling residents locked in miserable exile by the world-wide naval power of Britain. There was the Russian Regiment which had been formed into a supporting unit of the police. There was, also, still the Shanghai

Volunteer Corps but without the backing of regular units it was a forlorn hope that it would be mobilised if the integrity of the foreign area was threatened.

In America the alarm felt by Britain and America over the course of events in Asia and the increasing hostility of the Japanese was expressed by President Roosevelt, who told Congress, 'Never before has American security been so seriously threatened.'

Chungking, far from us, remote in wild Szechwan, was being regularly bombed by a hundred or more Japanese planes at a time and much American property was destroyed.

I was regularly sending cables to the *News-Chronicle* in London of Japanese warlike preparations in East Asia and I knew that Japanese censors in the telegraph office were scrutinising them.

The Vichy régime in France had been forced to allow the Japanese to occupy several naval bases in Indo-China, an event which the French people in Shanghai must have viewed with considerable shame but which they covered with a veneer of hostile aloofness.

And then, in February, 1941, about 40,000 Japanese troops sailed for southern Indo-China to occupy the country and construct air bases near Saigon and the naval bases at Saigon and Camranh Bay.

I had my first brush with the Japanese censor when I sent off a cable reporting a massive movement of Japanese transports from Shanghai southward, probably to Hainan island. He rang me up and said that the message could not go. I was careful and calm.

'All right,' I said, 'drop it. It doesn't matter.'

He seemed surprised but pleased that I had not insisted on my rights and expressed his thanks with many hisses.

'Right you bastard,' I said when I dropped down the phone. 'We'll see.'

I took the message along to the British Consulate-General where I knew the radio operator. After much persuasion I got him to send the message addressed to the *News-Chronicle* but also marked 'Attention Foreign Office'. Whether or not the report ever got to the *News-Chronicle* I never found out.

On Sunday, December 7th, 1941, I attended the night show at the Roxy cinema in Bubbling Well Road. I reached home at about 11 p.m. and was in bed shortly before midnight.

A few hours later – it was still dark and I had no idea of the time – I was awakened by a series of explosions each one following the other in rapid succession. I was not worried as about a week before a large godown near my apartment building had gone up in flames and the sound of exploding kerosene tins had been like that of gunfire.

I remained in bed and listened. Suddenly I heard the sound of several people mounting the stairs of the building near my door. There was the babble of excited – and frightened – voices.

I got up, donned dressing gown and went outside. No sooner had I got to the stairs than I met a resident hurrying down, very frightened.

'What's the matter?' I asked him.

'There's battle going on in the river,' he said, shivering violently. 'Come, go into my room and look at the river.'

He grabbed my arm and rushed me into his spacious flat across which I strode to the balcony and peered into the darkness. I could see in the distance the glow of a large fire, the seat of which was hidden by the massive Jardine building on the Bund. The explosions were loud and coming in rapid succession. I heard the staccato bark of rifle fire.

I looked at the consulate buildings where lights were coming on in the residence of the Consul-General.

I had a sense of foreboding. In Shanghai it could have been a battle between the police and armed robbers. These were frequent but they were never as noisy as this event.

I grabbed a phone and dialled the desk at the Central police station.

Paddy Self answered. I recognised the voice.

'Ralph Shaw, *North-China Daily News*, here,' I said. 'What's all the racket about on the Bund?'

His reply staggered me. I remember his exact words, spoken calmly, no histrionics, no alarm: 'Japan has declared war on Britain and America. They've occupied the Bund. We can't get through down there.'

'Well, what's all the noise about?' I replied, asininely, the purport of his information not having registered in my mind.

'They're attacking something. We can't get down. There's a hell of a lot of firing going on.'

There was the sound of an aeroplane. The gunfire proceeded and the crack-crack-crack of the rifles.

I suddenly realised that I, a Briton, was now an enemy of Japan. I was 10,000 miles away from home. There was no hope of escape. The Japanese were all around Shanghai. I was caught like a rat in a trap.

Yet outwardly I was calm. I had no idea what the future held in store. I could only guess that from that time on my life would change completely.

I returned to my flat where I dressed and waited for the dawn.

The firing died down and then stopped. Then there was silence, broken only by the sound of vehicles from time to time moving along the Bund.

At six o'clock I tried my radio. XMHA was silent. So was XMHC. I turned the dial and picked up the German station which was blaring out long fanfares prior to the news in English.

The announcer was excited. Japan was at war with Britain and the United States. There had been an aerial attack on Pearl Harbour and the American fleet had been destroyed. An attack had been launched on Hong Kong which was proceeding successfully. Further operations were under way in South-east Asia.

As news flash succeeded news flash I prepared myself for a visit to the office to see actually what was happening. There had been no mention of events in Shanghai. Were we going to publish or not? I had my doubts but I was determined to find out.

Before I left I saw columns of thick, black smoke pouring from the incinerator chimney in the British Consulate. There was no sign of Japanese troops anywhere.

I walked to the office the usual way which took me along the Bund. It had its normal appearance and there was no evidence anywhere of the pre-dawn battle although I noted that the shipping wharves seemed unusually deserted.

There were few people in the office when I arrived and I went straight to the fifth floor where there was no sign of Hoste or Peyton-Griffin. I rang up the police for the latest news and a voice speaking Japanese answered. Hastily I put down the phone.

I then rang up the Reuter office close to the Bund to try and find out what all the noise had been about earlier on. They told me.

I should have noticed when I walked along the Bund. Had I looked closely I would have seen that the British gunboat, *Petrel*, was no longer there. She had been sunk – by the concentrated gunfire of several Japanese warships.

Later, I heard the story of the *Petrel*. A boat containing a high-ranking Japanese officer and some naval ratings had gone upriver to demand the surrender of the *Petrel* and the American gunboat, *Wake*, further upstream. These were the only two British and American naval vessels in the harbour.

They got short shrift from Lieut.-Commander Robert Polkinghorn, a Cornishman and Royal Naval Reserve officer in com-

mand of the gunboat. Through a loud hailer he refused point
blank to surrender and said that he would open fire if any
attack was launched on his vessel.

The Japanese sent up a Verey light and this was the signal for
the guns of several warships lower down the river to pour a hail
of concentrated fire on the *Petrel*. From the river bank Japanese
marines opened up with rifles and machine-guns.

The *Petrel* did not have a chance. A spotter plane overhead
guided the gunfire and though the British gun-crews aboard the
gunboat were quickly in action the little ship was soon burning
furiously from stem to stern. That was the fire I had seen earlier.
Soon the *Petrel* was sinking, guns still firing, ensign flying.

Polkinghorn gave the order to abandon ship. He and his men
jumped into the muddy, swirling waters of the Whangpoo.
There were few serious casualties. He and his crew were made
prisoners as they reached the Bund wharves. They were quickly
taken away under heavy guard.

The *Petrel* sailors were placed in a prison camp where they
were joined by a force of American marines, who had been left
behind on guard duties at the Peking Legation and in Shanghai.

As for the *Wake* it was a case of capture. An attempt to
scuttle the gunboat failed. The Japanese boarded it and, later in the
morning, I watched the sorry spectacle of the *Wake*, Japanese naval
ensign flying from its stern, make its way downriver over the large
patch of oil which marked the watery graveyard of the *Petrel*.

The crew of the *Wake* joined the British sailors and the marines
in the prison camp which was located on the Pootung side of the
river in the heart of the countryside.

In the office we were milling around with no prospect in view
of what was going to happen. Several members of the editorial
staff had turned up and we were discussing the morning's
events with fear in our hearts.

I went down to the second-floor business offices and there
found most of the staff standing about aimlessly in groups.
Harry Morriss was there but there was no sign of R. W. Davis,
his right-hand man, or of his brother, Gordon, who was no
doubt more concerned about the fortunes of his own firm.

And then the phone rang in Davis's office and the printing
manager, Haslam, took the call.

It was from Major Kenneth Bourne, the Commissioner of
Police. He wanted an urgent printing job to be done – several
thousand posters which would tell the population that the
Japanese forces were going to march from Hongkew into the

Settlement proper at 10 a.m., that the people were to remain calm and that the protection of lives and property had been assured by the Japanese high command.

At 10 a.m. we all gathered to watch the Japanese forces, headed by men of the Naval Landing Party, march along the Bund, short, squat men, steel-helmeted and in full war kit. The occupation of the international district was under way, a move which, according to Harry Morriss, was a flagrant breach of international treaties guaranteeing the neutral status of concession areas everywhere in China.

Squads of Japanese marines or soldiers were placed at street intersections and the building shook as squadrons of tanks moved in behind the marching men.

Shortly before noon a Japanese officer accompanied by eight soldiers arrived in the building and entered the second-floor section where he looked around as if trying to spot a senior man amongst us.

'Who is man in charge?' he asked.

Immediately, Harry Morriss pointed a finger at me and said, 'He is.'

'You rotten bastard,' I thought. 'Why pick on me?'

The officer came up to me and said that the Japanese forces were going to seal the building – every office. I would accompany him. I did.

We started from the top floor and worked our way down. Every room was sealed with heavy tape. I was informed that this was not to be broken or there would be heavy punishment. We cleared out the Chinese staff, who were told to go home, and then entered the editorial department where I watched with some misgiving the act of sealing the office occupied by Hoste and me. It was there that I kept copies of my cables to the *News-Chronicle* and of editorials and stories I had done which were decidedly not pro-Japanese.

The entire operation took about two hours and the officer told me that from that time on the *North-China Daily News* would cease publication. The entire building, he said, was now under the control of the Japanese military forces and any attempt to remove anything from it would bring heavy punishment.

We gathered on the second floor which was the last section to be sealed. As we milled around in the spacious corridor, the officer addressed us:

'All men now go home. All finish. No fear.'

My life in enemy hands had begun.

Prisoner

Life started peacefully under the Japanese. I and my colleagues on the *North-China Daily News* were out of work but the *Shanghai Times* continued to publish under direct Japanese management and the *Evening Post and Mercury* was kept going.

Powell's Weekly Review was closed but Powell, to my surprise, was still free. If there was one man the Kempetai wanted to get their hands on it was him. So was Elroy Healey of XMHA, silent but still a marked man.

The big public enterprises such as the gas company, the power company, the tramways, the telephone company and others, all foreign-owned, were taken over by the Japanese but Britons, Americans and other enemy nationals working in them kept their jobs. An instant clear-out of these technical men would have caused havoc in the essential services.

All other enemy concerns, including the banks, the merchant houses and the industries, were occupied by the Japanese. Some continued to operate, others were closed down.

Within a few days the British Residents' Association, under the chairmanship of Hugh J. Collar, a director of Imperial Chemical Industries' operations in China, started a relief scheme for families in need. Those of us who had lost our jobs were given cash payments monthly in Central Reserve Bank currency, which was the Japanese puppet money in the occupied areas of China, and a shop was opened in the grounds of Holy Trinity Cathedral where we could buy cracked wheat and other supplies provided by the Swiss Red Cross organisation.

The Americans, the Netherlanders, the Greeks, the Norwegians and others started similar relief schemes.

Within a week of the take-over we were told that we should report in alphabetical order of surnames to Hamilton House, a large office building in the central district, to be registered by the Japanese Enemy Aliens Office.

I went along and was received politely by an English-speaking

Japanese official who gave me a form to fill which I did, deliberately leaving blank the questions to be answered about former military service. I was issued with a red armband on which was printed the letter 'B' and a number. This had to be worn every time I went out to show that I was 'B for British' and an enemy of Dai Nippon.

The Americans wore their 'A' armbands and the Netherlanders sported their individual numbers under the letter 'N'.

We could still visit the cinemas, where Hollywood releases had not been banned. The only difference was that the newsreels were Japanese and reported the successes of the Japanese forces everywhere in East Asia.

At the Uptown I sat next to two Eurasian girls, not enemies of the Japanese because they did not wear armbands. We watched a newsreel showing a squat Japanese searching three British or Australian soldiers captured in the Malayan campaign.

The girls decided that they were British.

'My goodness, how tall they are,' said one girl, admiringly.

'All Englishmen are tall,' said the other girl.

My bet was that the prisoners were Australians. These two girls needed instant optical attention for they must have seen the Durhams and the Seaforths fairly recently in the city. A tall man in those mobs was a rarity, indeed.

Life wasn't too bad, though the cabarets and night clubs were off-limits. We had to be in our homes before midnight. There was a curfew for us and to be caught out after that time by one of the many Japanese patrols was asking for trouble.

Frequently the Japanese cordoned off a district in the city and anyone unlucky enough to be inside the area when the barbed-wire barricades enclosed it had to remain there until it was opened again. Many times armband-wearers found themselves completely sealed off from their families for periods of twelve hours or more – sometimes through the night. While the Japanese did not molest enemy aliens accidentally caught in the dragnet – their prey was the Chinese underground patriot – the alarm and despondency of waiting families often led to nervous breakdowns and more patients for the hard-pressed British and American general practitioners permitted only to serve their respective communities on a welfare basis.

The Swiss Red Cross was supplying funds distributed by the various residents' associations for our needs. We signed forms guaranteeing to pay back the money when hostilities ended, but none of us had any idea what the future had in store.

After several weeks of inactivity the Japanese decided to show the world how magnanimous they were in Shanghai where not one enemy national, according to the *Shanghai Times*, had been maltreated. A press conference was staged at Hamilton House and neutral correspondents thronged the large hall where army, navy and civilian administrators spoke of the Bushido spirit which guided all Japanese actions.

Powell and Healey, for whose safety all of us feared, had been invited to attend. They were singled out by the military spokesman, who said that, despite their previous anti-Japanese activities, there they were – free, in good health, evidence of the kindliness of Dai Nippon.

It was a hypocritical performance – bereft of any genuine intention. A week later, early in the morning, Powell was dragged from his bed and taken to the Bridge House, the torture chamber of the Kempetai.

Then Healey disappeared. The news spread and a feeling of alarm gripped all of us. Who would be next on the Kempetai list? The honeymoon period was over. The Japanese were showing their teeth and, from their record of cruelty in China, we knew that many of us were going to suffer indescribable ill-treatment.

Every day the news spread of more arrests. Percy Finch was taken. A few hours later an armed patrol picked up Peyton-Griffin. I went to see Hoste in the French Concession and we agreed, fearfully, that we were probably on the black list. All we could do was wait, tense, racked daily by terrible fear, sleepless in our beds as the sound of footsteps anywhere sent us into cold sweats and heart-pounding terror.

'Tommy' Thompson of the British-American Tobacco Co. was hauled off.

He survived the Bridge House where he underwent the most fiendish of tortures, including the excruciatingly painful water treatment. He was shipped home after the war, a wreck of a man – one of thousands whose lives were blighted forever by the inhuman savagery of the Japanese.

Powell also survived – but not for long. The Kempetai torturers wreaked their vengeance on the brave American and subjected him to atrocious assaults, beating him unmercifully, inflicting on him all the methods of interrogation which were contained in the Japanese army training manual.

They included kicking, usually in the genital region, beating – anything connected with physical suffering. Interrogating officers used violent torture. There were threats of execution.

Most common forms of torture were the water treatment, burning, electric shocks, the knee spread, kneeling on sharp instruments and flogging. Excruciating pain was inflicted on victims and thousands died throughout South-east Asia. It is impossible now, so many years later, to appreciate what these unfortunate and innocent victims of Japanese brutality suffered.

Powell, a permanent invalid, was later shipped home to the United States aboard a repatriation vessel following an agreement on an exchange of enemy nationals held by the Americans and the Japanese.

Gangrene set in and Powell had part of a leg amputated. He never recovered and died shortly later, courageous to the end. We heard that not once had he flinched, not once had he asked for mercy during the most barbarous of the Japanese tortures.

Healey never reached home. The Japanese, angry that Alcott had eluded them, subjected his successor at XMHA to treatment which plumbed the depths of human depravity. He went insane and died bloodied and crippled in his rat-hole of a cell in the Bridge House.

Peyt came out in better shape though he had undergone savage treatment. He had been placed in a cell contining about twenty people, including a Russian Soviet woman who suffered degrading indignities which included the insertion of sharp objects in her vagina, violent electric shocks applied through her nipples, the pulling out of her finger- and toe-nails and blows which had broken her jaw.

He told me how the men in the cell had made a screen so that the poor woman could use the slop bucket in the corner in some privacy and how they tore up their shirts when her menstrual period arrived. She was still in the cell when Peyt was released. He had no doubt that she would not come out alive.

Finch was battered, too. He told me with rare Yorkshire humour when I called on him about a week after his release that he would rather have spent three weeks in Blackpool but beggars couldn't always be choosers. Nevertheless I could see that he would never forget the horror of his incarceration. No one who had been in the Bridge House would ever be able to escape the screaming nightmares from which all its victims were doomed to suffer.

Percy left Shanghai in an exchange of British and Japanese personnel arranged by the Swiss Red Cross. We called the ship, the *Asama Maru*, the Wangle Maru, for it was plain to see that many of the taipans who found places aboard were in no danger had they remained in the city. Nor would they be able to help the British war effort at home in any way.

Peyt was offered repatriation but refused. He was living with a Russian woman who would have had to stay behind. He chose to remain at her side. He had guts, for he knew that the Japanese might not have finished with him. There had been many cases of re-arrest of men who had been in the Bridge House. As it turned out, he was later interned in a camp run by the Japanese consular police and emerged in 1945 to edit the first post-war edition of the *North-China Daily News*.

Sapajou became the cartoonist of the German newspaper. It was either that or starvation as a stateless Russian. More than a thousand White Russians had lost jobs in British, American and Netherlands firms closed down by the Japanese and their plight was pitiful – worse than that of the Jewish refugees, most of whom were still in the Wayside camps supported by donations from international Jewish charities.

After the war there was no job on the *North-China Daily News* for the Russian cartoonist and, after a poverty-stricken existence in a Hongkew hovel, kept alive on the hand-outs of friends, he ended up in a transit camp for stateless refugees in the Philippines. A sick man, he died shortly afterwards.

The months sped by. Cut off from the imports that once made our lives if not that of gourmets at least deliciously variable, we began to drink soya-bean milk and groundnut 'coffee'. We ate fish instead of meat. We made substitute 'meat' soups with soya sauce and local vegetables. The Red Cross cracked wheat provided the morning 'porridge', became the 'barley' in soup, filled our stomachs in place of bread, liberally smeared with lard instead of butter or margarine. There was intense excitement when we found on the black market a tin of pre-war sausages made in Shanghai by the British firm of Duncan, Main and Partners. A can of Hazelwood jam sold for four times its peacetime price.

To Peyt and the drinking fraternity the closure of the Shanghai Club and the gradual evaporation of all imported liquors was a bitter blow. Red armbands were prohibited in the bars and the alcoholic drought soon had disastrous effects on the morale of the regular topers, who developed hallucinations in which gallons of Johnny Walker or Gordon's gin cascaded from the fountain in the Bund Gardens only to be swallowed before they could reach the precious nectar by enormous frogs, toads, pink elephants and red rodents.

209

Peyt liked his gin and bitters. I managed to procure for him several bottles of a Shanghai product made in a vodka distillery. He thanked me profusely and bestowed on the product three stars but I fancy this was because he had forgotten the taste of the genuine stuff.

'Tommy' Thompson, to whom I also gave a bottle, likened the liquid to congealed rhubarb juice in that four glasses gave him the 'screaming shits'. From an engineering point of view he maintained that the man who brewed it could have made more money by selling it to the French bus company to propel their vehicles instead of the charcoal burners they were using. I offered to take the stuff back but he wouldn't hear of it.

Sir Victor Sassoon's fleet of double-decker and single-decker buses vanished from the city. Petrol and diesel oil were no longer obtainable so that the trams took over in the Settlement the burden of carrying practically the entire population. Charcoal saved the French buses but the trams were more reliable in that there was less risk of them asphyxiating their passengers and crews.

The trams played a prominent role in the Japanese propaganda programme. When Hong Kong fell a lavishly decorated and illuminated vehicle ran up and down Nanking Road and along the Bund.

I doubt if there was a Briton on the streets. It was humiliating for us, who had been the master race in the city, to see the evidence on a former British-owned street-car of the loss of the Crown colony.

'Can't compare with the Blackpool illuminations, at least,' said Frank Fearon as we watched the coach and trailer cross Garden Bridge.

When the battleships *Repulse* and *Prince of Wales* were sunk off Malaya two street-cars were decorated and a band was placed aboard one of them.

The naval débâcle left us stunned and miserable. We had supreme confidence in the Royal Navy and the amazingly easy Japanese triumph at sea filled us with sorrow and foreboding about our ability ever to recover the initiative in the Far East.

Malaya collapsed. Singapore fell. Borneo was invaded and surrendered. The Netherlands East Indies were occupied. In the Philippines the American forces, including the marines who had been in Shanghai, were defeated. It was the blackest chapter in British and American history.

When the warmer weather arrived I decided to learn Russian

and got myself a *Teach Yourself Russian* paperback. I took this daily to the Bund Gardens where I sat in the sun and murdered the Slavic sounds.

There I met and made friends with Whoosh Marttens, a German national of extremely liberal views. I called him Whoosh because of his prowess in swishing his arm through the air at remarkable speed to catch flies, the wings of which he removed before throwing them to the frogs which inhabited the little ornamental pond at the entrance to the park.

Marttens changed wives every seven years. He said he preferred frogs and toads to women but a man had to get it off occasionally and, having read in a scientific book that metabolic processes changed human beings completely every seven years, whatever wife was in his menage at the end of a stretch of seven had to go.

'I'm in my rights. She could not be the same person I married. The book says so,' he told me.

Marttens and I discussed the war. He had the utmost contempt for the Japanese, which he showed every time the Emperor's soldiers visited the park, but admitted that Hitler had been wise to bring Japan into the Axis alliance to contain Russia in Siberia and to weaken the Allied forces in Europe.

He was convinced that Germany would win the war even with America involved and despite the Fuehrer's decision to attack the Soviet Union.

'This time there won't be any 1918. You had Japan on your side then. You have lost every battle so far. We've thrown you out of Europe and the Americans won't be able to prop you up there because they'll need every man in the Pacific,' he said.

I admitted that his argument seemed sound but neither he nor anyone else could convince me that we'd lose. True, the Germans and the Japanese were in the ascendancy. They wouldn't be when it was all over.

'Give me the facts. What are the grounds? I want to know your reasons,' he replied.

'Tell you what,' I said. 'I'll bet you five dollars C.R.B. that we win the war. I'll come and collect here in the park – on this very seat.'

Marttens, wherever he is now, owes me five dollars Central Reserve Bank currency – worth today, I suppose, minus nil. But I'd love to collect. It was more than a year after the war had ended that I visited the Bund Gardens. The genial German was not there. He might have been immediately after the Japanese surrender for he was an honest man. But all Germans were rounded up and most of them were shipped back to the Fatherland. They'd gone when I got back to Shanghai.

Our governments had decreed that we were enemies but Marttens and I never spoiled our regard for each other by allowing deep-rooted faith in our national causes to end up in heated animosity. Had we been facing each other in uniform then he would have shot me or I might have killed him. All of which shows the futility of war. We were good friends. We had the common sense to 'fight' with words and to leaven our verbal assaults with extraneous jocularity. We laughed the long hours away in that little garden. His presence there lightened my gloom. I hope that mine in some way made his life happier.

The Buddhist abbot was not so pleasant. In fact he was downright abusive but I'm glad I met him.

Every afternoon I watched the plump, bearded figure of a European clad in the monastic robes of the Buddhist faith walk round and round the outer path of the garden. He had deep-set, piercing eyes and a hooked nose which denoted Semitic descent. Around his neck were amber beads. He walked sprightly and softly on sandals. His hair and beard were greying and I guessed he would be about sixty.

He took no notice of Marttens and me until, one day, he heard me exclaim fervently:

'Well, Britain has not lost a war yet. We'll win this one.'

He stopped, turned and looked at me. His eyes bored into me. He advanced.

'I hate the British. You, young man, should be ashamed of your race. You will not win the war.'

I was speechless. So was Marttens.

There followed a tirade against the perfidy of the British race, of their hypocrisy, their dishonesty, their exploitation of others, their cruelty, their bumbling inefficiency, their inability to succeed without the help of others, their overwhelming but groundless belief in their greatness, their insularity, their obvious inferiority compared with the Germans, their . . . All that and so much more abuse delivered in sharp, stinging tones, heartfelt, angrily showered on me in accented English – a German, perhaps, or some other European race nearby.

I was cowed. His voluminous flowing robes, stirred by the river breeze, puzzled me. His air of authority overwhelmed me. His appearance of venerable sagacity, his beard, his flowing locks, the hypnotic gaze of his eagle eyes kept me silent, open-mouthed, stunned.

'One day I will walk in the ruins of London. I will see you a conquered race. You deserve all that the future is going to heap on you.'

Without addressing Marttens he turned, looked at me angrily and walked away.

I asked Marttens who he was. He did not know.

I was going to find out and I did.

This was Abbot Chao Kung, resident of the Foreign Y.M.C.A. in Shanghai, better known in Britain as Trebitsch Lincoln, once a Church of England curate, former Liberal MP for Darlington, Monte Carlo gambler, failed businessman and ex-convict.

His story is in the files of the Fleet Street papers. A Jew, born in Hungary in 1879, and in 1914 the British postal censor. He offered his services as a spy on the outbreak of war with Germany but was turned down by the War Office.

Lincoln then crossed to Holland where he forged some documents and engaged in negotiations with the Germans. He sailed to America and in New York confessed to being a German spy.

He was extradited at the request of the British authorities, tried at the Old Bailey and sentenced to three years' imprisonment for forgery, deprived of his British citizenship and later expelled from the country.

He went to China where he became adviser to the warlord, Wu Pei-fu, and then entered a lamasery.

In the 1920s, Natzl, his favourite son, was found guilty of murder and was sentenced to be hanged in Britain. Lincoln rushed to Europe to see the young man before he was executed but he was still aboard ship when the sentence was carried out. He was not allowed to land and returned to the Orient, heart-broken, bitter, a sworn enemy of the British people.

I saw him many times again in the Bund Gardens. He never spoke to me – ignored me completely. He died in Shanghai in October 1943.

The honyemoon period lasted until November 1942, when the Siberian winds from the north, sweeping southward over the central plains, brought the prospect of deep winter.

On November 4th I had gone to bed fairly early, comfortably warmed by the heat from the coke stove I had installed in the flat when lack of fuel had ended the central-heating system. I slept well.

At about four a.m. a thunderous banging on the door woke me. I sat up and peered through the darkness. My heart was pounding. I could hear voices and heavy boots in the hallway.

Then another rapid attack on the door as if it was being kicked by several pairs of boots. I jumped up and without putting on my slippers stumbled over to the electric light switch and flicked it on. Then I turned the key in the door and opened it.

I was roughly thrust back by an arm and into the room poured five men – all in Japanese uniform. As I stood by the table an Army officer, sword at his side, placed a scrap of paper on the polished surface and, in good English, told me to read it.

It told me that, instantly, I was to be interned. I would be allowed to take with me bedding and some clothes, toilet articles and a quantity of food – nothing else. The last sentence said: 'Protection of your life and property assured.'

I was not reassured. Every nerve in my body had been jarred and I shivered uncontrollably as if in the grip of malaria, which I had contracted several months earlier and which, in high fever and teeth-chattering spasms, racked my body.

But I was cold from fear – terribly afraid. I was certain that I was on the Bridge House list. Could I ever stand the torture undergone by Peyt and Finch? Would I emerge alive?

I looked around the room. Three men of the Japanese naval landing party were barring the door, rifles in hand. With them was a naval officer, hand on sword in its scabbard.

Then the army officer spoke.

'You get dressed,' he said, not unkindly I thought. 'You get washed and get dressed. Quick!'

I turned and entered the bathroom, my senses bludgeoned into fear-ridden obedience. The officer followed me in.

'I want to use the toilet,' I said, calmly, quietly. 'I only want to use the toilet. Can I use the toilet?'

The officer nodded his head and, leaving the bathroom door open, walked into the living room. As I flushed he re-entered and carefully watched me wash and shave – I dared not take my usual morning bath. He seemed to be in a hurry.

About fifteen minutes later, a bundle of bedding slung over my shoulders, a carrier bag in my hand containing toilet articles, I walked down the stairs between two of the sailors. There were two men behind me and the army officer led the way out of the building.

As we left I saw the Chinese watchman, tense and downcast, looking at me. I could feel his sympathy.

We tramped to the end of Jinkee Road where it joined the Bund. We would have to turn left to reach the Bridge House just over Garden Bridge. We turned right and walked towards Nanking Road. And there at the intersection my heart bounded with hope for I saw two more Europeans, Jack Liddell of Liddell Brothers, the big import-export hong, tall and distinguished looking, and the elderly head of the Thomas Cook organisation, 'Johnny' Green, similarly equipped with rolls of bedding waiting under armed escort for my party to catch up.

Green looked apprehensive but Liddell seemed cheerful enough.

'Good morning,' he said. 'We're going on a Cook's tour, it seems.'

Green smiled wanly. I attempted to put on a brave front and replied: 'Where to, I wonder?'

We soon knew. We were taken to the offices of the Standard Oil Company and there we were locked up in a large, ground-floor room for hours as more and more men joined us – Britons, Americans, Netherlanders mainly.

Our freedom was at an end. We made light of our predicament. At least we knew that the Bridge House was not our destination –too many for that. We joked to keep up our flagging spirits. There were a few Japanese soldiers by the door but they made no attempt to keep us quiet.

Late in the afternoon a fleet of Japanese army trucks drew up outside the building. We were sorted into groups of about twenty and marched out to the vehicles with two or three guards among us.

As we were driven through the city we could see the Chinese crowds watching us curiously. We saw many Europeans. Those with red armbands stopped and we could sense the fear they felt as they watched the procession.

We reached our destination – a large Chinese estate guarded by high brick walls into which we were driven through a covered passage cut through the wide brickwork of the wall facing the road. We tumbled out and took stock of our surroundings.

The grounds were vast, enclosing several Chinese-style buildings and a maze of courtyards in which, evidently, a former mandarin had maintained an establishment of women – wife and concubines – an army of servants and a regiment of gardeners and other servitors. There were two main buildings reached by flights of steps from the lawns in front and the small garden plots.

The buildings on the right were occupied by the Japanese. We could see soldiers standing on the steps and a young officer addressing them.

Where we had landed there was an air of emptiness. This was the main block containing, perhaps, twenty or more halls built around two large courtyards, tiled and ornately decorated with dragons. The halls had no doors, only decorated screens of wood which could be moved fan-like to bring open-pattern coolness in summer. The buildings had two storeys with balconies overhanging the courtyards.

We soon discovered that the estate had been the headquarters of the Fourth Marines in Shanghai. There was still the Leatherneck insignia in the main hall. They had built a system of modern lavatories and shower rooms. Away from the main conglomeration and behind the Japanese-occupied building there was a magnificent kitchen and dining hall equipped with long tables and trestle benches. There were four huge ranges with large ovens. By the wall were four rice boilers and an upright boiler.

At the rear was a huge yard, concreted and empty. It had been the vehicle compound. Access was by way of a large gate, wide open. A senty stood there, for there was no wall around the compound, only a barbed-wire fence behind which was a Chinese-squatter shanty-town.

Over to the right of the Japanese building was another large yard, cindered and desolate. This had been the marines' sports ground.

As more and more lorries arrived with their loads of bewildered humanity those of us who had been there for several hours watching the proceedings from the main steps started cheering and ribbing the newcomers.

The Japanese soldiers watching us enjoyed the joke and joined in the merriment as we shouted, clapped and cheered.

And then we were all in – 350 of us: Britons, Canadians, Australians, New Zealanders, Americans, Dutchmen, one Hong Kong Chinese, one Russian Jew with Norwegian nationality, some Greeks and, among them, one lone and miserable Turk.

Colonel Odera, whose prisoners we were, addressed us in the large courtyard.

We were in the custody of His Imperial Japanese Majesty's army. We were not to be afraid. We would be well treated. We should not try to escape for this would mean heavy punishment. So long as we behaved ourselves and obeyed orders all would be well.

The colonel, who seemed to be a retired officer brought back for war service, said he was sorry that Japan and England were at war. He had been on a training course in England and he had a

216

great respect for that country. He was a short, stocky man. His moustache, of the type later to be sported by Royal Air Force 'wizards', ensured that, henceforth, he would be 'Old Handle-bars'.

His address was translated by a younger officer, Lieutenant Honda, who was going to remain with us throughout our imprisonment. He spoke English with an American accent, and it was he and not the colonel, who was also in charge of prisoners of war from the services, who made his quarters in the camp and with whom we had daily contact.

We learned that we were 'prominent citizens', which surprised many of us, particularly the ex-American Navy bar-keepers, the policemen, the warders from the jail, the hard-up inmates of the local Salvation Army hostel.

As 'prominent citizens' we had the equivalent rank of sergeants in the Japanese army. We were entitled to five cigarettes a week.

Cigarettes! The original coffin-nails. Five sticks, green with mould, as old as Tutankhamun himself and probably discovered in his tomb. We called them Kamikazes for it was suicide to light one and take a drag. Your lungs pumped like a blacksmith's bellows to produce hacking coughs. We barked like consumptive seals. Our faces screwed in first-swallow agony. We went pale around the gills. But we survived.

Bulpin, the camp comic, suggested that they were made of the original tobacco old Walt Raleigh had brought back from America.

Brezowar, the camp barber, ex-American Navy and lover of 'black gals', chewed them and spat with unerring aim into a large tin a stream of bilious-green juice which 'Doc' Sturton said had the destructive power of dragon's blood.

Nevertheless, deadly or not, we smoked them. They were better than tea-leaves, toilet paper, dried grass or the sundry garden substitutes we had to use later on.

Prominent citizens it soon became evident we were. We were probably the only prisoners of the Japanese who had nine – no less! – excellent Chinese cooks.

Their presence was a tribute to the genius, the brass-necked salesmanship of a man who should have been President of the United States.

His name was Anker B. (for Bullshit) Henningsen, born, he said, in 'the asshole of the world', Butte, Montana, of a Danish father and an English mother. He ran in Shanghai the great Hazelwood canned-food empire, the Chocolate Shops and several other enterprises that provided him with a palatial home in the city, a ranch in California and a penchant for sybaritic living.

He was elected the American camp representative, which meant that he was the go-between who, with Hugh Collar, the British representative, conferred daily with the colonel or Honda.

It was lucky that Odera and the tall, rangy American had much in common – a love of the luxuries of life. We were fortunate in that Henningsen had been vaccinated with a gramophone needle and could talk the hind legs off a jackass. He had winning ways – even with the enemy. Poor old Odera had no chance. Henningsen could have sold him the Brooklyn Bridge for cash and a promise of future delivery back in Osaka.

Within a few days Anker had pulled off his deal. The nine cooks, all from the Hazelwood kitchens, were allowed in the camp every morning to feed us three meals that would have done credit to the Cathay or the Hungaria.

I wonder how many prisoners anywhere were fed on chicken, beef, pork, duck and ice-cream! For many of us the meals were superior to anything we'd had in our homes.

Not only that but Henningsen talked the colonel into delivering to the camp office, which were living quarters for him and Collar, a magnificent radiogram that had been in his home and almost a truck-load of records.

The colonel insisted that we should not listen to short-wave broadcasts and had the radio works sealed. A wire or two skilfully inserted by Geest, the radio expert, and we soon knew what was going on in Russia, in the Middle East and Europe.

Then came the hens from Collar's home, clucking happily and dropping eggs with gay abandon in the spacious grounds.

They were followed by rabbits on the job every minute, or so it seemed, to give promise of a never-ending supply of pie-potential offspring.

Then came the sow, huge and plump, almost reeking of the roast pork it was destined to be.

Best of all, to the colonel were delivered seven bottles of Johnny Walker, three of Martell brandy, one of advocaat and one of Gordon's gin, all from Henningsen's home stocks – the bargaining pieces for a better life for Shanghai's captive prominent citizens.

Collar did his bit, too. He was a rowing man from the Simon Langton School, Canterbury, and Oxford. He liked exercise. He got it by hacking away at the concrete in the former vehicle yard every afternoon when most of us were asleep on our camp beds so that after the soil appeared we could grow corn, potatoes, onions, tomatoes, and various greens.

Apart from the loss of feminine company we had little to complain about.

We organised ourselves into a well-knit community of workers – the kitchen staff, the vegetable peelers, the carpenters, the plumbers, the boot-and-shoe repairers, the camp-bed-canvas menders, the lavatory squad, the gardeners, the medicine men, the teachers, the herdsmen and the like.

The Swiss Red Cross provided us with a monthly comfort allowance in CRB currency. We got monthly food parcels sent in by contacts still outside and delivered by the Red Cross. We opened a canteen. We even started a camp orchestra.

Hanvey, ex-marine from Birmingham, Alabama, musician and one of the camp's two official buglers – the other was Albon from the police and an ex-guardsman – took over the conductorship.

I had played the violin in the school orchestra. I had had a go at the cello. The carpenters made it – hardly of Stradivarius quality – but it played.

Genius of the orchestra was Adolph Goldkette, an American who spoke fluent French, superb violinist and member of a world-travelled stage family whose best-known member was his brother, Jean Goldkette. His band in America had, at one time, vied with the Paul Whiteman orchestra in recording fame.

We organised a softball league – the Peelers, the Panhandlers, the Squitters (formed by members of the lavatory squad), the Nailers (carpenters), the Flushers (plumbers), the Scribes (office staff) and the Bone-Idlers (membership open to anyone).

Smith-Wright of the Shanghai Amateur Dramatic Society started theatrical activities. I took women's parts in several productions, notably in *The Importance of Being Earnest* by Oscar Wilde. I needed a pair of tits. I visited Monk Bares, bearded and busy over his sewing machine (another Henningsen contribution), and asked him if he could fit me up.

The old American sailor showed no surprise as he stopped his camp-bed-canvas repairs.

'What size?' he drawled. 'Russian or Chinese?'

We put on a variety show in which big Bulpin, Cockney ex-soldier and Shanghai policeman, Joe Orapello and I dressed in grass skirts and did a hula dance.

Orapello was hardly sylph-like. He was a New Yorker of

Neapolitan parentage, short and fat and in a grass skirt and bra could easily on a dark night have been mistaken for a barrel of lard festooned for a ceremonial opening.

We all wore fondooshis – the Japanese equivalent of adult diapers – a long and narrow piece of material attached to a long tape which we tied round our waists and into which we tucked the material after it had been pulled from the rear under our crotches to keep genitals decently hidden in summer heat.

At the concert the Japanese soldiers and about ten Japanese females – most of them nurses – were in the front seats. They went into hysterics during the act. So did everybody else. We were a riot.

I found out the reason after we had left the stage. My fondooshi had slipped to expose testicles and stalk which were rapidly revolving in an anticlockwise direction as my hips rotated Hawaiian-style.

The women, who had probably never seen balls in anything but a static position, were completely overcome by the gymnastic exhibition.

'They were going like a bloody Catherine-wheel on Guy Fawkes' Day,' said Tiny Pitts, who was also a prominent citizen.

On July 4th, 1943, we celebrated American Independence Day with a softball match – the U.S.A. versus the British Empire.

We packed our team with Canadian Bob Ralfe and some local Britons, who had grown up with the game in Shanghai. We also bribed Webber, the chief cook, to lace the tea – no coffee in the camp – of the American team with what he called 'jollop' – bowel-looser.

'They'll shit showers after that lot,' he assured us.

Whether or not Webber's purge was the cause the Yanks lost the match – even after Henningsen had laced the gloves of the British lads with rotten egg yolks which made catching difficult.

The disgrace was too much for poor Orapello, manager of the Yankee side, who went into mourning add organised a slap-up funeral for the following day. The 'corpses' were to be a bat and ball as symbols of American shame.

'I wouldn't mind being licked by the New York Yankees,' said Joe, 'but a goddammed bunch of Limeys . . . holy shit, I'm mortified.'

The funeral was conducted Chinese style with poor old Joe decked out in widow's weeds leading a procession of crestfallen Yanks all 'weeping' and wailing as they followed the trestle on which the bat and ball reposed under a wreath of weeds.

The honour guard was presenting bats over the grave in the garden and Hanvey was about to blow a bugler's farewell when Honda came flying through the gate, screaming with fury in a mixture of Japanese and English.

'Fuck me,' said chief mourner Orapello, 'here comes trouble.'

Honda, whose sense of humour (if he had one) never showed itself all the time we were in camp, stopped the proceedings immediately and the bat and the ball were saved from ignominious oblivion.

We never beat the Americans again because 'Wild Bill' Hallett, Joe's assistant in the canteen, took over the job of umpire which meant that impartial adjudications fled for ever from the cinder field.

The *North-China Daily News* provided several prominent citizens: Hoste, Cal Hirsh, Julian Bates and me.

I worked in the office with Henningsen and Collar. I took a shorthand note of the news in English from the Soviet station at Vladivostok and went round the rooms to read it out. Old man Cook, who spoke fluent Russian, helped me with the pronunciation of places on the eastern front and Mischenko of the police, who spoke English, Russian and Japanese, came in as adviser on Japanese pronunciation.

Russell Brines of the Associated Press, who had been captured in Manila, took on the job of teaching the Limeys the intricacies of American football so that, come next July 4th (if we were still there), a 'Rose Bowl' classic could be played. The elaborate technology of the Yankee game was too much for us. How anybody could have developed such a mathematically complicated exercise from the simple bull-rush Rugby I had played at school amazed me. And, in any case, a cinder field was hardly the sort of place on which to be up-ended violently, arse over tip. After three sessions the number of people limping painfully in the camp suggested that we were patients in a casualty clearing station.

We left the game in the sole possession of the Yanks.

Living up to the status bestowed on us by the Japs had its hazards. There were those who had not realised that spitting was not commensurate with good breeding. Nor was it a healthy exercise.

'Doc' Sturton decided to do something about it – to drive the lesson home to the peasants.

'If you expect to rate as a prominent citizen, then do not expectorate,' he told us in the hall.

Sturton, the missionary medic, the leprosy specialist, and Dr Dunne, who was a partner in an American practice in Shanghai, were the camp doctors. They started a clinic in the main hall with Red Cross medical supplies – limited but useful – and organised a team of British and American ex-service medical personnel as pharmacists and nurses in the clinic and the small hospital it became necessary for us to have.

Bouts of malaria hit me badly. I was carted off to the hospital many times and liberally dosed with quinine.

While life was not a bed of roses, we were comfortable enough. Compared with the mass of prisoners taken by the Japanese elsewhere we were the luckiest people alive. It seemed too good to be true. It was.

We lost the Chinese cooks. They got marching orders. Looking back, it seems to me that Colonel Odera must have been hauled over the coals for bestowing such a luxury on us.

Still, the Red Cross was delivering parcels to those of us who had contacts outside. Men like Jack Huxter, manager of the Mercantile Bank, who could produce tinned sausages, dried egg, butter, jam, biscuits, canned fruit juices, tinned cheese, milk powder, canned fruits and vegetables and many other commodities for the 'short order' cooks to prepare in the kitchen.

There was Eric Moller, head of the Moller shipping interests, similarly supplied. Willy Burns, the dour Scottish shipbuilder, had his shelves stacked with cans. There were many other food millionaires which made the less fortunate residents without outside contacts – and I was one – green with jealousy.

Moller owned the most magnificently bizarre mansion of any taipan in the city. Day in and day out builders were adding minarets, gargoyles, Buddhas and other extras to give it a Disneyland, fairy-tale appearance. Hordes of Chinese women would congregate by its massive gates to burn joss-sticks and kowtow before two enormous Buddhas he had placed there. The place reeked of Hollywood Technicolor and Wizard of Oz fantasy.

The reason for the non-stop construction was that Moller, a superstitious man, had been told by a Chinese soothsayer that if he ever stopped building then he would surely die. He became the best customer of the city's brick-and-mortar boys and the fabulous Moller 'Madhouse' attracted thousands of visitors daily.

There must have been an element of truth in the soothsayer's prophecy for Eric Moller was killed in an air crash in Singapore shortly after the Communist takeover in China had decreed that his home should be seized and he banished from the city. All building activity then ceased.

Moller's artistic extravagance had its counterparts in the camp on a less elaborate, though no less inspiring, scale.

The American Navy, it seemed, had been manned by a horde of peripatetic art galleries, men tattooed from arsehole to breakfast time.

Monk Bares was an example of the tattooer's witty craftsmanship. Under his left nipple the needle had implanted the word, 'Milk'. Under the right nipple: 'Beer'.

Compared with Pop Daley, a huge Irish-American, he was as barren of decoration as a barn. On Pop's enormous chest there was tattooed a whole fleet of sailing ships under full sail.

Nevertheless, Pop was way down in the league compared with the masterpiece occasionally exhibited by another former gob, whose name has slipped me. Proudly he would lower his pants and expose his hairy arse. Thereon – on both cheeks – were realistic pictures of foxhounds in full cry after the fox the only part of which was visible was its bushy tail protruding from the orifice between the cheeks.

The monotony of camp life was frequently relieved by Henningsen's practical jokes.

There was a young American in the camp office, Arnold Kiehn, born in China of missionary parents, who had by a series of daring smuggling operations in Japanese territory built up a considerable fortune on which to start legitimate business activities in Shanghai.

He had sent in by his secretary, a Portuguese girl, a corduroy cat-suit to keep him warm in winter. It was fur-lined completely inside and this gave Henningsen the gem of an idea: why not create a grizzly bear pet?

So the one-piece garment was turned inside out and Kiehn, who was stocky and broad-shouldered, donned it and became Henningsen's 'pet'. With a woolly balaclava helmet almost completely obscuring his features and his slouching body covered entirely by long fur he was ready for the exercise.

Late at night with only the fire-watchers on duty – older inmates of the camp excused manual work – Henningsen tied a long piece of rope round Kiehn's neck and led him forth from the office.

The first man they met was John Harvey, shipbuilding engineer, tall and somewhat short-sighted.

'Evening,' said Henningsen casually. 'Nice weather.'

'Evening,' said Harvey. 'Not bad at all.'

'Grrrh,' growled Kiehn, padding a few feet behind at the end of the rope held by Henningsen.

'Evening,' said Harvey calmly. He should have been in hysterics – terror-stricken.

'Blind as a bat,' said Henningsen. 'God help us if we ever have a fire. He'll think it's bright starlight.'

He spotted little Timmy Gwynne, a small, elderly Welshman making for the toilets in his pyjamas.

Quickly he released Kiehn from the rope and the burly, fur-covered American padded softly behind Gwynne to take stance by him at the stand-up urinals.

Waiting in the shadows outside with Henningsen we doubled up with mirth when the little Gwynne burst through the door at breakneck speed, dashed down the alleyway as if Satan himself was in pursuit and vanished into his room.

Out came Kiehn all fur and frivolity. He told us what had happened.

Poor Timmy was in the middle of his pee when he noticed something big and furry next to him. Kiehn uttered a fierce growl, rubbed his fur all over Gwynne's pyjamas and that did it. Gwynne uttered a strangled cry, stopped the flow half-way and took off like a rocket.

'Could have given the poor old sod a heart attack,' I told Henningsen.

'Another sight like that and I'll have one myself,' said Anker B., holding his sides.

'Let's take some of the bullshit from du Berrier,' giggled Henningsen.

Hal du Berrier was a young American, moustached on the lines of Ronald Colman, a fervent Francophile who maintained that he was entitled by virtue of aristocratic French ancestry to be addressed as Count.

'Cunt more like it,' said Bulpin, who was proud of his plebeian birth.

'Probably escaped from a hole in his dad's french letter. That's the nearest he'd been to France.'

It was decided that Kiehn would enter du Berrier's room, hover over him on his camp bed, growl and rub his long hairs all over his face.

We hid outside the room which contained about ten people, including Goldkette. Kiehn entered. We heard loud growls.

Then there was a yell. Out came Kiehn to vanish quickly into the darkness.

A few seconds later we saw du Berrier's figure outlined in the doorway. He looked this way and that, peering first to the left along the balcony and then to the right. We saw him scratch his head. A moment later he was joined by the slender figure of Goldkette whose French, unlike that of du Berrier, was impeccably Parisian.

'Jesus Christ,' said Goldkette, 'did ya see it? What in hell's name was it?'

He was frightened. Splendid musician he might be but he was a simple soul, impressionable, superstitious.

Hal du Berrier was calm. Unlike Goldkette he was not convinced that a great, hairy monster was running wild in the camp.

The next morning the story of the 'escaped bear' went the rounds and there were many, including Goldkette, who were convinced that a wild animal had visited the camp and that something had to be done about it before it gobbled up one or two prominent citizens.

I was approached by du Berrier in one of the courtyards. He asked if I had heard of the night's events. I said I had. He thought Henningsen was the master-mind. It was him he was gunning for.

I promised him my assistance and he then produced from inside his sweater a small alarm clock. This, he said, was the pride and joy of Goldkette. He treasured it. He doted on it. To him it had greater value than the Crown jewels.

Would I hide this somewhere in the camp office? It was timed to go off in an hour's time and he would see to it that Goldkette, who was running around with murder in his heart, would be there to hear it and, probably, to murder the entire office staff.

I took the clock. I went to the office and did my betrayal act. Henningsen was there with Kiehn. I told them of du Berrier's plot.

'The ornery bastard,' said Henningsen. 'We'll fix him.'

There was then set in motion an elaborate scheme that could only have been devised by a genius like Henningsen. The clock was placed well out of the way up the office chimney. Its alarm was 'defused' and it reposed there awaiting the arrival of the angry Goldkette.

Soon enough, Goldkette arrived for an interview with the American camp representative. Henningsen, serious of face as we busied ourselves with seemingly urgent business asked what the matter was.

225

Goldkette, deadly serious, said that some goddammed swine had stolen his clock. If he ever laid hands on the culprit then homicide would be done. He wanted that clock back.

We were making herculean efforts to keep straight faces. Had I looked at Henningsen, sitting behind his table with the most comically consulting-room expression on his rugged face, then I would have gone into hysterics. He was a superb actor.

'Look here, Goldkette,' he said. 'This is serious. We don't want any goddam thieving in this camp. This has got to be stamped out. I'm going to put my best operator on the job. We'll have the bastard. Don't worry.'

Anybody else but Goldkette would have realised that his leg was being pulled. Henningsen told him to wait while he fetched E. C. Baker, chief of the camp police (the ancient fire-watchers).

'Doughy', well primed by Henningsen, arrived with the American camp representative to face Goldkette. His presence carried some authority for he was a real policeman, an assistant commissioner in the Shanghai Municipal Police.

They sat facing the white-faced musician. Henningsen told the facts to Baker, who asked Goldkette some pertinent questions. The New York Homicide Bureau couldn't have looked more convincing. Goldkette told all.

'Right,' said Baker, not daring to look at Henningsen, 'I'm going to put Operator 29 on the job. He's my best man – solved some of my best cases. If there's anyone who can get your clock back then it's good old 29. Sorry, I can't tell you his name. He works in secret.'

A much happier Goldkette left the office, convinced that Operator 29, whoever he was, would soon have the clock and culprit in safe custody.

I met a puzzled du Berrier some time later. I told him that the alarm had failed to go off and that, when I got the opportunity, I would re-set it, let him know and he could get Goldkette in again.

He seemed dubious but I assured him that all would be well.

In the meantime Goldkette had been called in again to face Henningsen and Baker. He was told that investigations had proceeded smoothly and that good old Operator 29 had not let them down – genius that he was. It was fairly certain that the clock had been located and that, if Goldkette prowled around in the vicinity of his room at about one a.m. the following day he would hear something to his advantage.

He took it all in and said that would remain wide awake and alert.

At midnight Kiehn avoided the prowling Goldkette, slipped quickly into the room and placed the clock under du Berrier's bed.

At one a.m. the silence of the night was shattered by the alarm bell. Goldkette, on the balcony, leaped from his perch on the railing and dashed into the room – just in time to see du Berrier, wildly terrified, trying to stuff the clock and its strident bell under his pillow.

Murder was almost done – but not quite. The members of the room, awakened by the din of the bell and the wild cries of Goldkette as he tried to strangle du Berrier, rushed over to pull off the maddened musician. He was finally pacified and retired to sleep with the clock clutched in his loving arms.

I met du Berrier in the courtyard some hours later.

He gave me a baleful look.

'Judas Iscariot,' he hissed and walked on.

Our saddest day was when a large number of the Americans left the camp under a repatriation scheme arranged by the Swiss authorities.

They were jubilant over the prospect of seeing America again. Henningsen was going. So was Kiehn.

For a week before the departure date I was typing for Kiehn on thin rice paper a list of everybody in the camp. We had the background of every man. Those who had been tortured in the Bridge House had told their stories. We recorded them. Every scrap of information that would be useful to our governments was placed on record.

Kiehn, the currency smuggler, had a brilliant idea. He got Ginger Stephenson of the police, a fine carpenter, to make two canvas deck-chairs, one for him and one for Henningsen. These were to be taken aboard the repatriation ship so that, in comfort, the lonely hours could be whiled away in sun-bathing, snoozing, reading or just idle dreaming.

Stephenson was another Chippendale. The chairs were identical except that one of them had a hollow arm into which had been placed a steel tube containing the rolled-up rice paper information. There was no sign of a join in the wood. Both chairs looked exactly alike.

Henningsen was tickled pink with the idea of owning his own leisure chair. He didn't know that he was going to get the one containing the secret information. Only Kiehn, Stephenson and I were in the know.

The day before the Americans were due to leave camp the Japanese paraded them in front of their building. On the lawn all the baggage they were taking with them was searched. Each man stood behind his pile and Kempetai men, brought in from Hong-kew headquarters, subjected each item to a minute examination.

My heart pumped when I saw one of the Japanese pick up Henningsen's chair, turn it over carefully, tap it here and there and run his hand over the woodwork.

Stephenson, who was standing next to me, had his fingers crossed. Henningsen, who knew nothing, was not worried at all. Kiehn, standing by his side with the other chair at his feet, must have been sweating blood. His face, however, showed no sign of emotion.

And then the Japanese carefully placed the chair on the ground and commenced to pick up other pieces of baggage. The test was over. The danger had passed.

When the Americans left the camp in Japanese army trucks the camp orchestra turned out to give them a rousing send-off. There was a stentorian cheer as the last vehicle slowly went down the main drive and through the wall-passage. With their feet dangling over the tailboard were Henningsen and Kiehn waving madly.

I gulped with emotion. There were tears in my eyes. I had lost two good friends, particularly Kiehn, who had promised me that if we survived the war then there would be a place for me in his future operations.

Once the Americans had left the camp administration became totally British with Yorkshireman Bill Wright joining Collar as joint camp representative. Many Americans had been left behind. They were mostly ex-servicemen who had married Chinese women and had families in the city. They also included Paul Hopkins, head of the Shanghai Power Co., and Bishop Ralph Ward, of the American Methodist Church, whose names were removed from the repatriation list by the Japanese.

Conditions soon deteriorated as food became scarcer and the Japanese stricter. We were given regular doses of bowing practice because we had failed to show total respect to the Emperor. Morning after morning, Honda or his junior, 'Dog Face', had us doing obeisance facing in the direction of Tokyo – body at the correct fifteen-degree angle, chin in, hands smartly at sides. They punched us, slapped us and generally worked off their anti-Western spleen on such towering goliaths as 'Tiny' Pitts, Daley, 'Lofty' Trodd and the ex-policemen whose size served to increase the inferiority complex they already possessed in good measure.

We were an ingenious lot. We constructed an amazing variety of electrical gadgets which included swizzle-sticks to boil water in thermos flasks, heaters, electric kettles, foot-warmers and the like. The result was that the Japanese electricity bills soared. So they started a system of instant searches of various rooms.

They never found anything. Our ingenuity foiled them. We had constructed secret hiding places. In the American room there was a fantastic secret chamber in the fireplace which for well-oiled inventiveness deserved a Nobel prize.

The policemen in Room Ten were almost caught out one day when the Japs came down without warning. An electric kettle plugged into a wall bracket was steaming merrily when in walked 'Dog Face' and ordered the men to line up. With great presence of mind 'Tam' Wimsett, from Halifax, Yorkshire, whose overalls were wide, draped them over the kettle so that the steam rose with ever-increasing heat up his leg. Bravely he stood there for several minutes while 'Dog Face' looked about the room. 'Tam' had his back to the wall so that the flex was hidden. He was in agony as the spirals of steam from the boiling kettle rose within his voluminous overalls to bring great beads of sweat on his brow as he fought back the pain.

After 'Dog Face' had departed 'Tam' was treated by Sturton for what his room-mates described as 'stewed balls' – a condition, they said, brought on by the Yorkshireman's foolishness in placing the kettle in the wrong leg of his overalls – the side on which his testicles dangled.

'Only a gormless Tyke would be so daft,' said Bill Pike, his room-mate.

Fuel supplies were cut short. We were making briquettes for the kitchen from coal dust mixed with a paste we made from the rice remnants in the steamers. But we were running out of wood with which to start the fires in the morning.

R. Manly-Allatt, ex-Royal Marine and employee of a local import-export firm, kept us going for a time with the Japanese flagpole. During the early morning hours he would swarm up the pole and lop off six inches or so. After chopping we had enough to set kitchen operations under way.

Operations had to cease when the Japanese noticed the shrinkage and Honda made it known that the most severe punishment would be meted out to the person, or persons, decapitating the pole. To his credit, Manly-Allatt said he was ready to continue the shortening process but was dissuaded from doing so by Collar, who pointed out that though the Japanese did not possess the normal quantity of grey matter it was fairly certain that the flagpole would be under constant surveillance following Honda's warning.

The Japanese were certainly easy prey for practical jokers like Bulpin, who was captain of my room. This meant that at roll call he had to bring us to attention by yelling out 'Kiotsuke', which was the Japanese army command for 'Shun'.

Every morning and evening Honda or 'Dog Face' gravely saluted Bulpin as he yelled out 'Quaker Oats' and bowed. 'Quaker Oats' or 'Kiotsuke', it sounded the same when delivered in a blend of Cockney and Japanese. The Japanese would have been none the wiser had Bulpin yelled out 'Carrots' or, as his successor, Ben Williams, did once: 'Bollocks'.

Bed-bugs were our greatest affliction. They bred in the woodwork at an amazing rate. Clever they were, too. They would crawl over the ceiling and take up a position over our beds. Then like a German Stuka, or a Japanese Zero fighter, they dropped at a fast lick to land on our camp beds where they sucked our blood and waxed fat and oily.

We had regular de-bugging sessions, throwing our camp beds for several seconds into a large fire in the courtyard. We could hear the bugs exploding, crackling like roast pork. But we never got rid of them. They swarmed everywhere in blood-sucking legions, miniature Draculas who cocked a snook at every ploy we used to exterminate them.

Another problem was the cracked wheat. This was crawling with insects.

It became the duty of some eagle-eyed prominent citizens, including several taipans who had never seen the inside of a kitchen in pre-war luxury, to spot and pick out the creepy-crawlers on a long table on which the cracked wheat was deposited. An amazing variety they unearthed. But many escaped their vigilance and finished up mashed and miserable in the morning porridge.

After Kiehn had left and his supply of goodies bequeathed to me had vanished I left the camp office and started work as a stoker in the camp kitchen. This meant rising on my duty days at 4.30 a.m., awakened by a fire-watcher who saw to it that I exploded into instant activity by stuffing a lighted Kamikaze cigarette into my mouth. Lungs screaming in agony I leaped out of bed, donned overalls and made my way in the darkness to the kitchen usually to be accosted by a prowling sentry by the kitchen door.

I answered his challenge: 'Shuiji-ba ichi mei' which meant 'Kitchen one man.'

It was a good job – kept me fit and assured me of some extra food at a time when rations were low.

The poor old pig had departed, slaughtered by Chinese butchers who had been brought in after Hanvey ('Ah've bin killin' hawgs since Ah was knee-high to a grasshopper') nearly wrecked the camp with his attempt to assassinate Rosie, as we affectionately called the animal.

According to Hanvey all that was needed was a hammer and a knife. You hit the pig on the head with the hammer, after which it was supposed to roll over unconscious for its throat to be slit. At least that's how it should have been.

Hanvey procured a hammer. He hit the pig between the eyes, but instead of rolling over it took off like a rocket and dashed through several rooms, knocking over beds and startled inmates. The terror-stricken animal, chased by a whooping crowd of prominent citizens, left a trail of havoc in its wake before it was finally cornered and reprieved for a day.

The Chinese butchers, brought in by the Japanese to save the camp further destruction, did an expert job and we had pork for a week or more.

The rabbits, unfortunately, contracted a disease and had to be put down.

The chickens, after ovulating magnificently for several months, became barren and they were killed to give us a plentiful supply of chicken dishes.

That, more or less, ended our supply of protein. We had cracked wheat, vegetables and rice with additions from the garden in season: onions, tomatoes, corn. It was not enough. There were heavy inroads into hoarded supplies from the monthly parcels and I was able to augment my diet by cooking powdered-egg-yolk dishes for Huxter, the bank manager. In them I put tinned sausages, tinned cheese, tinned salmon – anything Huxter delivered to me at the stove. God knows what concoctions I turned out but they filled the stomach and kept beri-beri at bay.

Some of the big police fellows had gone down with the deficiency disease. They were without parcel supplies and a regular diet of rice was not enough to provide the sustenance they needed. Sturton, who had lost the help of Dunne, on the American repatriation roster, importuned the Japanese for more medical supplies, particularly vitamins. He got some from the Swiss Red

Cross but they had to be hoarded carefully as all the signs pointed to greater privations to come.

The war was costing the Japanese heavily. They were still bogged down in China, and elsewhere the Allies, particularly the United States with its immense resources and technological superiority, were embarking on the long and bloody island-hopping campaigns which Japan, with its extended lifelines and meagre home economy, was unable to stem.

As food became scarcer so the monthly parcels from the outside contacts dwindled in size until, finally, they vanished altogether. Only our 'millionaires' – Huxter, Moller and company – managed to eke out our mainly vegetable-and-rice diet. The canteen under Joe Orapello was down to such items as soap, salt, sewing cotton, buttons and materials for repairing garments. Yet, in comparison with our servicemen taken prisoners by the Japanese in South-east Asia, we were still living in luxury.

We had our tragedies as time passed and as a meagre diet and lack of medicines took their toll of the weakest. W. J. Monk, a well-known British businessman, died from a heart attack. One of the former American sailors, cut off from his two bottles of whisky a day, wasted away and collapsed in the toilets. He died a few days later.

We lived daily in the fear that the Kempetai would take us from the camp for interrogation. This had happened many times. They came in a small British car – one of the spoils of war. Their arrival sent shivers down my spine. Who did they want this time? Woe betide the poor devil they came to fetch for he would be returned battered and bruised, an instant hospital case after delousing with anti-vermin powder in the camp clinic.

The fate of one man taken by the Kempetai, who inflicted on him the most devilishly inhuman torture, shocked the entire camp into a state of grief so deep that the memory of his suffering would never be erased from our minds.

His name was Bill Hutton. He was a big man from the north-east of England, a Shanghai policeman, cheerful always and brave. The cause of his tragedy was a Sikh policeman, number thirty-nine, one of the many Indians in Shanghai who had joined the Indian National Liberation Movement of Subhas Chandra Bose.

As well as the Japanese soldiers the Indian policemen, who arrived every morning, guarded the camp. They were well-known to the British policemen, some of whom, including Hutton, had been their officers.

Number thirty-nine, tall and bearded, made a complaint to Honda that two men in the camp, both former policemen, had attempted to induce him to take messages out to contacts outside.

There was an immediate order for a roll call. We were assembled in our rooms and the Indian, accompanied by Honda and 'Dog Face', carefully scrutinised every man.

He picked out two – 'Ragpicker' Watson, who had been in the Sikh section of the police, and Dick Ekin, another policeman from the north-east of England, similar in appearance to Hutton.

They were taken to the Japanese building and a message was sent by Honda to the Kempetai to come and collect them.

Hutton, who had been with Watson close to the Sikh guard on the front lawn, but who steadfastly maintained that he had never attempted to get a message out of the camp, realised that Ekin had been mistaken for him. He went over to Honda and told him that he was the man against whom the complaint had been made. The Sikh agreed that this was so. It was a brave act on Hutton's part for he had signed his death warrant.

The Kempetai arrived in the small British car. Hutton and Watson were bundled in and the vehicle was slowly driven down the drive on its way to the interrogation headquarters. I saw Hutton, smiling cheerfully, wave to us from the back of the car.

Nine days later, the car returned and drew up in front of our main hall. A Japanese in civilian clothes alighted and opened the rear door. There on the floor was Hutton, insensible, sprawled in a grotesque shape, head lolling over the footboard.

A sharp command from the Japanese, who was a plain-clothes Kempetai officer, and several of us carefully lifted Hutton from the car and placed him on a stretcher in the hall.

He was in a deep coma. He was emaciated, his eyes sunken, his cheeks hollow. His tongue, enormously swollen, filled his mouth. His lips, dry and cracked, were blood-spattered. His entire body appeared to be broken. He had the appearance of an aged man – a complete human wreck. He was unrecognisable as the tall, strapping specimen who had so cheerfully waved to us just over a week ago.

Honda arrived as Dr Sturton started his inspection of Hutton. The Japanese officer, shocked by the sight, giggled from the nervous tension within him. This was the oriental way. He appeared to be as horror-striken as we were.

Sturton's diagnosis was serious. The man was completely dehydrated. He was in a coma, almost at the point of death. Angrily, he turned to Honda and, pointing at Hutton, demanded to know why the man had been subjected to such savage treatment. It was inhuman – savage – uncivilised.

Honda made no reply.

Hutton was removed to the camp hospital and placed under intensive care. An examination of his body revealed that he had been trussed up with wire in the shape of a ball. The wire had made deep cuts in his flesh. He had had no food and drink. On one side of his genitals someone had carved with a knife the word 'War'. On the other side was the word 'Murderer'. His suffering had been unbearable until merciful oblivion intervened to save him from the savages who had literally crucified him.

He was fed drops of water from a teaspoon. Sturton tended him day and night. It was to no avail. Hutton died, still in a coma – yet another victim of the bestiality of the Japanese army.

Our grief, our burning anger produced open rebellion.

There had been a typhoon and a large tree had been blown down.

The colonel ordered us to drag it with ropes to the cinder field where it could be chopped and stacked for firewood.

We refused. A deputation was sent across to the Japanese building and it was pointed out that we wished to report the case of Hutton to the Swiss Red Cross. Collar told the colonel that our anger was understandable. He protested in the strongest terms.

Colonel Odera said he understood the effect Hutton's death had had on us. Nevertheless, the man had disobeyed camp regulations. He had been punished. We would have to obey orders or else stern measures would be taken to see that we did.

As we milled about the camp still refusing to work on the tree we could see Japanese soldiers armed with machine-guns taking up positions on the wide wall of the camp. Others carrying rifles took up posts surrounding our buildings. There was no doubt that they would open fire if the rebellion continued.

The Sikh guards, every one of them hated with vitriolic intensity, were withdrawn. It was a confrontation between us and the Japanese.

The colonel called Collar and Wright over. He made it known that we had only a few minutes to make a decision – either we worked or action would be taken.

We realised the hopelessness of our position. After a stormy meeting in the main hall we decided that orders would have to be obeyed or the camp would be filled with dead men.

The tree was hauled to the cinder patch and there we chopped it for fuel.

Watson was returned in fairly good condition. He had been beaten but it was plain that, unlike Hutton, he had not retaliated against the ill-treatment he received. That was Hutton's way. He had enormous courage, almost foolhardy courage. If he was hit then he punched back. To do so against the Kempetai was as good as ordering his own execution.

After the war Watson, Dr Sturton, Ronnie Hillman, the hospital nurse, and several others testified at a war crimes trial in Hong Kong against the Japanese who had killed Hutton. His torturers were sentenced – some of them to death.

The Sikh, number thirty-nine, was located after the Japanese surrender working for the Americans in Shanghai as a security guard. His body was found under a jeep. No one asked who had killed him. I had a shrewd idea. I think Watson knew the answer.

We lived on in greater privation until June in 1945 when we were told that we should be removed to another camp. Our destination was kept secret. All we knew was that it would mean a train journey and that, for a week prior to our departure, I would be working loading railway trucks with our possessions.

The war was going badly for the Japanese. That we knew. While Henningsen's radiogram had been dismantled by the Japanese, the Americans had built a secret radio in their room and the news of Allied successes cheered us. We knew the end was not far away but we also realised that we were hostages, special cases, and that we could be in great danger. Why, for instance, were we to be moved from Shanghai?

There were wives and families in other camps in Shanghai run by the Japanese consular police. They were civilian internees. We were not. We were prisoners of the army and, as such, in greater danger.

It was good to get outside the camp again. I enjoyed my trips in Japanese army trucks to the North Station where we loaded up with our possessions.

On one run we followed a lorry carrying young Germans in the direction of the Kaiser Wilhelm Schule.

They goaded us with shouts in their own language.

We yelled back: 'Your turn next, you bloody Huns.'

Germany had lost the war. Italy had collapsed. Japan was alone.

News of our departure spread in the city. There was a young young Chinese girl in the row of terrace houses outside the wall who was, we thought, working for the Chinese underground. We slit tennis balls and placed messages in them. We dropped the balls in her small garden. She picked them up and waved to us.

On the day we were to leave for the North Station we were lined up in two ranks on the lawn facing our main building.

The Japanese called the roll. There was one man missing. It was dour old Willy Burns.

Suddenly emerging from the hall there was Willy. Never was there such an apparition. Around his waist was a piece of rope from which dangled an amazing variety of pots and pans, clanking with each step he took. On his head was his beloved bowler. Over it he had jammed several more headpieces – a straw panama, a battered trilby and a cap.

We gazed in awe as Willy staggered down the steps on his way to join us.

Before he reached the bottom step Ashley Harman of the Power Co. had broken ranks. He marched up to Willy, bowed low before the canny Scot, who was going to leave nothing of value behind, and said loudly: 'Dr Livingstone, I presume.'

It lifted the gloom. We clapped and cheered as Harman gravely escorted the clanging and jangling Scot to a position in the front rank. Even the sour-faced Japanese soldiers detailed to escort us to the station had broad grins.

We reached the North Station, where we disembarked from the trucks and were formed up to march into the freight yard where our train had been assembled. There were hundreds of people on the streets including the Chinese wives and neutral girl-friends of many of our inmates. They waved. We waved back. Some of them were crying.

It was a nightmare journey. We were packed into coolie-class coaches with hard, wooden seats and issued with American Red Cross parcels as rations. This saved the Japanese the cost of feeding us and proved our earlier suspicion that the Red Cross parcels, which should have been issued immediately, had been deliberately stolen for Japanese use. What we were getting were the left-overs.

The problem was not food but drink. As the train slowly moved toward Nanking our thirst increased and we could hardly chew the American food which consisted of cheese, corned beef, Spam, chocolate, milk powder, instant coffee, butter and bacon.

We were packed solid and had little room to move. The seats were hard, unyielding. Soon we were suffering the torture of severe muscular pains. There was nowhere to lie down. We took it in turns to stand up and stretch our pain-racked bodies. All the while we were closely watched by armed sentries who stood at each end of the coaches.

At Nanking we were shunted on to the train ferry which took us across the Yangtse to the railway yard on the north bank where we saw several steam locomotives badly damaged either from guerilla action or bombing.

There, to our great joy, we were told to alight and, for half an hour or so, we were able to stretch our legs. Water was brought and we drank greedily and without thought of the danger of contracting typhoid or dysentery from contaminated supplies.

I remember the train stopping at Tsinan, where a crowd of curious Chinese were kept back by the Japanese soldiers as we piled out of the coaches to collect more water from a hillside farm trough. After that – oblivion.

I went down with dysentery and with a temperature soaring to more than 102 was placed on a luggage rack over the heads of my fellow prisoners. Later, I was moved to the coal truck behind the locomotive together with several Japanese guards suffering from malaria and emerged at the end of the five-day journey looking like a nigger minstrel – but still alive thanks to the constant nursing of Dr Sturton, who worked indefatigably to ensure that not only the prisoners were kept supplied with medicines but sick Japanese as well.

If ever there was a man who deserved a hero's accolade it was Sturton. Without sleep, racked by the hunger and thirst that afflicted all of us, he never failed to make constant journeys up and down the train with his meagre supply of medicines to attend to our needs which, with every slow and painful mile we covered, became more and more exacting.

I owe my life to Sturton. So do many of our Japanese guards, who would surely have died had it not been for the missionary's inspiring display of his genuine love for mankind which made no distinction between friend and foe.

Our destination was Fengtai, the large railway marshalling-yard complex near Peking. There, enclosed by electrified wire, we were placed in two enormous warehouses.

It was after we had found messages scrawled on the walls of the warehouses that we discovered the prisoners of war in Shanghai had been there before us. They told us that they were on the way to Manchuria, only about sixty miles distant at Kalgan, probably to work in the coal-mines there.

We had no doubt that Fengtai was only a transit stage and that, shortly, we would be boarding another train to follow the servicemen whose camp commandant was Odera and who had met us at Fengtai station.

We quickly organised camp routines but without the amenities of our Shanghai camp life became austere, makeshift. We dug deep latrines where the almost-overpowering smell of ammonia in time dulled our senses close to unconsciousness. We ate camel stew made from the carcases of animals that had died at the end of long treks from the Gobi desert.

August arrived and still we had not been moved. It was summer but in sight was the golden autumn of North China – and the bitter sub-zero winter of that near-Siberian region. Sturton was worried. We could not possibly survive a northern winter. Surely, he said, a move to better quarters could not long be delayed.

It was not – but when it came its impact was unbelievably overpowering, so fantastically unexpected was the shape it took.

It was heralded by several nights of feverish activity in the railway yards. We could hear trains being assembled by shunting engines and then the powerful chug-chug of main-line monsters as they hauled the trains into the distance. And then, one morning, silence – not one sound from the vast maze of railway tracks which made Fengtai one of the most important communication arteries of China. It was as if every coach, every wagon, every locomotive had been taken away on some enormous transport operation. Indeed they had, as we discovered later.

Mischenko, whose Japanese was fluent, said he had heard the sentries talking about a big battle in Manchuria. This, he said, could only mean that the Russians had attacked the Japanese or, less likely, that the Americans had staged a landing there. The camp wiseacres – the pundits who professed to have analytical knowledge of the ways of war – told him that he was spreading bullshit in huge spadefuls. It was probably a gigantic military exercise.

Perhaps two or three days later in the silence which now seemed to have become a permanent feature of the Fengtai complex, we heard the sound of a plane in the distance. We saw approaching at a fairly low altitude a bomber. We took it to be Japanese. And then, as it roared nearer and finally passed over the railway yards, we saw the American insignia on its wings. We scattered for cover. Lying flat on the ground we waited for the bombs, but none came. Nor was there any anti-aircraft fire. Our courage flooded back and we all raised ourselves to watch the plane as it roared on toward Peking.

Suddenly, a shout from one of our men. We looked into the

sky, blue and unclouded, and over the tall towers on the great city wall of Peking we saw parachutes opening – seven of them, coloured and shining in the brilliant sunlight.

It could not be an airborne landing, for there was only one plane and seven parachutes. On the ground there was the powerful Japanese North China army. Who would be fool enough to drop into the midst of Japan's biggest and best defended military region in China?

The truth emerged through Mischenko late at night. In the darkness he had stolen across to the Japanese quarters where he had heard through open windows a broadcast from Tokyo. He could not believe his ears. The voice that had emerged from the loudspeaker was that of the Emperor, the Son of Heaven.

The Japanese spoken had been archaic, difficult to follow, but the message had been clear and the command explicit – the Japanese armies everywhere were to surrender, the war had been lost. The Emperor's order was to be strictly obeyed. Every commander in the field would be personally responsible to the heavenly ruler to see that not one Japanese soldier, sailor or airman engaged in further operations against the enemy.

Mischenko burst into the warehouse in which I was quartered. We were talking in groups here and there. Others were either sitting or lying on their camp beds – sewing, darning, reading or just staring into space.

He shouted: 'Japan has surrendered. I've just heard the Emperor on the radio. It's all over, boys. We've won the war.'

The reception he got was typical of our state of mind filled with dashed hopes and the seeming endlessness of our captivity.

There were loud shouts of 'Bullshit!' . . . 'Pull the other leg, mate!' . . . 'Old Misch has gone mad!' . . . 'And I'm to be Queen of the May' (from Bulpin) . . . 'Get stuffed!' – 'Piss of, you Russian twerp!' . . . and many more in similar vein.

But Mischenko stuck to his guns. As we gathered round him, gradually absorbing the excitement that flowed from him, his fervent appeals to us to believe him gradually sank home.

There was no sleep for us that night. Collar and Wright had been approached by Mischenko. They believed him. We were all for sending a deputation across to the Japanese side to demand instant freedom. But, as Collar pointed out, there was no confirmation of what Mischenko had reported. We sat around for hours excitedly discussing what should be done. Finally it was decided that come the dawn a deputation led by Collar would see the colonel and find out the truth.

Long before roll-call the deputation, watched by the entire camp, walked across to the warehouse occupied by the officers. The Japanese sentries in their tall towers by the electric wire were still at their posts, armed. They watched us but made no move to send us back into the vast concrete buildings from which we had emerged. They looked crestfallen and dejected.

We watched the deputation enter the warehouse. We waited, tense and silent, as an hour passed by. And then another thirty minutes. Suddenly, at the door, we saw Bill Wright. He waved his arms in joyous abandon. He shouted. We couldn't hear him. But we had the feeling that the news was good.

As the deputation reached us Wright raised his arms for silence. He looked wonderfully happy.

'Quiet, everyone,' he said. 'Quiet. Hugh Collar has something to tell you.'

Collar waited a few moments for the hubbub to subside. He stood on a box. Without a trace of emotion he spoke:

'We have spoken to the colonel. It is true. Japan has surrendered. The war is over. We have . . .'

He could not proceed.

An immense cheer that must have been heard in Peking seven miles away burst forth. Wild cheering continued. Amid the din Bill Wright frantically waved his arms for silence. It was a hopeless effort. Mass hysteria had taken over. Someone started to sing 'God Save the King'. The cheering died away and, filled with intense emotion, the entire assembly stood stiffly at attention and the inspiring words of the British national anthem were carried away on the still air.

Then the Americans took over with the 'Star Spangled Banner'. We didn't know the words but we hummed the tune and remained at attention.

Captain Calafatis, leader of the twenty or so Greek sailors amongst us, led his men in singing the Greek national anthem.

The Dutchmen sang their anthem and as the last notes died away pandemonium ensued. We cheered, clapped, sang and danced like wildly excited children.

All the while the sentries watched us. There was no sign of any of the Japanese officers across the yard in their quarters.

Finally, a hoarse Bill Wright got us quiet. He pointed at Collar, still on the box.

'As I said,' Collar continued, 'the war is over. We have made several demands. There will be no more roll-calls. In future we

waited

we must. The sentries stay in perimeter. I will be let you the meantime, we stay here. That is all. stay here.

camp discipline. In the meantime, we swept through me. My eyes weeping. The Greeks, highly were wet, listening to The Dutch, phlegmatic, volatile, a group listening to Winkelman, son of General Winkel- the Dutch commander-in-chief whose forces had been overrun by the Germans in 1940.

So this was the end of my misery. I had come through un- scathed. I was a free man again.

It was a com... the ... Americans, so far a... slander, so far a... days were still g...

there was no interfe... there but still auth... dejected Collar and Wrigh... with to our side of t... across and probably st... younger invincibility, kep... Japane one evening we we... Late into Peking. All ou... moved by the younger men wh... trucks by I was asked to join... quarters at the chance.

...walked ... Honda, ... the myth of

There were was... Waves of tear... We shall maintain our... know what the next move will... withdrawn but they will be on the... camp. He is responsible for our protecti... until we ... the colonel has made it clear tha... He held up his hands as the cheering... the Japanese. However ... shall manage our own... He quietened down...

...that we were to be ...would be loaded in ...also unload it at our new ...join ne 'furniture removers' and I

... into Peking where we humped jumped made several journeys into Peking where we humped We ..., kitchen equipment, kit bags, food stocks and other camp beds, into two Japanese-owned hotels which, we were commodities to be our new quarters pending the arrival of transport told, were to be our new quarters pending the arrival of transport ... were to take us back to Shanghai.

It was back-breaking but we worked with enthusiasm, stripped to take us back to Shanghai.

It was back-breaking but we worked with enthusiasm, stripped to the waist, dripping with sweat but filled with exhilaration as we surveyed the carpeted magnificence of the two-storey hotels in to the ... we were to live as free men.

We returned to the camp in the early hours for the final clean- which ... and were told that the move-out would be up of the warehouses and were told that the move-out would be that evening. About thirty of us piled into the trucks arrived. About thirty of us piled into that evening.

It was dark when the trucks arrived. We looked like fugitive Robinson Crusoes – tattered, the first one. We, looked solidly against a lone Japanese bearded, unkempt – paced solidly against a lone Japanese soldier who stood by the cab, rifle in hand. We ignored him. He didn't exist any more.

242

The first truck entered the city through one of the gates in the massive wall. It was hot and in the light of the street lamps we could see the citizens seated on chairs fanning themselves on the pavements. Everywhere there were Chinese flags to celebrate victory. Some shops were festooned with lanterns and bunting.

We drove slowly between the crowded pavements. We heard a shout and then more. There was suddenly a great surge toward us from both sides. People ran into the road, blocking our entry into one of the main boulevards. And then the sound of clapping as the crowd recognised us as Westerners, allies, prisoners of the hated Japanese.

The Chinese are not a demonstrative race but our presence must have sent the blood racing through their veins. The clapping grew in intensity. More and more people poured out of the houses and shops to swell the din. Hands were outstretched to us as the Japanese sentry vainly tried to bully the crowd with shouts. They yelled back at him. Great handfuls of rice were showered on us – a sign of enormous joy.

We felt like heroes. We waved wildly, cheered and shouted. And still, as the lorry slowly forced its way through the crowd, the clapping went on – on and on and on as the news spread of our arrival.

Finally, we reached the hotels. Japanese soldiers pushed back the Chinese and we entered the two buildings. I started work immediately, lugging heavy pots and pans on to one of the large balconies that fronted the main road.

Stripped to the waist we appeared on the balcony. Below us a sea of Chinese faces looking up at us. They clapped incessantly and we raised our arms in acknowledgement.

The gifts started pouring in early next morning. In never-ending relays members of the Chinese community entered the hotel foyer and left there a veritable grocer's shop – Peking roast ducks, golden brown and crispy, chickens cooked a hundred-and-one ways, roast pork, roast goose, spiced ham, pao-tse (steamed buns), sweetmeats and, to the joy of most of the camp who had almost forgotten the taste of alcohol, bottles of Chinese wine, of mao-tai, kaoliang, vodka, Japanese beer and sake.

The liquor started the debauch. Scenes comparable with the wildest of the Roman orgies sent the horrified missionaries amongst us in deputation after deputation to Collar and Wright to demand it to stop. They might just as well have tried to stop the torrent of water rushing down the Yangtse.

What the men wanted was women. There were plenty of

willing females in Peking but they were not allowed in the hotels. There were, however, other ways of securing their entry other than by the front doors.

Bulpin was a big, hefty lad. So were several others. They formed the rope gang, lowering over the high wall surrounding the hotel a long, stout length of manila hemp the end of which was grasped by the waiting girls. The rest was easy.

Up the wall went the girls in droves as Bulpin and crew tugged at the rope. The girls, all Chinese, were carefully lifted down, taken into the hotel and paired off. There was a certain amount of bargaining as not one member of the camp possessed any money, but items of clothing, particularly woollen sweaters and the like, were handed over.

The trouble was that the younger members of the camp and, in particular, the ex-American navy boys couldn't wait to get at it and weren't at all bothered about privacy.

A missionary leaving his room quivered in horror as he tripped over a fat arse going hell for leather over a delicately shaped damsel, head pillowed on a woollen garment and her own pants.

Another 'God-botherer' was forced to step over at least six couples performing in the reception hall.

Not only that but one of our bishops who wanted to take a bath discovered that the tub was occupied by a young man, who had only the previous Sunday read the lesson, and a buxom wench.

Gradually the great build-up of steam subsided and the girls, hugging their great assortment of clothing, left through the front doors, past the wide-eyed Japanese sentries, who grinned and pinched their backsides.

Apart from the missionaries and the religiously inclined it was generally agreed that never had there been such a welcome celebration since Mafeking had been relieved.

Looking back, it seems strange that I did not take part in the orgies. The reason is that though I was still virile and never short of the morning erection I was hypocritically inclined to hide my baser nature from those I wished to impress – the missionaries, for example, or the public-school types who, I thought, might include me among the untouchables.

Early in the afternoon the biggest hand-shaking marathon of all times commenced when three American officers, immaculately garbed, shining like new pins, tall and stalwart, walked in to be saluted by Odera and Honda in the foyer.

The senior man was tall – Major Wheeler. He was the man in charge, the dispenser of authority, the military autocrat who, to our delight, ordered the colonel and Honda to follow him up the stairs.

He led the way followed by two younger officers, one of them dark-haired, brown-eyed and olive-skinned. In the rear were Odera and Honda who was smiling oriental style to cover his embarrassment as his former prisoners watched his humiliation.

There was a mad rush to shake the hands of the Americans as they mounted the stairs. Grinning broadly, patting several of us on our backs, they submitted to the incessant pumping. They were a sight for our camp-bleared eyes – the first of our combatants we had met since Pearl Harbour. Their presence brought universal joy. They had fought the war for us and had won. They were there to free us. They were the bosses now – not the Japanese.

In the main dining hall upstairs the three Americans took seats at a table facing Odera and Honda for whom there were no chairs. We loved it. We crowded into the room to see what was going to happen. The tall colonel started the proceedings by questioning Odera in English. Honda translated.

Odera, hemmed in by us, started to bluster and then to order us to leave the room. He was cut short by the American officer.

Sternly, looking straight at Odera, Major Wheeler said, 'I am in charge here. I give the orders. These men may remain.'

As we cheered Honda translated and the colonel, his shoulders sagging, face revealing the humiliation of his position, nodded his head in abject submission.

This was an interrogation of the two officers – not a third-degree ordeal on the Japanese pattern but strict enough for all that with the American officer making it plain that he wanted straight answers, no lies, no hiding of the facts.

It was rumoured that somewhere in Peking the Japanese were holding several Americans among whom were the survivors of the air raid on Tokyo early in the war carried out by planes under the command of General James Doolittle.

Some of the planes had crash-landed in Chinese territory occupied by the Japanese and the survivors had been summarily executed by the Japanese. Some, so it was reported, had escaped death but had been savagely tortured and were now languishing in a Japanese prison.

The Americans were determined to discover the whereabouts of any of their men, or allied nationals, still being held by the Japanese who, it was feared, would kill them and dispose of their bodies to avoid exposure.

Gradually, Major Wheeler wormed the truth from the colonel.

There were several Americans being held in Peking prison. It was fairly certain they would need intensive hospital treatment.

Dr Sturton was called in. The American flair for all-embracing organisational cover was displayed in a series of short, sharp sentences from the American colonel whose agile brain had foreseen all the contingencies he was likely to face.

The doctor would take charge of a makeshift hospital to be located in the Peking Hotel. A Japanese army truck would be requisitioned and manned by younger members of our camp to bring out stretcher cases if there were any from the prison. In the meantime, our problems would have to be discussed later when the most urgent matters had been successfully dealt with. The time had come for action. We would help Sturton and his assistants to fix up the hospital. Then we would wait at the hotel for his orders. A liaison officer from his team would remain with us.

From the liaison officer I learned that he was one of the seven parachutists whom we had seen dropping over Peking. He was a young Greek-American, whose fluency in the language of his parents made him the idol of the native-born Greeks in the camp.

I was astounded to learn that these seven Americans, armed only with revolvers, had dropped a few hours after the Japanese surrender on the Japanese fighter airport outside the city to take over the entire North China region in the name of the United States and their allies, the Chinese – an astute, but dangerous, move to foil any Soviet attempt to move an army down through Kalgan from Manchuria and to prevent an attempted take-over by the Chinese Communists backed by the Russians.

The danger was that the Japanese were unpredictable and could easily have slaughtered every man once they came into the range of machine-gun or rifle fire. Each man in the team had known this – but nothing would have stopped them from taking on the mission. Not one of them had done a parachute course so if they did manage to find the Japanese friendly there was always the chance of injury on landing.

I asked the young officer what his thoughts had been when he jumped.

'Well,' he said, 'my chief worry was that the Japs would open up on us. Once the 'chute had opened I felt okay but the nearer I got to the ground and saw the Japs watching us at the airport then, brother, I said to myself "What the hell am I doing here?" '

It was one of the bravest acts of the war. The Japanese belief in their own invincibility and the disgrace of the Emperor's surrender had resulted, as the Americans in Free China well knew, of massacres of Allied prisoners and of continued resistance from fanatical suicide squads. There was no way of ascertaining what the reception would be in Peking.

I was on duty in the Peking Hotel hospital at night when the first casualties of Japanese brutality arrived to join the camp sick cases we had carried there.

The first man was an American, young but lined and wrinkled. He had a Spanish or Portuguese name. He was a mental case, his mind a black jungle of imbecilic vapourings caused by unbearable torture. We learned that he had tried to escape from a prison camp. He had been caught. Japanese vengeance, sadistic and savage, had made him a slavering idiot.

We picked up an American naval officer from Wake Island who had been abominably tortured but who had never lost his capacity to defy his captors in defiant retention of every faculty – a brave man who had survived days and days of excruciating agony bound in a leather strait-jacket on which had been poured water so that in the sun, where he lay totally exposed, it would tighten to chest-suffocating intensity.

There was a group – seven or eight – of civilians from Wake Island, every one a mental case. God knows what they had seen or suffered. They could not tell us. Not one was capable of coherent thought. One man, huge in girth he must have been on capture, could only ramble incessantly about his home in Idaho and the great potatoes one day he would gorge himself on when the war was over.

And then they found the men in chains in the rat-infested dungeons of Peking prison. They were suspended by their arms, their bellies enormously swollen by the ravages of beri-beri. My memory is not clear now on how many we rescued – perhaps two or three, maybe more.

I remember helping to lift one of these human skeletons from a truck on to a stretcher.

Weakly, he whispered, 'I'm from Texas. Where you all from?'

These were the survivors of the first air raid on Japan carried out by sixteen small American planes under the command of General James Doolittle on April 18th, 1942. Involved in the operation which was launched from the aircraft carrier *Hornet* were eighty officers and men.

The force of B-25s was supposed to land at Chuchow airfield

247

in Free China after the raid but a series of disastrous events forced several planes to cⁱash-land in Japanese-occupied territory.

Lieut. William G. Farrow's plane landed south of Nanchang where the crew was captured by puppets. Farrow and Corporal C. Spatz were executed. Other members of the crew were imprisoned including Corporal Jacob deShazer.

Another officer, Lieut. Dean Hallmark, was executed. Robert Meder died in prison from maltreatment. Lieut. Chase Neilson was in prison for forty months.

It is likely, on reflection, that two of the men we picked up in Peking were deShazer and Neilson.

Corporal deShazer who, like Neilson, was subjected to inhuman treatment by the Japanese, was a deeply religious man who, in true Christian charity, forgave his captors after the war and became a missionary in Japan.

My frustration showed itself in Peking when a French family named Millereau invited me and two or three others to dinner at their home in San Tiao Hutung to celebrate the defeat of Japan and our release.

The father was French, a long-time resident of Peking. His wife was Chinese. They had three gorgeous daughters including one ravishing beauty, Yolande.

The three girls called at the hotel to pick us up. We walked across a park. Yolande was with me. Innocently, she placed her arm through mine and I could feel her lithe, supple body. That did it. I got a mountain of an erection. As we walked in a group my mind ran through my repertoire of advances. How could I let her know I was as stiff as a ramrod? Now, what move could I make so as to let her hand feel it 'accidentally'? Could I bump into her and press it home? Suppose I just grabbed her little hand and plonked it down there what would she do?

I did nothing. An inner voice told me that not one of the girls was likely to respond with anything else but revulsion. They loved to be in our company – Westerners – after the Japanese had almost denuded the city of European young men in their own social group. They were Catholics. To them the honour of the family was all-important.

I suppose had I stayed in Peking long enough I would have made an attempt to woo Yolande. But within a week of my meeting her I was on my way to Yunnan province, close to the Indo-China border.

An American C-47 cargo plane arrived with men and supplies – the forerunner of the airlift of personnel and equipment needed to prepare billets for a large force of battle-hardened marines lifted from the bloody island-hopping campaign in the Pacific.

I met the pilot of the C-47. He gave me an idea. We had been told that transport to get us back to Shanghai would not be available, perhaps, for three months. I was chafing at the bit. I did not relish the thought of kicking my heels in the city, beautiful though it was.

My intention was to land in some place where, with a bit of luck, I might be able to get back to England and start work as a newspaperman again.

I asked the pilot if there was any chance of a 'ride' out of Peking.

'Sure,' he said, 'but you'll be on your own when you get to Kunming. We stop there.'

I had no hesitation.

'I'll take the risk,' I said. 'When do we start?'

'We'll pick you up in the truck at seven tomorrow morning. Travel light. We've got one or two other passengers.'

I said farewell to my bug-ridden camp bed. I made a pile of my blankets and eiderdown, threadbare and filthy, my old camp working clothes and other possessions which I could not possibly have taken with me. I made a bonfire and watched them disintegrate.

I had one good brown suit, a decent shirt and a tie which I had carefully kept for my release. I looked fairly presentable when I boarded the truck the following morning. A crowd of my camp friends gathered to see me off. I felt sad to leave them and there was a lump in my throat when Albon, the bugler, blew a fanfare as the truck started on its journey to the airport.

It was my first flight and I enjoyed every minute of it. particularly the generosity of the crew who showered on me and the other passengers cigarettes, chocolates, sweets and as many boxes of K rations as we wanted.

One of my fellow passengers was Dr J. Leighton Stuart, released from internment at Weihsien, near Peking. He was principal of Yenching University, an American missionary college. A short time later he was to become the American ambassador in China.

We touched down on the vast runway at Kunming built by the Americans using Chinese labour, including thousands of women coolies whom we saw breaking stones.

No sooner had I stepped out of the plane than I was surrounded by a large crowd of American officers and enlisted men who patted me on the back and quickly made it known that I was to be their guest.

Our first call was at the mess for breakfast – as many fried eggs as we wanted, bacon, waffles and maple syrup, coffee ... and Atebrin tablets, the latest antidote against malaria.

From there to the quartermaster's store where a short, fat enlisted man heaped on me a G.I. uniform, including raincoat, boots and underwear.

I protested that I was not American and that, in any case, I did not need so many items of clothing.

'The war's over, brother,' he said. 'Nobody else wants it. Take it. Why waste it?'

We were then taken to the airfield hospital where we found that we had been allocated beds. I looked the American nurses over. One of them was in the Jane Russell category. I wondered if there would be any chance of inducing one, or more, of them to be cooperative but I had my doubts. Friendly they were – but they looked so damnably efficient, so medically dedicated, that I wondered if sex played any part in their lives.

On each bed was a Red Cross package, a brand new safety razor, a packet of blades, chewing gum and cigarettes. A card contained the message: 'With the compliments of the American Red Cross Club. Happy landing.'

I was touched – even more so when a woman in Red Cross uniform handed each of us another card which would permit us, free of charge, to use the facilities of the Red Cross Club in the town, including the restaurant.

I was somewhat disappointed when the Jane Russell among the nurses was not the one on night duty in our ward. Nevertheless, the duty nurse was young and attractive enough. In the next bed to me was Leighton Stuart. He prayed on his knees before he pulled back the mosquito net and tucked himself in.

'Good night,' he said, looking at me from inside the screen. 'Sleep well.'

'Goodnight, Sir,' I replied, 'I'm sure I will. What a day it's been.'

'It has,' he said. 'Thank the Lord.'

I was wearing hospital pyjamas and there was quite a gap at the fly-front. It gave me an idea.

The nurse turned down the lights in the ward and sat herself down at a table at one end of the room. From the bed, through the mosquito net, I could see her crossed legs – shapely, enticing in nylon-clad symmetry.

After about an hour, she rose and took hold of a torch. She visited each bed in the room and, shining the torch through the netting, looked at the occupant.

When she came to me I pretended to be fast asleep. I was lying on my side, eyes firmly closed, breathing heavily. I heard the click of the torch and then another click as she switched it off. I reckoned she would be around again in another hour. I made my preparations.

The next time she approached my bed I was flat on my back with my legs spreadeagled over the top of the bedclothes which, I hoped she would believe, I had kicked down the bed during sleep. The fly-gap in my pyjamas was wide open. Jutting from the gap was my penis, thick, taut and over-sized. My eyes were closed. I pretended to snore softly. I could feel my rod jerking as I heard her reach the side of the bed.

I heard the click of the torch. Just one. She hadn't switched off the light. I daren't open my eyes. For several seconds nothing happened and then the bed was shaken. I pretended to wake up with a start.

As I opened my eyes I could see the beam of the torch focused on my pyjama fly-front. Then the beam moved up to my face. A voice, soft and husky, spoke:

'Young man, cover your tummy. You'll catch a chill. It's dangerous.'

There was a click and the light went out. I couldn't see the nurse's face. I bet she was smiling.

I covered up and went to sleep.

After about five days in the hospital I was taken to a rest camp up in the hills overlooking the town. The place was filled with convalescent cases from the campaign in the Pacific, in the China and Burma theatres. Many of them used crutches. Others limped around with the aid of stout walking-sticks. Most of them had been wounded but there were some who had gone down with malaria, dysentery, typhoid and other diseases.

I was given a room to myself, a small cubicle in the centre of a long row of similar cabins. The air was crisp and fresh. There was greenery everywhere outside the buildings – beautifully kept lawns, tall trees and flower-beds.

From time to time I ventured into town and found Kunming, high in the hills, an invigorating and attractive place. Opium was its chief commodity. The poppy flourished everywhere and the provincial governor, Lung Yun, who ran his own private army, had made a massive fortune out of the drug which was openly smoked everywhere.

Even young boys and girls could be seen on the streets smoking the opium dross left over from the divans. No matter that the Nationalist government had made use of opium illegal; Lung Yun, who was virtually emperor of Yunnan, was far too powerful to be challenged by Chiang Kai-shek. And, if the truth was to be told, there were not many Nationalist officials who did not use the drug.

Early one morning a whirlwind blew into the rest camp in the form of Major George Jacks of the British Army, in civilian life a Hong Kong businessman.

Jacks was a short, stocky chap, moustached, powerfully shouldered and full of the old-boy, old-chap, my-dear-fellow vocabulary of the British commissioned man.

He told me that he was going to take me over. I was British and, as such, could no longer enjoy American hospitality. If I would gather my belongings and dump them in his jeep then he would transport me to the British Consulate in the city, where I would be taken care of.

I said my farewells to my American friends and joined Jacks in the jeep, which he drove along mud roads, through paddy fields, up hill and down dale at such a violent speed that I was as near to a heart attack as I have ever been – absolutely petrified as the vehicle skidded, jumped, slewed, screeched and rocked for miles until the consulate buildings came in sight.

I made a vow that if George Jacks were the driver then I would never travel in another motor vehicle.

The consulate provided enough evidence to show that we were, indeed, the poor relations of the Americans in China.

Food was rationed, for supplies never arrived regularly and there was margarine instead of butter. The everyday filler was porridge with some bacon now and then.

I was given a camp bed and quartered in an office room outside which was the veranda fronting the entire length of the building.

I started to help the overworked staff by typing letters and reports for them. This they appreciated, for the building was continually besieged by Overseas Chinese from Hong Kong, Malaya, Borneo, Singapore and Burma trying to get back home after spending the war years in China.

Among the colonial subjects were many pretty girls.

There was one girl in particular who took my fancy, chiefly

because she was so tall. She was about five feet eight and her legs were long and slender. She had the patience of Job, waiting hours on end on the verandah outside my room for the opportunity to press her case for repatriation, via Hong Kong, to Penang where her family lived.

She spoke good English and one afternoon I invited her in to escape from the blistering-hot sunshine which, day after day, she endured in her mission to shake the dust of China from her feet.

She thought I was a British consular official. I told her that I was not, that I was in the same boat as she – a reluctant lodger at the consulate waiting for some miracle to happen so that I might find myself in the middle of Piccadilly Circus or, better still, in the bar at The Bell in Fleet Street.

She sat on a high-backed chair, crossed her long legs and exposed a tantalising expanse of stockinged thigh, smooth, silky, seductive. She told me her story.

She was an Overseas Chinese with dual nationality. Her family had sent her to Nanking to continue her studies. She had fled with thousands of other students from the Japanese to Free China. She had been in Chengtu and Chungking and was now working for the Americans in Kunming as a translator. She was twenty-five and had not seen her family since 1938. She was desperate to get back home.

My eyes were glued on her legs. She noticed that my gaze never wavered from her thighs and she attempted to pull her cheongsam down.

'Please don't do that,' I pleaded. 'You have lovely legs.'

I launched into a heartrending tale of camp life without the sight of women, of the frustration, of the longing for feminine company.

It was a good ploy. I was excusing my lecherous behaviour by blaming camp celibacy, draping myself in a cloak of hypocrisy – inviting her to believe that I was a decent young man normally but that long isolation from women and her beautiful figure had triggered off a sensual explosion within me.

She smiled and said that she understood. She added that she was sorry for me, that my suffering in camp must have been unbearable.

I put on one of my best histrionic performances and, near to tears, stammered that I only wanted to forget the torture I had been through.

'You poor thing,' she murmured, lifting one leg high so that stocking-top and bare flesh were visible.

I pretended to be overcome by a tidal wave of passion. Her eyes were riveted on me. She followed my every move. I could read her mind. Here with this European she could learn what a man was likely to do if he was excited sexually by a woman. She was the exciter. She was enjoying her power to make me lose self-control.

I sighed loudly and squirmed in my seat.

'Gosh,' I said, 'you are beautiful. You have lovely legs. I'm excited. I can't control myself.'

I took a quick look outside. There was a group of Chinese at the other end of the verandah. They didn't look as if they would be coming my way.

The girl had not changed position. Her leg was lifted high and she had clasped her hands on her knee to take its weight. She was cooperative.

'What do men like in a girl?' she asked. 'I know they like legs. What else?'

'Well,' I replied, 'I like to see a girl's breasts. Some men like buttocks. Some like to see a girl's underwear. Some like hair. There are many things.'

As I spoke my hand drifted down to my flies and I began stroking the bulge there. Her eyes followed every movement.

'Please excuse me,' I said hoarsely. I was really excited. 'I can't help it. I am too excited.'

'It's all right. I understand.'

That was it. She was willing me to go on. My hand was going faster over my fly-front. I had a rock-hard erection. She moved her legs, stretched them out in front of her. Her dress was high. She had lovely, long, slim limbs. She held her cheongsam and kept it high over her thighs.

I groped for the buttons, undid them and brought out my penis.

I watched her eyes. They opened wider. Her mouth opened. Her gaze never left my rod, taking in its shape, its length, its thickness . . . every detail as I moved my hand over it.

'Show me your legs! Show me more!' I exclaimed.

She lifted her dress higher so that I could see the 'V' between her thighs.

My hand went faster and faster. I groaned and jumped. I thrust legs apart and the semen gushed in deliciously body-shaking spurts to the floor.

My passion deflated I became extremely self-conscious. I apologised profusely for my action.

254

'I don't mind,' she said. 'It's natural. You have suffered a lot.'

I got a piece of paper and wiped the floor. It left marks but who would know what the cause had been?

'How would you like a cup of tea?' I said. 'Don't go yet.'

I went along the verandah to the living quarters, put a kettle on and brewed up. I carried the tea, cups and saucers, sugar and milk to my room where she sat still on the high-backed chair. But her dress was pulled down. I had a packet of biscuits which I had brought from the American rest camp. I opened them.

We sat and talked for about an hour. She asked me about life in camp. I laid it on thick and heavy. She told me how homesick she was and asked me if I could possibly help her to get some form of transport down to Hong Kong. I said I would try. I asked her to drop in on me every time she came to the consulate. Then we parted.

As she left I apologised once more for my actions.

'I'm glad,' she said. 'I wanted to help you. I know how you feel.'

The Penang girl paid regular visits and I wooed her with cups of tea and biscuits – not the rationed British tea-leaves but a bag-full I had obtained from the American commissariat as a free gift from a corporal who told me his dad had been born in Liverpool.

I could see that she was eager to indulge in some form of sexual play. One day she arrived carefully made up and she took every opportunity to show me her lovely legs. I would have been a complete clot had I not encouraged her.

She was honest. She told me that she was a virgin and would be until she got married. She didn't mind being kissed and cuddled but she could not let me have my way with her. It all sounded so naive, which, indeed, it was. I played along with her – told her that her presence excited me, made me desire her, encouraged me to embrace her but that I would always respect her wishes. She had no need to fear me.

I got her by the typewriter table, pulled her toward me and kissed her. When my hand slid up to her breasts she pulled back.

'Don't do that,' she said. 'I don't like it.'

It didn't worry me that much. There was not much to grab hold of.

So I just pulled her to me again and planted my lips on hers. She responded and pressed her body into mine. She wanted to feel my hardness. I brushed my taut rod against her.

I got hold of her arm and guided her hand down to my fly-front. She did not resist.

255

I placed her hand over my penis. She kept it there. Her fingers moved so that she could feel it, test its thickness and its length. As she moved I sighed and shivered. She looked at me curiously. She continued to let her fingers roam up and down the front of my trousers, thin, summery, American-army issue. I could wait no longer.

I opened the fly-front, drew it out and immediately placed her hand round it. She gasped, moaned and shivered violently. She was excited, that was certain. I drew her in and kissed her, my hand roaming up and down her back from buttocks to shoulders.

'Move your hand,' I gasped. 'Move your hand. Hold it tight.'

She did. Up and down her hand went in slow, sinuous rhythm. She pushed me to one side so that her eyes could follow the movements. Her head was lowered, her gaze constantly on the weapon which jerked spasmodically as she reached the tip and then retreated.

With a great gasp I started shuddering. The sperm flew out. Still she held me and still her hand moved. But it was all over. I grabbed her hand and held it.

I did a quick mopping up operation and then burst out laughing.

My hilarity was contagious. She started to laugh and in a few seconds we were literally rolling about, holding our sides, the tears just streaming down my face.

That was the last time I saw her. Whether or not she ever reached Penang I do not know. On the following day I was destined to meet a man who changed my plans completely and whose friendship I shall always value.

I met him on the consulate verandah. He was a light-haired, well-built Englishman, broad-shouldered and tall. He introduced himself as Harry Martin of the British Ministry of Information in Kunming. I told him that I was a newspaperman and he told me that he, too, was a journalist – a Fleet Street man seconded to the MOI for duty in China.

I aksed him what paper he had been on. Several, he said, but the last one had been the *Daily Mail*. I told him my history and he listened intently.

For a few moments he was silent. Then he spoke: 'What are you going to do?'

'I want to get back to England,' I said. 'I'll have a go at getting a job in Fleet Street. My China experience should stand me well.'

'Well,' he said, 'they're looking for an editor up in Chungking. Strikes me you're just the man for the job. You know China well. You can't go wrong. Are you interested?'

He explained that the headquarters of the MOI were in Chungking, where an Australian, Stanley Smith, ran a large organisation which distributed news to the Chinese press, compiled a daily bulletin of news, maintained liaison with the Chinese government, educational institutions and the like, broadcast regularly over the government radio station, supervised the work of British Council staff and performed a hundred-and-one other tasks to maintain British influence in China.

My job, he said, would be to edit the bulletin and take charge of the news side of the operation.

I told him I was interested. If the job was going then I would like a shot at getting it.

'Right,' he said, 'I'll get on the blower to Stanley Smith right away. I'll let you know.'

Martin did not waste time. The following day he told me it was all arranged. Smith was interested. I would be flown up to Chungking by the RAF and I'd be met at the airport by an MOI representative.

I was met at Chungking by a station wagon sent from the MOI headquarters in the charge of a China-born Briton, Harry Crosland, dark-haired, moustached and, I was glad to discover, a real pre-war Shanghailander.

Crosland was the transport man. He spoke many dialects of Chinese, had a Chinese girl-friend whom he later married, had been tried and tested on the Burma road and was as tough as they came in a region where strength and stamina often meant the difference between death and survival.

The last time I saw Harry he was directing the morning streams of workbound humanity across the Star Ferry in Hong Kong in the blue uniform of a ferry company inspector.

Crosland told me that he would be taking me to meet Stanley Smith. He looked me over carefully. I had on my brown suit.

'Nice suit,' he said. 'That's a bit of Shanghai tailoring.'

Final Fling

I was an instant success with Stanley Smith, a tall, fair-haired Australian who received me at the headquarters of the Ministry of Information near the British Embassy compound. He operated from a room in a large Chinese house which was being used as a hostel for MOI employees.

I found Smith a genial host, who plied me with questions about my imprisonment and career as a newspaperman in China. He was a man of quick decisions, a shrewd advertising agency man who knew all there was to know about publicity.

He told me that I was the second fattest ex-prisoner he had seen and that his fears about my health had dissipated as soon as he had seen me walk into his sanctum. I would be all right. The job was mine. I would be preparing the daily news bulletin down at Chung Hwa road, reading the English news each evening for the government radio station, XGOY, preparing a weekly English radio feature over the same station -- and, in general, keeping the Chinese pressmen happy and pro-British.

Smith introduced me to a trim, petite Chinese girl, May Wong, who, he said, would fix me up with accommodation for the night in temporary quarters pending my assignment to a less-crowded hostel. She was shapely and I liked the look of her legs. She had had a college education and, like many other patriotic Chinese, had fled from the excesses of the Japanese army in occupied territory.

Lunch was a bit of a problem. I sat with all the hostel employees and Smith at a large table in the spacious dining hall and, for the first time for three years, was served waiter-style by a white-clad Chinese boy. There was still the urge to grab everything eatable on the table and it took all my will power to keep my hands on my lap.

There were several English girls with us, but my eyes were on May Wong and several other Chinese girls whose trim figures and legginess I found more stimulating.

Among the men was Jack Crawshaw, dark-haired, moustached and suave, who told me that he was a native of Keighley, Yorkshire, though he had been working as art editor on the *Sunday Mirror* for many years. There was little of the dour Yorkshireman in his demeanour. Long years in London had given him a man-about-town polish and there was scant trace of the broad vowels of the moors and dales in his speech. I liked his jovial approach to life.

Jack was the cause of my Chungking downfall, though I must admit his intentions had been hospitably honest. He suggested that as he and I had much in common with Keighley, we should visit the Royal Air Force officers' mess and 'meet the lads'.

Disaster struck quickly. For the first time in my life I was afflicted by Cal Hirsh's muscular inertia – a sort of paralysis that crept up on you and laid you low gracefully in a ballet-like slide from whatever you were sitting on so that you reposed on the floor in wide-eyed stupefaction, unable to move a muscle, yet capable of sight and comprehension.

The cause was a local spirit brew called Hunter's gin, delivered round and about in large stone bottles similar to the old ginger-beer containers back home. The brewer, so I was told, was a Russian named Molotov and while he did not claim to have invented the 'cocktail', I had little doubt that his explosive product would have been just as lethal had it been lobbed undiluted into the Hun hordes.

Imported liquor was almost unobtainable. Scotch whisky, brandy, gin – even beer – were in such short supply that a bottle of John Haig could be sold for an astronomical price. War supplies, flown in over the Himalayas, had precedence. No wonder that the chaps I met in Chungking were afflicted with gargantuan thirsts.

The only safe way to drink Hunter's gin was to dilute it with canned fruit juices. Taken neat, the stuff would have skinned you alive. Crawshaw was used to it. So were the Air Force boys. I was not.

The first glass, handed to me by Squadron Leader 'Tubby' Wills, was liberally topped up with orange juice. Foolishly, I downed the contents in one gulp and went into a foaming fit, breathing fire and brimstone through a mouth that felt like the firebox of the Royal Scot on the express run from Euston to Glasgow.

It seemed I was the guinea pig. I'd been away from liquor since 1942 – serious drinking, that is – and they wanted to see what Mr Molotov's infamous concoction produced in me. Madness. Mayhem. Or Melancholia.

The evening was uproarious. As the gin released my inhibitions, I lapsed into broad Yorkshire and Crawshaw and I did our 'slaughterhouse act', quite off the cuff, bawling at each other across the table as the RAF types rolled in the aisles.

I was Enoch. Jack was Albert. We were two abattoir employees about to slaughter a bullock. We were using methods of which the Royal Society for the Prevention of Cruelty to Animals would have disapproved.

"Od t'bugger dahn while Ah take a swipe at 'im,' I yelled, indicating that I was the chap about to swing the poleaxe.

"Ave yer got t'bucket fer t'blud, Albert?'

'Eeeh, bah goom, mind 'is bollocks,' yells Jack alias Albert. 'Bollocks?' I yell.

'Yer daft bugger, bullocks don't 'ave bollocks.'

'Ooh 'eck,' yells Albert. 'Ah'll tell thee, Enoch lad, then this bugger's getten a couple o' lovely boils right by 'is arse.'

And so on until, finally, the poor animal is despatched, skinned, chopped and delivered 'ter t'butchers at back o' t'fuckin' tramsheds'.

It was about 11 p.m. that I was smitten by Cal Hirsh's muscular inertia. Several strong men delivered me to the hostel and dumped me in a temporary bedroom in one of the offices in the courtyard.

After breakfast the next morning, Smith called me aside and asked me to wait for him while he cleaned up some papers in his room. He had a large American car, and we drove downtown in it for general introductions to all and sundry in the offices.

I met a Tamil-Ceylonese, J.P.S. Rajasooria, who had previously been editing the bulletin, Jock Murray of the *Daily Mirror*, P. A. (Pan) North, a full-time consular official who looked after all the accounts, Jimmy Yapp, a South African Chinese, Harry Crosland, an Anglo-Burmese named Lubeck, recently arrived from the Chengtu office, and a bevy of Chinese and Eurasian girls in the typing pool whom I weighed up carefully and to whom I gave full marks for attractiveness.

Rajasooria took charge of me. He was extremely friendly and he guided me through the intricacies of preparing the bulletin and of sending news items from Britain to the Chinese Press. I caught on quickly and within a day or two I was handling the operation quite successfully.

A room had been found for me at Smith's hostel and there, to my delight, I found a radiogram and some good dance records, the sound of which quickly drew the girls from their rooms. I made a discovery.

They were all mad on ballroom dancing, but although they could shuffle along, they were ignorant of the variations and good ballroom technique. I took my chance to show off.

I did a quickstep with an English girl and found she could follow every step. We had an appreciative audience and it was generally agreed that I was really a good dancer and, as such, a popular newcomer in their midst.

I offered my services all round and took the girls, one by one, through quicksteps, waltzes and foxtrots. May Wong danced quite well and I liked the feel of her. I pressed her close to me. She did not object. I was not lecherous. I never was when I was showing off on the ballroom floor. Lechery would follow.

May told me there was a good cabaret near Chung Hwa road called the International. I suggested a night out dancing and she agreed. What I didn't know was that May was the delight of Smith's eye. He was married and had a wife and family in Australia, but the union was on the rocks. May filled the gap. In fact, she became Mrs Smith and the last I heard of her was that she was living with him in the Bahamas – happy and content and in luxury.

Smith was an astute businessman. After leaving the MOI, he started a business in Hong Kong and within a short time was knee-deep in money. He told a friend of mine in Hong Kong: 'I'm a millionaire in any man's currency.'

In Chungking, however, he had not reached that fortunate position, though he was no pauper. What I had failed to realise was what everyone else knew: that when males are thrown together with females thousands of miles distant from wives and families then the sexual urges operate on both sides to create a condition of cohabitation.

Like a blind man, I sought social enjoyment in May's company at the hostel and though there was never any hint of sensuality between us – not on her side, any way – it was evident to others that I was treading on dangerous ground.

I had one more success with Smith before disaster struck me with the force of a typhoon – and remained with me in whirlwind force until I left the war-time capital to return to Shanghai.

Smith called me at the hostel one evening, very worried. Admiral Lord Fraser was paying an official visit to Chungking and was having dinner that night with Generalissimo Chiang

Kai-shek in the hill fortress outside the city occupied by the Chinese leader and his wife.

Pictures of the great event were needed. This had been overlooked and no arrangements had been made. Our photographers were Chinese and it would be impossible for them to get anywhere near the Generalissimo without passes stamped by an army of officials. Even then there was no guarantee that the guards would permit a photographer of their own race to get anywhere near Chiang.

He asked me if I would get in his chauffeur-driven car with one of our photographers and see to it that we gained access to the dining room and there let the flash-bulbs pop to record the event for posterity.

I jumped at the chance. I had never seen the Generalissimo or his wife. The driver was nervous. So was the photographer. They assured me that we would not get beyond the outer wall – if even we landed the car there. The entire road leading from the city outskirts to the retreat contained practically the entire Chinese army. They were sure to turn us back without passes.

I said we'd have to risk it and told the driver to press on regardless (a war-time phrase I had just picked up).

Progress was slow. Every fifty yards or so a gun-toting, bullet-loaded soldier or policeman waved us down. I had in my pocket an old Royal Army Service Corps weekend pass and each time one of the villainous-looking guards stopped us I flashed the piece of paper, pointing to the official stamp under the signature of my old C.O. At the same time I told the photographer to explain that I was a representative of the Lord High Admiral who was at that very moment the honoured guest of the great and exalted Chinese leader. And, by the beard of the ancient and much revered Confucius, the 'Gissimo' would certainly have his bloody guts for garters if I was not permitted to join the salty one within a matter of minutes.

The old official stamp did it. There was no more potent dooropener in China then than the chop – the Chinese equivalent of the rubber stamp. A businessman carried his own chop. So did officials. You could see them everywhere unloading the chops – in wood, ivory, jade or other delicately carved product – from some inner recess in their gowns along with the padded ink container. One press, one quick contact with the paper and there was the chop, usually in brilliant red.

Mine was sombre black, but it did the trick. I was waved on – and on and on and on – until we reached the massive wall of the fortress high up in the hills. There a colonel, armed with revolver in holster, came out from a guardhouse to look us over. He saw me and addressed me in impeccable American.

He was tall and lean and wiry. His uniform was spotless and he shone like a new pin – a change from the uniformed hoboes who had been impeding our progress for ten miles or so. I told him I was from the British Embassy and could we be permitted to enter the house to take a few pictures of the Generalissimo and Lord Fraser at dinner.

He politely invited us to wait in the guardhouse while he went inside to see what could be done. I gave him my name and said he could confirm the object of my mission from Stanley Smith down at the hostel. He didn't seem to be worried and left us.

After ten minutes or so he returned and said we could enter the house. He accompanied us and, deferentially, led us into an ornately decorated dining hall where at the head of a large table sat Chiang Kai-shek. On his right was Admiral Lord Fraser. On his left sat Madame Chiang, slim, beautifully made up – a most attractive woman.

I looked at the trim military figure of the Generalissimo. He was in uniform and his chest was loaded with decorations. He was then in his fifties, eagle-eyed and vigorous, small in stature but authoritatively impressive.

He was engaged in animated conversation with Lord Fraser, who was in uniform, and Madame Chiang was acting as interpreter for the Generalissimo could not speak English. As we moved round the table he broke off talking for a few moments and looked at me. I bowed. He smiled a welcome afid dropped his head forward in acknowledgement of my greeting. Then he returned to the subject of his discussion with the admiral.

A party was in full swing in the grounds of the British Embassy when I returned to report that my mission had been completed successfully. Smith, in jovial mood, drink in hand, patted me on the back vigorously and made it known that for a man who had been a prisoner of the Japs only a few weeks back I was a corker – a real professional.

From that time onward our relations were doomed to deteriorate. The reason was the aphrodisiacal effect of Hunter's gin, of which I was imbibing gallons weekly. As in Shanghai so it was in Chungking. Alcohol stimulated my testicles, pickled them in lustful juice, directed my thoughts always to legs, tits, bottoms and other parts of the female anatomy so that I was in constant erectional excitement.

When Smith flew over to have a look at conditions in Peking prior to setting up an MOI branch there I ventured with May Wong and several others to the International Cabaret for a night out. We had a pleasant time and I don't think that sex reared its erotic head. Nevertheless, it was a mistake. A short time later I was installed in another hostel with Rajasooria, Lubeck and a most comical character from Manchester, Henry McAleavy, a representative of the British Council fluent in Mandarin Chinese whose bosom companion was a Chinese girl, Jane Chu, with whom he worked and who shared table with us.

These sort of liaisons were commonplace. Crawshaw, for instance, was often in the company of another Chinese girl named Rose. Sadly, she tried to commit suicide when the Fleet Street man returned home after the post-war rundown of the MOI services in China.

So far as the Americans were concerned, their constant association with Chinese girls led to friction with the Chinese student element, who staged violent demonstrations in which jeeps were stoned and several girls were forcibly dragged from the vehicles. Others were warned that they would be punished if they were seen with Americans. Vigilante squads roamed the streets and many girls were publicly degraded for disobeying the call to all Chinese womanhood to avoid association with the 'barbarians' from overseas.

One after the other, I took various Chinese girl members of the MOI staff down to the cabaret where I stoked up with Hunter's gin and soon I earned myself the reputation of a haam shup gwai, literally a salty man, a womaniser. Belly-rubbing was a popular Shanghai cabaret pastime. I introduced it to our hostel parties in Chungking and the news got around that I was a real horny sod who was ready to prod any dancing partner with his gin-pickled cucumber. It was true.

The ladies did not seem to mind. In fact they spread the news around that I was a sexy devil. Inevitably fact was embellished with fiction and it was rumoured among the menfolk that I had the ability to 'make a girl come' if she danced with me. Quite untrue, though I never denied the story.

I got into serious trouble one night when my rampant rod was seen by a British member of the staff unashamedly exposed under a table in the International cabaret. What had happened was that, stimulated to lecherous heights by the gin and the beauty of a cabaret girl with whom I sat, I had whipped it out and placed her hand on it. Astonished by my audacity in a public place she had quickly departed from the scene, but before I could replace John Thomas he had been spotted by the snooper who soon made it known that I was 'a bloody sexual pervert'. Indeed, I wasn't. I was merely over-excited and, perhaps, a little indiscreet.

It was made known to me that this sort of behaviour was not British and that, in future, I had better pay more respect to the flag under which I served.

I almost blotted my copy-book once again after a party given in a restaurant by a cropped-haired former lorry driver, P. C. Shao, who had made a pile of money by operating his own vehicles on the Burma road.

I had toothache and it dampened my spirits considerably. Next to me was a Chinese girl translator, who lived in the Chung Hwa road hostel. She suggested that if I filled my mouth with warm Shaoshing wine and kept it over the tooth it might help. It did. I drank her health gambai fashion – bottoms up. She responded. The wine flowed copiously and the host usually toasted each of his guests in this fashion – no heel taps. The guests responded and then toasted one another similarly. Long before the last course all the guests – men and women – were merrily overboard in alcoholic enjoyment. I loved Chinese parties.

After this particular one we decided to finish off with coffee in the living quarters above the Chung Hwa road offices. The girl entered her room there. I noticed that she staggered somewhat and that she had left her door wide open. I saw her open the top drawer of her dressing table, take out a powder puff and dab it over her face. Then she weaved unsteadily to her bed and flopped out on it.

That rang the bell in my balls. 'Get weaving, you bloody fool. Nip in, lad. She's pissed. She won't scream.' I heeded the tempter within.

In the full view of the assembly I made a beeline for the girl's bedroom, stepped boldly inside and surveyed her recumbent form.

I clambered on the bed, placed my arm over the girl and drew her toward me. I leaned over her and kissed her passionately. She thrust me back.

'Don't,' she said, 'I am repulsive to men.'

She had a complex, a clever girl, not pretty but attractive enough of figure to lure me on. She was devoted to study. Her English was excellent. She believed that men regarded her as a sexless blue stocking. She needed the fire to be lit within her.

'Not true,' I whispered in her ear. 'Every woman is beautiful. You do not repulse me.'

The wine was talking. I was stoked up with sensual dynamite.

I bent over her and kissed her again. This time she responded and my tongue went in and out of her mouth. I fumbled with the fasteners of her cheongsam and laid bare her bosom. Her breasts were small but I noticed the nipples were thick and erect. I placed my mouth over her right nipple and let my tongue rove over it. She shuddered and I pressed my body into hers.

Then I held her hand and guided it to my fly-front. She felt the stiffness there and squeezed strongly. Normally, she would have screamed the place down, but the Shaoshing wine had destroyed all inhibitions so that both of us were threshing all over the bed in the grip of feverish – and drunken – passion.

And all the time the inmates of the hostel and our visitors from the restaurant party watched the performance through the wide-open door of the girl's bedroom.

I didn't rape the girl. Nor did I manage to expose John Thomas in lecherous tumescence. Someone entered the room. I think it was Rajasooria. Whoever it was handled the situation most diplomatically. I remember the words 'Come and have some coffee, old boy.' On reflection it was a typically astute move to get me out of what threatened to be an unholy scrape.

Each morning I drove to the Chung Hwa road office very early to take a shorthand note of the All-India Radio news broadcast. There were two camp beds there for the Chinese radio operators who worked the sets. Poor chaps. Regularly an American army captain and I long before dawn bundled them out of their beds to make room for us and a couple of girls from the cabaret whom we screwed all ways and paid off. As a mark of our appreciation of the willingness of the two Chinese lads to vacate their beds we offered to pay for them to have a session with the girls. We were surprised when the offer was refused.

'They only use it for pissing out of,' said the captain.

Muscular inertia was striking me more and more as every night after my broadcast I visited the cabaret to prop up the bar there along with American and British servicemen, Chinese officers, civilians from all over the world and a varied assortment of cabaret hostesses.

I watched a burly American marine, all biceps and bullshit, down his fifth glass of Hunter's gin neat and then subside like a descending balloon into a grotesque position on the floor from which, eyes staring upward, he regarded us all in speechless para-

266

lysis. We just left him there to recover. A long process. . . .

I was delivered by jeep to my hostel several times to be deposited in the porch like a sack of coal there to repose until life returned to the 'corpse' and bludgeoned muscles gradually regained enough power to carry the body unsteadily to bed. And, on awakening, not one recollection of the previous night's debauch - the mind a complete blank. As an anaesthetic Mr Molotov's fire-water was unbeatable, which was all to the good, for God knows what excesses had been committed under its lecherously drunken influence.

Somewhere in this world – if he's still alive – is a former Nationalist Chinese general who had me for some hours as his bed-companion in a rambling mansion about fourteen miles from Chungking. How the hell I got there I haven't the foggiest idea. I must have met him in the International bar and struck up a bibulous friendship with him. All I can now recollect is that shortly after dawn I awoke in a large bed fully clothed with a great weight on my chest. There pinned neatly across my coat were three rows of medals. Next to me as I gazed blearily through bloodshot eyes I saw a great mountain. I looked again. The mountain gradually assumed the shape of a vast stomach, a huge bladder of lard belonging to a Chinese gentleman of enormous proportions lying flat on his back, snoring stertorously. He was in uniform and the stars he wore indicated that he possessed high rank.

Startled by the discovery that I was not at the hostel I jumped out of bed and made a quick reconnoitre. The bedroom was large and the scrolls on the wall indicated that it was Chinese-occupied. I saw a window through which I looked into a large courtyard. There was a servant woman swilling pans by a pump. She did not see me. I was bursting for a pee. Where the hell was the bathroom? I looked under the bed. No commode.

Then my gaze alighted on a glass water-jug, half-filled, placed on a chest of drawers. I grabbed it quickly for I could not dam the flood much longer, heaved the water out of the window, opened my flies and with a great sigh of relief filled it to the brim. I should have sent its contents after the water. I didn't. I was in such a hurry to leave the place that I placed the container back on the drawers, heaved myself through the window and made my way across the courtyard to an open door leading to the street.

I hope the general when he recovered consciousness did not take a swig from the jug. If he did then all I can offer his family is my sympathy. Potent stuff was Hunter's gin. I also hope he managed to explain the loss of his medals which I carried away as souvenirs.

On another occasion I awoke in darkness early in the morning to find myself sprawled on the cobble-stoned front entrance of the French Embassy. I was horrified to see that I had several companions – huge rats which were gambolling all over me. I jumped up in great alarm. They were not pink in colour. They were real enough. If ever there was a city that required a Pied Piper it was Chungking. The place was lousy with rats – millions of them, big and fat, fed on the thousands of corpses left lying around after the fierce Japanese air-raids. As I walked the quarter of a mile or so to the hostel I saw that the streets were literally alive with rats, racing across the road right under my feet. I tucked my trousers in my socks, pulled my coat collar up round my neck and prayed that I'd complete the journey in one piece before this legion of rodents decided to attack me.

Hostel life had its amusing moments. There was Lubeck, who drank mao-tai with every meal, as fiery as Hunter's gin but more refined, and who required a saucer-full of chopped red-hot chillies handy to dip into as others might need peanuts.

Perhaps his diet was the cause of his nightly excursions into the city in search of feminine company. He made no bones about it. Night after night he returned with women – usually Chinese – and accommodated them in his room where he proceeded to let off steam. And boiling hot it must have been fired as it was with his daily dose of chillies. His performances, though I never saw one, were often watched by McAleavy and another British Council Chinese scholar, John Blofeld, both of whom were to make their names as authors. They stood outside his window quietly and were much impressed by his constant success with the female sex.

McAleavy, too, was a source of constant amusement, particularly when he took a great tome in Chinese to the lavatory at about eight o'clock in the morning and stayed there for hours engrossed in the ideographs of a language that sent most Europeans trying to learn it stark, staring bonkers.

At about midday the womenfolk in the hostel were running around in a frenzy. There was only one toilet and the calls of nature, as everyone knows, are more frequently heard by the female sex than males. If there were any burst bladders then McAleavy must shoulder the blame.

Like most professorial types McAleavy had bouts of absentmindedness. He had many friends among the Chinese and they often called on him at the hostel.

We were at dinner one night when three young Chinese in grey gowns dropped in. Henry looked up from his plate and greeted them warmly. He asked them to seat themselves down at the other end of the room where there was a large settee and several big armchairs. They looked perturbed.

A few minutes later five more arrived – three girls and two men – and McAleavy assured them that as soon as he had finished his meal then he'd be with them. Would they please join the others at the other end of the room? They did so. They looked completely nonplussed.

Four more arrived, including two women. McAleavy went through the same routine and smiled blandly at the twelve Chinese seated, silent and morose-looking, on the settee and the chairs.

Suddenly Henry flung down his knife and fork and exclaimed, 'My God, I invited them to dinner!'

He had – several days previously. He had completely forgotten it. They were members of the government theatrical troupe with whom he conversed in fluent Mandarin.

'Mac', as we called him, extended his profuse apologies to his guests, whose stomachs must have been rumbling like thunder. What he said in Chinese I don't know but they seemed happy enough when he led them out of the hospital like a Cook's tour operator to fill up at his – or the Council's – expense at some local restaurant.

His usual top garment was a corduroy windcheater which had a large circular yellow patch on the back. I found out how this had been acquired.

Chungking was renowned for the vagaries of its electricity supply. One minute there would be brilliant illumination and then, suddenly, the light bulbs would flicker and fade to a dim, red glow. On such occasions, which were frequent, we used to turn a knob on a booster and hope for the best. Sometimes we improved the glow. More often than not we didn't. Out came the candles and we lit a dozen of them, or more, to pierce the gloom.

'Mac' was entertaining a group of Chinese students one night when the lights went low. He could hardly see the boys and girls in front of him as he stood with his back to the mantelpiece. In came the number-one boy to light the candles which always reposed on the mantelpiece ready for such an emergency. 'Mac' continued with his discussion.

Suddenly he stopped.

He sniffed the air, nostrils quivering like a bloodhound on the scent.

'Do you smell anything burning?' he asked the students.

They sniffed and said that they did not.

'Mac' went on with his dialogue.

Then disaster. The Mancunian burst into flames. The entire rear portion of his windcheater began to resemble a Sheffield blast furnace.

There was a mad rush by the students, who roughly seized 'Mac', turned him round and commenced walloping his back as if they were beating a dirty carpet.

From that day forth the windcheater carried the yellow patch – a reminder of the disaster that might have been and the bruises that the scholar carried for weeks afterwards following the muscular rescue act of the students.

Those were the days when, officially, the Chinese Communists and the Nationalists had buried the hatchet to present a united front against Japan. There was a large contingent of Communist journalists, men and women, staying in a hostel in downtown Chungking. It was well known that they were carefully watched by Chiang's secret police but this did not deter McAleavy and other Westerners from visiting them openly.

We were invited by the Communists to have dinner with them at their hostel. McAleavy led the party, of which I was a member.

They received us graciously and entertained us with songs and the Yangko dance before we sat down to a splendid meal.

A small chap, who was evidently their leader, addressed us in English and, full of smiles, told us that in our honour he had managed to procure a bottle of 'foreign wine'. He placed it on the table. It was bilious green in colour and when I sipped it I thought it had the taste of boot polish.

When we had all drunk most of it the little chap asked us, again in English, what we thought of the wine.

McAleavy took on the role of spokesman.

Did anyone there speak French, he asked.

There was a general hubbub round the table.

'No,' said the leader, 'we do not know French.'

'No matter,' said 'Mac'. 'The wine . . . it is delicious. It reminds me of my student days at the Sorbonne in Paris when we used to sit at the street cafés and drink a similar wine. It was called Urine de Cheval.'

The Chinese clapped their appreciation of the compliment as I

down to Shanghai as the government moved its seat to Nanking. Bahadur Singh, Rajasooria and several others were flown out by RAF C-47s and I looked forward eagerly to joining them in the city I loved and which I knew so well within a matter of weeks.

In the meantime, I managed to obtain sensual satisfaction from helping two schoolgirl sisters with their biological studies.

Next door to our hostel was a large house, the occupant of which was a Chinese general out somewhere facing the Communists. His wife, a most attractive Chinese woman whom we often invited over to our parties, had set off for her home in Shanghai. She had left behind in the charge of house-servants two daughters, a girl of fifteen and another about a year younger. They were good-looking, bigger built than their mother, more amply breasted and, like all Chinese girls, the possessors of satiny smooth, shapely legs which were amply displayed by the foreign-style dresses they wore.

From somewhere or the other these girls had obtained a microscope – probably purloined by dad on one of his campaigns. Over the garden wall they told me about their acquisition and of their amazement at its magnified revelation of the seething contents of such things as frog-spawn, saliva, skin particles and the like. They couldn't take their eyes from the thing.

They invited me over to have a look at the contraption. It was the real thing, a splendid piece of German workmanship which, on the market, would have cost a fortune.

It gave me an idea. Carefully – very carefully – I extolled its educational value to them. They listened to my every word. This was the sort of machine, I said, that would teach them the facts of life. For instance, if they could obtain the material they could see how babies were made.

What material?

Well, if they would excuse my frankness, a man's sperm, the fluid which inside a woman fertilised the ovum and turned into a baby in the womb.

Oh no, they didn't mind my frankness. They did biology at school (an American mission establishment) and they knew all about pollen and the birds and bees.

Well, I said, pretending to be bashful, I could act as the guinea pig. I was a man. I had sperm. It could be released for microscopical examination.

There was, naturally, some girlish reticence, embarrassed glances and a blush or two but I pressed my case. My object was scientific, I repeated. I wanted to improve their knowledge. As I

273

spoke, the thought of what might be had given me a fine erection.

We talked in their bedroom where there were two single beds and a table in a corner of the room on which stood the microscope under a bright table lamp.

I sat on a chair in front of the table and, as the two girls listened carefully from leg-revealing perches on the beds, I lectured them on the sexual responses of the male. I carefully explained that a man's penis became erect when he was excited and that sperm could only be ejaculated when the penis was big and stiff.

They asked me what made it stiff.

Well, I said, bidding Mr Hyde not to show himself too soon, a woman excited a man. It could be a woman's legs or her breasts – anything. When a man was excited by the look of a female then blood filled his penis. It became big and stiff. It was ready to push into her and disgorge its sperm for the purpose of fertilisation.

I said that, if they were really interested, then I would demonstrate, but that they had better be very circumspect about the event as some people might not understand that it was all being done for educational advancement.

They responded so quickly with an affirmative answer that I suspected it might be sexual precocity rather than educational eagerness. Probably it was a bit of both.

I stood up. I undid my flies and exposed my manhood in full erection. I looked down at it. I looked at the girls. They were wide-eyed, held spellbound by the sight.

I told the girls that they would have a job to do. They jumped up eagerly and I told them to get a piece of paper and hold it steady underneath my rod. This would catch the sperm, I said. They could then spoon some off and put it on the slide.

I commenced to play with the glans, explaining that this was the sensitive part. I wanted one of them, preferably the bigger girl, to hold me but I fancied I'd better be patient. So I rubbed away, fixing my gaze on the big girl's legs. She noticed where my gaze was fixed and shuffled forward so that she was very close to me. They held the paper steady by its four corners and kept it steady under my jerking rod. Their eyes never left it.

Suddenly I got that wonderful feeling of imminent ejaculation. Out it came in great spurts to drop on the paper.

'Ai yah!' exclaimed the big sister. She looked at the younger girl. They seemed to be in a trance.

'Catch it all,' I shouted. 'Catch it all.'

They bent down and made great play of holding the paper steady as I shook off the final drops.

'Now get a spoon or something and put it on the slide,' I said. 'You'll see what sperm really is.'

The big girl got a matchstick and a glass slide. Carefully she scraped off some sperm and smeared it on the slide. She flicked on the table light.

Excitedly she placed the slide in the microscope, glued her eye to it and peered as she twisted the gadgets that brought the specimen into magnified focus.

Her sister was too impatient to wait. She tugged at the big girl's sleeve.

'Let me have a look. Let me have a look,' she said excitedly.

In the meantime I was wiping off, buttoning up and, bereft of lustful liquid, cursing myself for being a bloody fool with these two adolescents.

Evidently what they saw on the slide satisfied them, kept them in a state of joyful exuberance and angry exchanges as first one and then the other pulled and tugged in order to get an eye fixed on my contribution to their education.

Finally, the big girl asked me to have a look.

I put my eye to the contraption and looked down. Either it was out of focus or I was going blind. I saw nothing except a sheet of glass reflecting the light of the lamp. They assured me that there was sperm to be seen and wonderful it was. I peered again and tried to manipulate the focusing screws. I did get a glimpse of minute worms wriggling and then all was lost again. I was no scientist. Anyway, I didn't care. I'd got rid of my steam. I wanted to get back to the hostel.

There followed four more 'laboratory' sessions. The girls seemed always to be in the garden with their eyes on my side of the low wall. I had no doubt they were looking for me in the hope that I'd again produce the slide specimen – or, rather, as I certainly realised, whet their sexual curiosity by exposing my rigid rod in front of them.

The slide and the paper and the microscope formed the excuse. We played the game of pretence. It made the whole experience far more exciting.

After some persuasion I got both girls to feel me. Their fingers savoured thickness and length. They just loved it. I got the big girl to masturbate me while the younger one held the paper underneath.

Then, on another occasion, they would change places and the

275

small edition would rub away to produce, with gasps of delight, the seminal fluid.

And then out came a confession. Mine wasn't the first erect penis they'd seen. Right opposite their bedroom window was a long, narrow window belonging to a room in our hostel. I looked out and saw that it was part of the toilet. I had never noticed it before – at least from my present position.

Daily, or almost daily, they told me, they had watched a European lift up the lower window and handle himself. They couldn't tell who it had been for the upper part of his body had not been visible.

Our next-door neighbours vanished from the Chungking scene after the arrival of the father, who had been posted to Nanking. This meant that the girls would join their mother in Shanghai, where the family originally came from, and attend school there. I never met them again. I wonder if they managed to milk some other male down there in the interest of biological research.

I was walking down one of Chungking's many hillside streets a few days later when, in the distance, I saw a stocky, broad-shouldered man in American officer's uniform approaching me. The gait was familiar. And, as he drew nearer, a great surge of excitement swept through me. There was no mistaking that face. Of all people it was Arnold Milton Kiehn, Henningsen's 'grizzly bear', my friend from the camp.

Arnold, immaculate in his uniform, did not at first notice me. His eyes were elsewhere.

'Kiotsuke!' I yelled.

'Bango!'

He hadn't forgotten his camp Japanese. He swivelled his gaze to me and a broad smile swept over his features. We shook hands warmly. He asked what the heck I was doing in Chung-king. I told him and enquired about his movements. It was a re-union that changed the pattern of my life.

For an hour or so I chatted with him in his room at the Victory Hotel. We were excited, for there was a commond bond of affection between us. He told me that he was going down to Shanghai to start his business there again.

'How would you like to join me, Ralph?' he asked. 'I need somebody I can trust.'

'Doing what?' I enquired. 'I'm a newspaperman, not a business-man.'

Arnold smiled.

'What does that matter? You can always learn – and you'll make more money. Think it over. Just let me know and the job's yours.'

We left it at that. My idea was to continue in the MOI and stick to journalism. The pay was good in sterling. There were many fringe benefits.

Within a few days Arnold had departed for Shanghai, but before he left he showed me the lining of a couple of his uniform jackets. There appeared to be a great amount of padding. There was – stacks and stacks of dollar notes of various denominations. He was a walking bank. All the notes were neatly sewn in. I could have retired on those two coats. It showed me that Arnold trusted me, regarded me as a true friend. He was up to his old currency-smuggling tricks again. Ah well, good luck to him. He had guts. I remembered the loaded deck-chair in the camp and his coolness during the Japanese examination of the repatriates' baggage.

One month later Stanley Smith called me into his room at the hostel. He was nervous. He seemed to be unable to find words to express himself. Eventually he got it out. The war was over and they were cutting down the MOI operation in China. I was the newest recruit and, regretfully, there would be no place for me in the streamlined office they would be running in Shanghai. Eventually, the entire MOI set-up would be closed.

I did not quibble. There was Arnold Kiehn's offer. I would take him up on it.

I sent a telegram to Kiehn in Shanghai. His reply thrilled me: 'Delighted. See you in Shanghai.'

Everything was quickly arranged. I flew down by Royal Air Force to Kiangwan and from there was driven to the new MOI office in Shanghai located in the vast Jardine Matheson building on the Bund.

From there a fairly short walk to Hamilton House where Arnold had a private, air-conditioned office on the ground floor. We drank coffee over at the Metropole Hotel and discussed, over cream cakes, my prospects. First of all, there was salary. How would five hundred American dollars a month suit me? I gasped. It was more than I was getting from the British government and there was no doubt that the Almighty Dollar was, at that time, the mightiest weapon in the world, far more powerful than the shaky pound, which was soon to be devalued.

I accepted without demur.

What about accommodation?

Well, I had nowhere to go but that didn't worry me.

In that case, Arnold said, I had better reside in one of his apartments. He had a place, small – living room-bedroom combined, kitchen and bathroom and storeroom – in Clements Apartments in Rue Lafayette. That could be mine. Naturally, I'd pay the rent which wasn't much.

What about the job?

He was vague on details. His idea was that I would be his trusted henchman, a sort of personal assistant to whom he could delegate confidential matters.

It was good to be back in Shanghai. It was still the greatest city in the Far East, apart from Tokyo. Hong Kong was still the same old sleepy, colonial outpost it had been when I had first seen it in 1937. Its phenomenal growth into the sky-scrapered metropolis it is today was then a few years off. Shanghai, for me, was the only Mecca.

Today, if you asked me what was Kiehn's business I would have to reply honestly that I don't know. He had offices here, there and everywhere and employed a sizeable staff in each office – three in Hamilton House, a large space in the Hong Kong and Shanghai Bank Building and one or two others elsewhere. Nor did I ever find out what my job entailed. I did nothing and got paid for it.

Life was pleasant. The cabarets were still open. I re-visited the Palais and the other Blood Alley joints. The Majestic and the Little Club now catered for civilians but echoes of the old days were provided by the white-clad American sailors who still sought the favours of the Russian 'countesses' back at the tables after the occupation. Jock's Bar, apart from the absence of the Seaforth lechers in their kilts, was no different.

I took an Indian official there one evening and introduced him to the girls whom he fell for in a big way. He took one of them upstairs and mounted her in one of the cubicles. It cost him about four hundred American dollars to rid himself of gonorrhoea – pox doctors charged exorbitant prices. I had penetrated one of my old girl-friends there and had emerged unscathed but I decided I would not take the risk again and gave poor old Jock a wide berth from that time onward.

Arnold lived out in his old home in Hungjao tended by a faithful manservant. He had his polo ponies and his cars – a Buick, several Jeeps, a Dodge, a Chevrolet and a small truck. His wife and son were still in America. I wondered how he was coping with his sexual needs, which, as I well knew, were as powerful as mine.

There were enough females in the city to fulfil even the needs of a regiment of Arab sheikhs. As it was his choice surprised me.

There was living at a large residence in Hungjao complete with swimming pool and tennis courts and spacious grounds an Indian woman, Rajkumari Sumair, reputed to be a member of the family of the Maharajah of Patiala. There was no doubt that she was intensely desirable, lithe as a panther, wide-eyed and beautifully figured. She could have emerged from the pages of the *Kama Sutra* so powerful was her sexual magnetism.

Arnold fell – head over heels. I did not blame him though I felt that Sumair's expensive background, her top-class social breeding and her coterie of exclusive friends, including a young Polish baroness, were far removed from Kiehn's austere missionary background.

Arnold and Sumair lived together although he retained his own Hungjao residence. From that time on it was perpetual party time – dancing, drinks, eats, tuxedos and evening gowns, jewels and diamond shirt-studs at number 555 Hungjao Road, at the Mandarin Club, the Hungaria, Maxims, everywhere where the prices were high and the service ultra-exclusive.

Ambassadors, consuls, high-ranking service officers, rich business tycoons and beautiful girls of many nationalities flocked to the parties which became the high spots of Shanghai's effervescent night life.

I donned white sharkskin tuxedo and danced my best. I drank my fill and thanked my stars that Hunter's gin had not penetrated beyond Szechwan province. I played with Russian, Chinese, Polish, American, British, French and other tits in the soft, warm moonlight by the lake and the sighing trees. I stroked nylon-clad legs in Arnold's jeep while pretending to give sundry females driving lessons. I kissed passionately my dancing partners by the tennis courts. I was handled with varying degrees of enthusiasm by young ladies stoked up on wine and my nipple-tweaking. Life was grand. Joy abounded everywhere unconfined by my previous poverty-stricken state.

But the day of reckoning soon arrived. I had no idea where Arnold's money was coming from. I knew it was going out in enormous amounts and at a remarkable speed. On one occasion from Feldger, the jeweller in Yates Road, I had carted away on payment of several thousands of American dollars a set of necklaces and bracelets in solid gold, heavy and beautifully

279

wrought. Some time later Arnold gave me ten thousand American dollars which I handed over to Feldger in exchange for a magnificent diamond ring. Sumair received them – and a Dodge limousine complete with chauffeur.

There was a nasty moment and, for me, an embarrassing interview when, unexpectedly, Kiehn's wife and son, Michael, arrived from America. I found them a charming couple, particularly the boy, who then loved his father.

Arnold refused to see them. He booked them in the Park Hotel and made it clear that he wanted them to go, as soon as possible, back to California.

I met them in his office at the Hong Kong Bank and there, sadly, had to explain to Mrs Kiehn that a reunion was not possible. Arnold had told me that, even before the war, he had come to the conclusion that they were incompatible and could not live together.

It was a tearful, heart-rending meeting and I felt sorry for Mrs Kiehn. There it was, however, and nothing I could say would change Arnold's mind. They left for America shortly afterwards.

Then my salary payments ceased for months on end. True, I wasn't doing much but the agreement had been made between us for regular handouts of five hundred dollars a month. Other members of the staff were similarly left unpaid. From time to time Arnold made up the arrears but then regular payments dropped off again. I began to get worried. The Chinese dollar had dropped to an all-time low. A box of matches fetched one thousand dollars. People going to the market carried cash in kitbags – bundles of two-hundred-and-fifty-thousand dollars. Salaries were paid in several millions of dollars – equal to less than a hundred American dollars.

All the while Arnold remained cheerful and assured us that we had nothing to worry about. We had faith in him. At times he was in the money. Then he paid out. In the meantime, he kept his two establishments in Hungjao and the parties continued.

I began to look around for alternative sources of income. I was lucky. Dr Hollington Tong, the Chinese Minister of Information, was a friend of mine. I spoke to him and he suggested that I should take over the column-spot in the daily, the *China Press*, which had been re-established after the war by the government and had a large circulation in central China.

It was a part-time post and I continued working for Kiehn in the Hong Kong Bank office where, daily, I typed my column piece under the heading, 'The Corner Seat'. There was a small picture of me at the top of the column. Payment was two million Chinese dollars a month – a pittance but I needed it to pay my rent and to eat.

In true Winchell or Cassandra style I bared my fangs and took great bites out of the establishment. The column became popular. I got a large mailbag each week and I was invited to take part in debates, round-table discussions and the like at the YMCA, the French Club and other establishments.

K. S. Chang, the *China Press* editor, big and beefy and much Americanized, gave me a free hand and insisted on one condition only – that I should use American spelling. It was the age of America. Traffic was now using the right-hand side of the road. The Chinese – and most others – were blowing themselves up with Coca-Cola or Pepsi-Cola. Bourbon was easier to obtain than Scotch. All the rickshaw coolies were using GI cast-offs and even the girls seemed to be adapting various items of American army uniform for adornment. I found it disconcerting, however, as a confirmed leg-ogler to see beautifully figured office girls, long-legged and nylon-clad, stumping around in great army boots. Leather was scarce after the occupation and shoes fetched a high black market price. Huge army clodhoppers, though hardly lady-like, were preferable to cardboard or cotton sandals which were about the only items of footwear available.

I fired my first broadside in the column when I watched a Roman orgy of the execution of two high-ranking Japanese army officers for war crimes.

I had no love for the Japanese. Their record in China was bestial and I had only recently been their prisoner. But the carnival that preceded the deaths of the two men completely sickened me and I determined that, if I had any influence, then such sights would not occur again.

The two Japanese, hands tied behind their backs, were placed behind the cab of a large army truck. Behind them, as they stared stonily ahead along the streets over which only a short time back they had swaggered as conquerors, was a posse of Chinese army gendarmes armed to the teeth. Sub-machine-guns, revolvers, rifles and even two hand grenades were pointed at the backs of the two men. In front of the truck was another vehicle carrying a detachment of soldiers. And in the rear were two other trucks each of them carrying about thirty armed men.

This cavalcade of death paraded through the town for several hours before arriving at the public execution ground on the outskirts of the city. Hundreds of thousands of Shanghai men, women and children lined the streets and were whipped into a frenzy of screaming hate as the doomed men, in full uniform, were slowly driven by.

I looked at the two men. They were brave. Their faces showed no sign of emotion. Amid the terrible din of curses from the men and screaming obscenities from the women they stared fixedly ahead. They held themselves erect. They were soldiers and they were going to die with the courage of soldiers. I was filled with compassion for them, though I had no doubt that their crimes called for the supreme penalty.

At the execution ground they were made to kneel with bowed heads. A gendarme, loaded Mauser at the ready, stood behind each man. On the word of command they placed the muzzles of the weapons against each man's neck and then, as another command was barked out, fired. Both the Japanese officers fell to the ground with half their heads blasted away.

And then pandemonium as the crowd in one massive surge broke through the ranks of soldiers on the perimeter and rushed to the spot where the bodies lay. I saw one woman dip her handkerchief in the blood of one officer and then wave it in hysterical madness as she screamed obscenities at the mutilated forms by her feet. Others joined her in kicking the dead men. In savage insanity a young girl bent down and exposed the genital organ of one of the officers. She pointed at the dead man's pubic region and a group of women rushed forward and joined her in an orgy of mutilation.

My column the following day asked the question: why had such a cultured people as the Chinese, renowned for their courtesy and humanitarian record, showed the world that they, too, could match the Japanese for savagery? Such scenes as those I had witnessed, I wrote, were an indelible blot on the good name of the Chinese nation. They were, in fact, inexcusable if only because they left the impression that the Chinese people were no better than the war criminals they were punishing for their bestial excesses.

There were no more public executions. Japanese war criminals ended their lives in Ward Road jail watched only by a handful of officials who recorded the fact that the sentences of the war-crime courts had been carried out.

The racial scene occupied my thoughts almost constantly. I abhorred racial discrimination in any form. I believed in the brotherhood of man and I could not stomach the bigotry of such people as the South African whites or their counterparts in the southern states of America. In Shanghai I vented my spleen on the members of the British-run Shanghai Club who still, unbelievably, barred membership to the Chinese.

But the old China hands stood firm. They would not budge an inch. Loss of their extraterritorial privileges had been a bitter blow and they were determined to show their contempt for the Chinese, whom they considered incapable of bestowing good government on the country in any shape or form.

If I failed to reach my target at least my barbs penetrated the thick hides of the taipans, one of whom in high dudgeon made it known to K. S. Chang that unless he silenced that 'bloody red, Shaw' then a lucrative advertising contract would not be renewed.

Chang told him what he could do with his contract – in fact, in real anger, he threatened to expose in the *China Press* columns the man's name and the purport of his visit to the editorial sanctum. The contract was never cancelled and the Shanghai Club committee, in stoical suffering, endured my ceaseless attacks until the triumphant Chinese Communists, successors to the more complacent Nationalists, not only turfed the bigots out of their racially exclusive edifice but out of China as well.

In my position as a columnist with a very large readership I found that corruptive forces were ever at hand. I was offered money to espouse this cause and that one. Industrialists offered me their products as gifts. I could have made a fortune quickly enough. I refused to depart from my principles and stayed poor. I do not regret my action for I firmly believe that the journalist, who has the power to shape the opinions of people, must stay incorruptible, must remain the possessor of absolute integrity.

I was not so inflexible when it came to sex.

My fame as a columnist had brought several young and pretty girls close to me. I loved the publicity that little picture at the top of the column meant.

There was one young Chinese girl – no more than eighteen – who constantly sought my company and daily phoned me at Kiehn's bank office. She said that my outspokenness on many subjects, particularly the racial issue, had filled her with admiration and that she wanted me to be her 'teacher', which, from a Chinese, was the highest compliment that could be paid.

Teach her I did. Regularly she visited the office in the evenings when everybody except me had departed. Kiehn had thoughtfully deposited a large and comfortable sofa in one of the rooms and it

283

was on this that discussions with the girl on philosophical topics gradually gave way to full-time use of the hand-maiden technique with the result that the evidence of my nightly ejaculations reposed in a jig-saw of patterns on the floor in front of the sofa.

Financial worries were severely cutting my costly excursionst to the top night-spots though the social life at Sumair's residence provided inexpensive enjoyment. From time to time I managed to drag some American dollars from Kiehn who was certainly in some sort of financial jam. Nevertheless, we had faith in his ability to overcome the crisis and his daily air of jaunty confidence reassured us.

Every morning Arnold read the Bible in the quietness of his office in the bank. This was a reflection of his strict missionary upbringing in China, though I doubt whether his father, the Rev. Peter Kiehn of the Church of Christ, would have approved of his personal life.

Nevertheless, Kiehn was a likeable chap, quiet-spoken, gentlemanly in his behaviour – the sort of man who inspired confidence in everyone with whom he came into contact. His circle of friends included many rich and influential businessmen in the city, some of whom, including Henningsen, had been his camp-mates. There was no doubt that they trusted him implicitly and were ready to back him with cash. Henningsen, in particular, placed several good money-making opportunities his way.

Kiehn's explanation of his inability to find ready cash was that he was unable to receive the profits of a silver mine he owned in Mexico due to a ban by the government there on the export of funds out of the country.

It was in Shanghai that I first saw the slogan which was to become universally adopted by politically inspired graffiti artists: 'Yankees go home' or 'Yanks go home'.

The cause was the rape of a Chinese girl by an American marine in Peking. It led to riots throughout China and I was involved in one in the former Avenue Joffre when a group of about a hundred students brandishing clubs stopped the pedicab in which I was riding and asked me if I was American. They were polite enough – typically Chinese. Had I announced that I was an American then they would have set on me without compunction and left my battered body in the roadway. I said I was British and proved it by flashing my resident's certificate which bore my picture and announced that I was a citizen of the United Kingdom. They inspected the certificate, politely bowed me on and went off in search of stray Americans.

Many Americans were attacked and beaten and much American property was badly damaged. Communist elements were blamed for the outbreak of violence but this was only partly true. Anti-American feeling among the younger people in China had been rising steadily since the end of the war and there was the feeling that the vast American involvement in the country presaged an extension of the former domination of successive Chinese governments by the Western powers. Victory had brought in its wake intense nationalism. The young people of China were demanding a strong and stable government and complete independence from any foreign entanglements. There were too many Americans in China for their liking – and their affluence at a time of a national financial disaster was too much to bear.

My economic situation had become parlous. Despite my faith in Kiehn and my friendship with him it was clear that I would have to do something to bring in more money every month. I did not want to return to journalism permanently in China for the papers there were undergoing a period of extreme hardship and they were paying pittances to everyone on their pay-rolls.

In desperation I went to see Henningsen to ask his advice. I was in for the surprise of my life.

I told him that Arnold was not paying salaries – obviously could not raise the money.

Henningsen – we talked privately in his office in the old Dollar building in Canton Road – expressed surprise that Kiehn, in whom he had placed full confidence in the camp and later in business in post-war Shanghai, had got himself into such a fix. Did I know the reason, for he was goddammed if he did when money was there in thousands for the picking.

I said I had no idea what had happened. It was true. I added that I had to get out, that to continue in the hope that Arno.d would regain his former wealthy status seemed to be plain wishful thinking and that my best bet seemed to be to return to England and enter journalism in London. That was if I could raise the cash to pay for my passage and some money to live on while I sought work.

Henningsen looked at me steadily.

'How much would it cost, Ralph?' he said.

I made a quick calculation but my arithmetic failed me.

Henningsen waited patiently.

'Look,' he said suddenly, 'how would five hundred pounds do? Would that cover everything?'

I said it would.

'Right,' he said, 'I'll give you five hundred pounds. Consider it to be a loan but if you can't pay me back then never mind. And if you breathe a word about this to anybody then I'll murder you. Understand? This is between you and me.'

When I tried to express my thanks he cut me short.

'Forget it,' he said. 'And get out quick. This country's going to the dogs.'

Of all the people I met in China – indeed, of all the individuals I have known in a lifetime of extensive travel in the world – Anker B. Henningsen stands supreme in my assessment of the qualities that they possessed. Shortcomings he must have had – where is the human being who is absolutely perfect? – but his goodness, his charity, his genuine concern for the welfare of others (I was only one of many helped on the way by this great American) shine like a brilliant beacon in a world seemingly dedicated to the principle of self-interest.

When I left China in the steamship *City of Khartoum*, I had said goodbye to Henningsen for what I thought would be the last time. Fate decreed otherwise. We met again in Hong Kong and our association continued until 1954 when I left the colony for other parts of South-east Asia. I have not seen him since, but the memory of his altruistic philanthropy will never be erased from my memory. He remains to this day the man I always regard as my greatest friend.

I arrived in Liverpool with my baggage and two large trunks filled with food, for I had heard that the British were still on war-time rations. It was all Shanghai black-market stuff and certainly all-American in content apart from a sackfull of rice.

From Liverpool to London and a happy reunion with Harry Martin back on the *Daily Mail* news desk as well as several meetings with Dickson Hoste in the bowels of Bush House in the Strand.

London I found dismally depressing after the epicurean gaiety of Shanghai. Bacon, cheese, eggs, meat, sugar and many other commodities were strictly rationed. I shone like a new pin in my Shanghai-tailored suits amongst the shabbily dressed citizens with whom I commuted daily in the capital. Spivs whistled at me in Piccadilly Circus when they saw my two Parker pens and the companion Schaeffer in my breast pocket.

But I was a welcome guest wherever I went because my thanks for hospitality was always a gift of food – a large can of cheese or bacon or, if there were children, a week's supply of rice.

There were joyful reunions with my father, who was living in Nuneaton in the Midlands, my brother in Surrey and a host of relatives in Yorkshire. But ten years' absence had rung the changes in my homeland. Many of my schoolmates had been killed in the war and I read with sorrow their names on the large memorial plaque in Big School where we had sat together for examinations, prep and other activities.

Fleet Street was not receptive to newcomers for its own men were returning from the services or from government service and newsprint was still strictly rationed so that daily issues were small. I had no wish to return to provincial journalism and even there jobs were scarce.

But what convinced me that the Orient was my particular paradise was the 1947 winter, which was one of the coldest Britain had experienced for many years. I remember walking in Bradford with chattering teeth and a face the colour of royal-blue ink. My toes had the icy consistency of today's fish fingers. My fingers were seared by pain. Fresh from the comfort of central heating and air-conditioned freshness in Shanghai I wondered how I had ever managed to exist up to 1937 in the antediluvian freezing chambers that served for homes in my native land.

Shortly before the end of December I was in Glasgow for the first time in my life ready to sail in the S.S. *Empire Brent* back to Shanghai. The call of the Far East was too strong to resist. There was no prospect of employment in front of me but, with typical Micawber-like optimism, I fancied that something would turn up somewhere and I was not wrong.

We spent several days in Hong Kong, and this gave me the opportunity to call on Harry Ching, the Australian-Chinese editor of the *South China Morning Post* there. Harry regularly read my column which I had kept going from Britain. He liked it. We talked for about half an hour and when I left the building I was the new night editor of the paper.

I had to take one last look at Shanghai, which was still the greatest cosmopolitan port in the Far East. It was agreed that I would spend two weeks there to 'wind up my affairs' and then return to Hong Kong to start work.

I found Kiehn still enmeshed in a welter of troubles but trying hard to re-establish his fortunes. I felt sorry for him and my affection remained unimpaired by his failure to pay me the salary he had owed me for so many months. I said goodbye to him and wished him well.

Early in the 1950s I met him again in Hong Kong after he had been expelled from China by the Communits, who had sentenced him to a long period in jail in the old Ward Road prison. Despite his suffering he was as cheerfully optimistic as ever, a regular reader of the Bible, certain that the Lord would bestow on him again the bounty of previous years.

He was busy making plans to set up business in Hong Kong. It was not to be. The American consular authorities refused him permission to stay and the colony government upheld the decision and ordered his immediate departure for the United States where, it was reported, his passport was impounded.

His passionate and tempestuous affair with Sumair had ended. She, too, had departed from Shanghai. I wonder now if Arnold was ever reunited with his wife and son away from the temptations of a city that corrupted many a saint. I hope so.

I sailed downriver for the last time in February 1948, in the Dutch liner *Tegelberg*. The parting with China was hard to make. I loved the country and its gracious people. Shanghai had changed me from a provincial yokel to a metropolitan sophisticate, a lover of the fleshpots, of good clothes, good food and of women whose goodness reposed in their willingness to accommodate my sexual whims.

The world has lost old Shanghai. No one should think that its passing should be the cause of lamentations. Its presence for a century or more was evidence of oppression, of cruelty and unforgivable discrimination. The foreigners have left the scene of their debauches. Their spirits, I am sure, in ghostly forays must be seeking out the scenes of their earthbound joys – alas, in vain, as the Leninist-Marxist thoughts of Chairman Mao have swept away the last lingering whispers of a hundred years of sensuality.

I can always console myself with the recollection that Hong Kong, in some part, took over the mantle of Shanghai in providing the pleasures of the flesh. But that is another story.